Rural Industry in the Port Phillip Region 1835–1880

Detail of *Near the You Yangs*, etching by Marion Ellis Rowan, *c.* 1880
Courtesy La Trobe Library, Melbourne

Rural Industry in the Port Phillip Region 1835–1880

LYNNETTE J. PEEL

MELBOURNE UNIVERSITY PRESS
1974

First published 1974

Printed in Australia by
Halstead Press Division, John Sands Pty Ltd
Artarmon, New South Wales 2064, for
Melbourne University Press, Carlton, Victoria 3053

U.S.A. and Canada: ISBS Inc., Portland, Oregon 97208

Great Britain, Europe, Middle East, Africa and the Carribbean:
International Book Distributors Ltd, 66 Wood Lane End, Hemel
Hempstead, Hertfordshire HP2 4RG, England

National Library of Australia Cataloguing in Publication data
Peel, Lynnette Jean
Rural industry in the Port Phillip region, 1835–1880/ [by] Lynnette J. Peel.—Carlton, Vic.: Melbourne University Press, 1974.
Index.
Bibliography.
ISBN 0 522 84064 7.
1. Agriculture–Economic aspects–Victoria–Port Phillip district–History. I. Title.
338.1099452

For C.W.P. and C.E.E.P.

Acknowledgements

This book is based on material in the collections in Melbourne of the Baillieu Library, La Trobe Library, State Library of Victoria, State Archives, University of Melbourne Archives, and Monash University Library; in Sydney of the Mitchell Library and the Archives Office of New South Wales; and in Canberra of the National Library of Australia. I am indebted to the librarians and archives officers in all these institutions for their willing assistance. I also wish to thank Lady Johnston, Mr H. Muir, Dr G. de Pury, Imperial Chemical Industries of Australia and New Zealand Ltd, the Victorian Crown Lands and Survey Department, and the secretaries of a number of shires within the region for allowing me access to their manuscript records. In the early chapters of this book I have drawn extensively on the *Clyde Company Papers* and I would like to express my gratitude to Mr P. L. Brown for his masterly editing of these papers and also for his willing assistance with more general information. Preliminary work was carried out at the University of Melbourne and the main research was made possible by a research scholarship from Monash University. I am particularly indebted to Professor A. G. L. Shaw and Dr D. Waterson for helpful discussion throughout the project and for criticism of the manuscript, and to Dr G. Serle for helpful discussion and for suggesting various sources of information to me. Mr G. Swinton and Miss S. Reid of the Cartographic Section of the Geography Department, Monash University, gave great assistance in drawing the maps, and Mrs B. Hadinek and Miss M. Quinlan in typing the manuscript.

Contents

Illustrations

MAPS

FIGURES

Conversion Factors

1 inch	=	2·54 centimetres
1 foot	=	0·30 metre
1 mile	=	1·61 kilometres
1 acre	=	0·40 hectare
1 square mile	=	259 hectares
1 ounce	=	28·3 grams
1 pound	=	0·45 kilogram
1 hundredweight	=	50·8 kilograms
1 ton	=	1·02 tonnes
1 bushel	=	36·4 litres
	=	0·036 cubic metre

Fahrenheit to Celsius $°C = \frac{5}{9}(°F - 32)$

In 1962 the Australian pound was converted to decimal currency on the basis:

£1	=	$2
1s	=	10c
1d	=	0·83c

Introduction

Early in the nineteenth century people emigrated from Great Britain, with its complex cropping systems and improved livestock, to south-eastern Australia where they soon displaced the Aborigines, who were nomadic hunters and gatherers.

One of the first actions of the newcomers was to portion the land among themselves. A characteristic of British agriculture at this time was its organization into individual units of production based on a family farm. On each farm the decisions about the methods and types of production were made independently by each individual occupant. Thus the agriculture of any given region farmed in this way was the composite result of the independent decisions taken on the many farms. As soon as the immigrants arrived, the possibilities for types of agricultural production within the area increased considerably. If the possible plant varieties are linked with the possible animal species then available to European man, the combinations available for systems of production are almost infinite. But in practice there are certain limiting factors in any rural situation which set the boundaries within which farm management decisions and actions will be confined. The more rigid the limitations imposed by these factors, the more uniform will be the agriculture in space and time. Thus the type of agricultural production within a region at any point in time can be envisaged as lying along a continuum between infinite diversity and complete uniformity, the actual position where it lies on this continuum being determined by the composite effect of a wide variety of limiting factors. Furthermore as time passes the limiting factors can change in nature or in relative importance and cause a shift along the continuum in either direction.

The greater the diversity in agricultural production from farm to farm and from year to year, the more the agriculture of the area is likely to change and therefore the greater will be its instability. Conversely the more uniform the agriculture is, the greater is its stability, as with a rice-growing area which has been producing rice and little else for centuries. Where there is an alteration in one or several of the factors affecting agriculture, the diversified unstable agriculture will be best able to cope with the changed circumstances because of the flexibility provided by the diversity. But the more stable and uniform the agriculture is, the less it will be able to cope with a sudden change or disturbance of the equilibrium. This will be illustrated below by the effects of falling prices and rust attacks on uniform and continuous wheat cropping. In some instances, for example in a stable largely rural economy, agricultural stability could be very desirable. Where the population is largely static, and a system of farming has been developed that provides the food and clothing needs of the people while still maintaining the soil fertility and other means of production, any change in the established pattern would probably be viewed with some concern. But in an economy where the non-rural sector is rapidly developing and possibly becoming more industrialized and where there is a rapid growth in the population, stability in the rural sector would probably be designated as stagnation.

The limitations on agriculture take many and varied forms but for convenience they can be brought together in a number of broad groupings. The first of these is the natural environment and includes the effects of terrain, soils, rainfall, temperature and natural vegetation. The second is demography—the size of rural and urban populations, the numerical changes in these populations, and the characteristics of populations, such as age and dependants. Thirdly there is the land system, the method by which the land is apportioned among the people, which particularly concerns such things as farm or plot size and the tenure under which the land is held. The land system is usually associated with the fourth grouping, the socio-cultural aspects of the community, and with the fifth, the politico-legal system. The traditions, laws and customs of a community and the way in which they are enforced invariably impinge on so basic an aspect of the community's life as its agriculture. The sixth grouping, the biological aspects of agriculture, includes the genetic and physiological factors in plant and animal production and such things as the incidence of diseases and pests. The seventh grouping covers the technical aspects of production, and the eighth the economic aspects of farming. This last grouping becomes increasingly important and beyond the farmer's control as the non-agricultural activities of the community absorb an increasing proportion of the labour and resources of the community, and agriculture correspondingly declines in importance. These are groupings only, but they do provide a basis for further examination.

1 : The Port Phillip Region

Navigators had debated for some years whether or not Van Diemen's Land was separated from New South Wales. Cook had sensed that it was; others thought not. In December 1797, when George Bass sailed from Sydney to explore the southern coast of Australia, the question was still unresolved. On this voyage Bass did not prove the existence of the strait, which later was to bear his name, but on 5 January 1798 he did discover Western Port Bay, 'a very extensive harbour'.[1] Ten months later he again sailed south, with Lieutenant Matthew Flinders, and succeeded in passing through the strait and circumnavigating Van Diemen's Land.

Thereafter several ships passed through Bass Strait, and Western Port Bay was explored further, but Port Phillip Bay remained unknown until 5 January 1802 when John Murray and his crew on the *Lady Nelson* sighted the entrance to the bay. Murray was under orders from Governor King to survey the southern coast, but adverse winds prevented him from entering the bay and he was forced to sail on. However, he returned on 15 February, entered Port Phillip Bay and anchored off the south-eastern shore. He then explored parts of the southern shores and took possession of the bay in the name of King George III. Meanwhile Flinders had returned to England where he was appointed commander of the 334-ton *Investigator* and instructed to explore the whole of the Australian coastline. Returning to Australia and exploring the southern coast en route, Flinders found and entered Port Phillip Bay on 26 April 1802, only two months after Murray had been there. He explored the bay, climbing Arthur's Seat in the south-east and the You Yangs in the north-west, and also landing at Indented Head (near Portarlington) on the Bellarine Peninsula.

The next party to enter Port Phillip Bay was under the command of Charles Robbins in the *Cumberland*. Charles Grimes, the surveyor-general, was on board and had instructions to make a survey of the shore, and during January and February 1803 the shores of the bay, and the courses of the Saltwater and Yarra Rivers to some miles above the site of the future city of Melbourne, were charted. In the north-west, Grimes and his men found a clear level plain to the mountains, which they supposed to be fifteen or twenty miles long.[2] The mountains came around closer in the north-east, and the eastern shore was timbered and swampy, while low, gently rolling hills could be seen on the south-west peninsula (see map 1).

In October 1803, two ships arrived directly from England to establish a convict settlement on the bay. The leader of the expedition, Lieutenant-Colonel David Collins, selected a site just inside the Heads on the south-east shore, but this was a scrubby sandy area with very little fresh water. The presence of Aborigines further

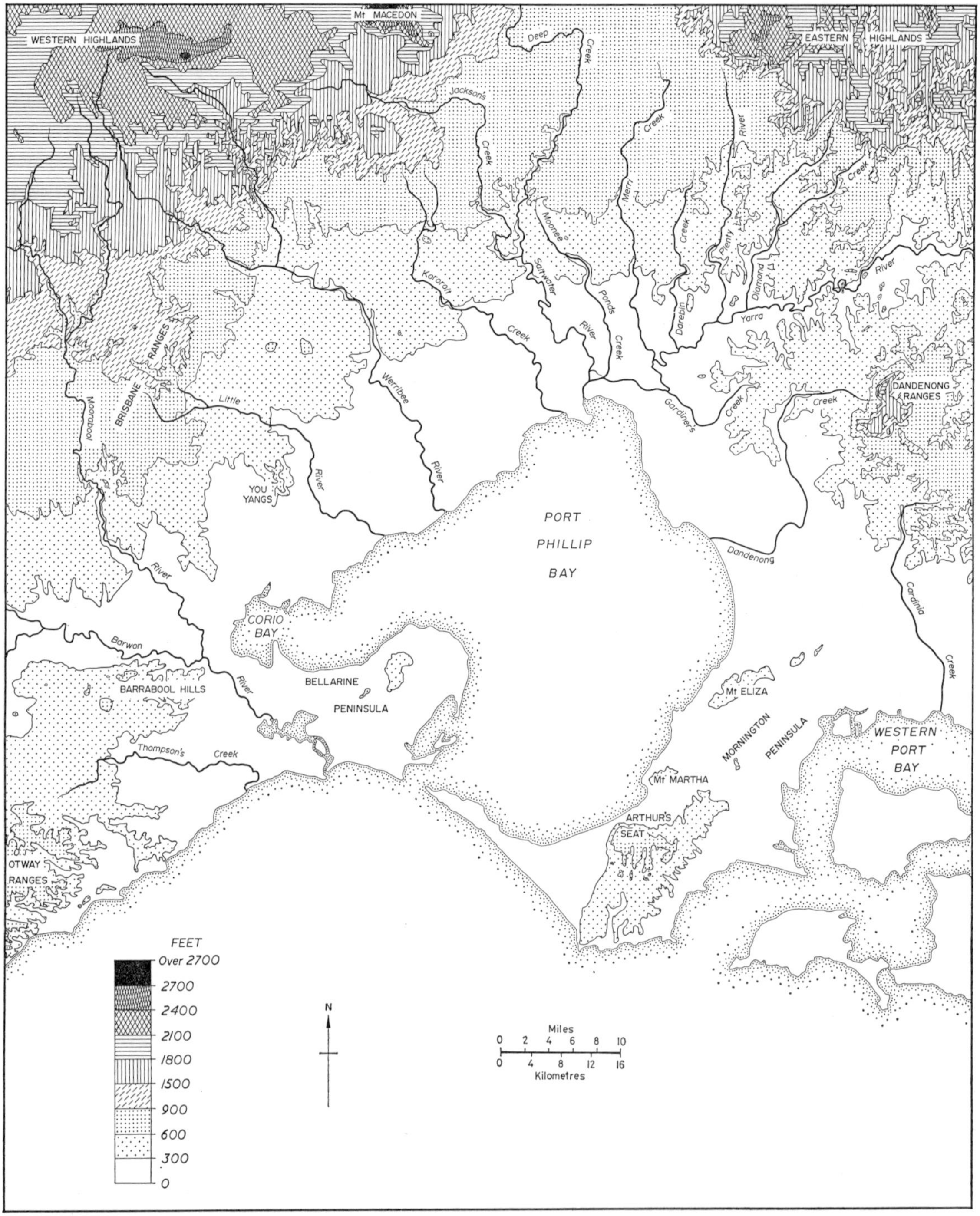

Map 1 Physiography

Military survey maps, series—4 miles = 1 inch, Melbourne and Queenscliff

disheartened Collins and the settlement was abandoned, the last persons leaving in May 1804.

Coming southwards overland from Sydney in 1824, Hume and Hovell found a route through the ranges, between the western and eastern highlands, more or less due north of the future site of Melbourne. After crossing the watershed they travelled some distance farther south until, from the top of one of the hills, they saw before them 'between the points south-east and west, alternate plains and forests . . . extending to the utmost verge of the horizon, and from N.N.E. to S.E. part of the Alpine Chain; while towards the south, the land gradually dips. Nothing could surpass the beauty of this view.'[3] On crossing the plains they found flocks of emus and wild turkeys. The kangaroo, however, 'was seldom met with'. Near the shore of the bay the water was covered with water fowl of various species including black swans, Cape Barren geese, and ducks.

After examining the north-western shore of the bay, the explorers returned overland to Sydney, where their reports of extensive tracts of fine country drew considerable attention. A decade later, in 1835, free settlers crossed from Van Diemen's Land with their sheep to found a permanent settlement. But before this the government did attempt another abortive settlement on the south-eastern shore of Western Port Bay between December 1826 and January 1828, mainly to forestall possible French occupation.

ENVIRONMENT

The plains in the Port Phillip region consist primarily of newer basalt (Pleistocene) overlying Tertiary marine sediments, although there are also limited areas of Pleistocene and Recent sediments. These basaltic plains form the eastern extremity of the Victorian Western District lava plains.

The highlands are mainly composed of Ordovician, Silurian, or Cretaceous sedimentary rocks with the exception of the You Yangs, Mt Macedon, the Dandenong Ranges and the three peaks of the Mornington Peninsula, all of which are granitic in composition (see map 2).

Much of the soil confronting the early settlers either set very hard in summer and was covered with stones, or consisted of poor swampy sands, or was hard, acidic and covered in timber (see map 3).

The two areas initially selected for cultivation when permanent settlement commenced were located on the cracking clays and other soils between the Plenty and Saltwater Rivers to the north of Melbourne, and on the cracking clays and loamy soils of the Barrabool Hills, immediately west of Geelong. There was little heavy timber to be cleared from these areas and the soils were reasonably fertile and not too difficult to work.

The heavier alkaline duplex soils were more difficult to cultivate, particularly in the more clayey areas, since the surface set very hard during the dry months. When the rains came, the soil softened and was workable for a brief period until further rain waterlogged the soil and it became too heavy and sticky for further cultivation; sheets of water often lay on the flat terrain, or in the crabholes, and drainage was a serious problem. Many of these soils on basalt also carried a heavy stone cover. Some of the hard-setting acidic duplex soils—loams and sands with yellow clay subsoils—found on the granitic and sedimentary formations, also had poor drainage.

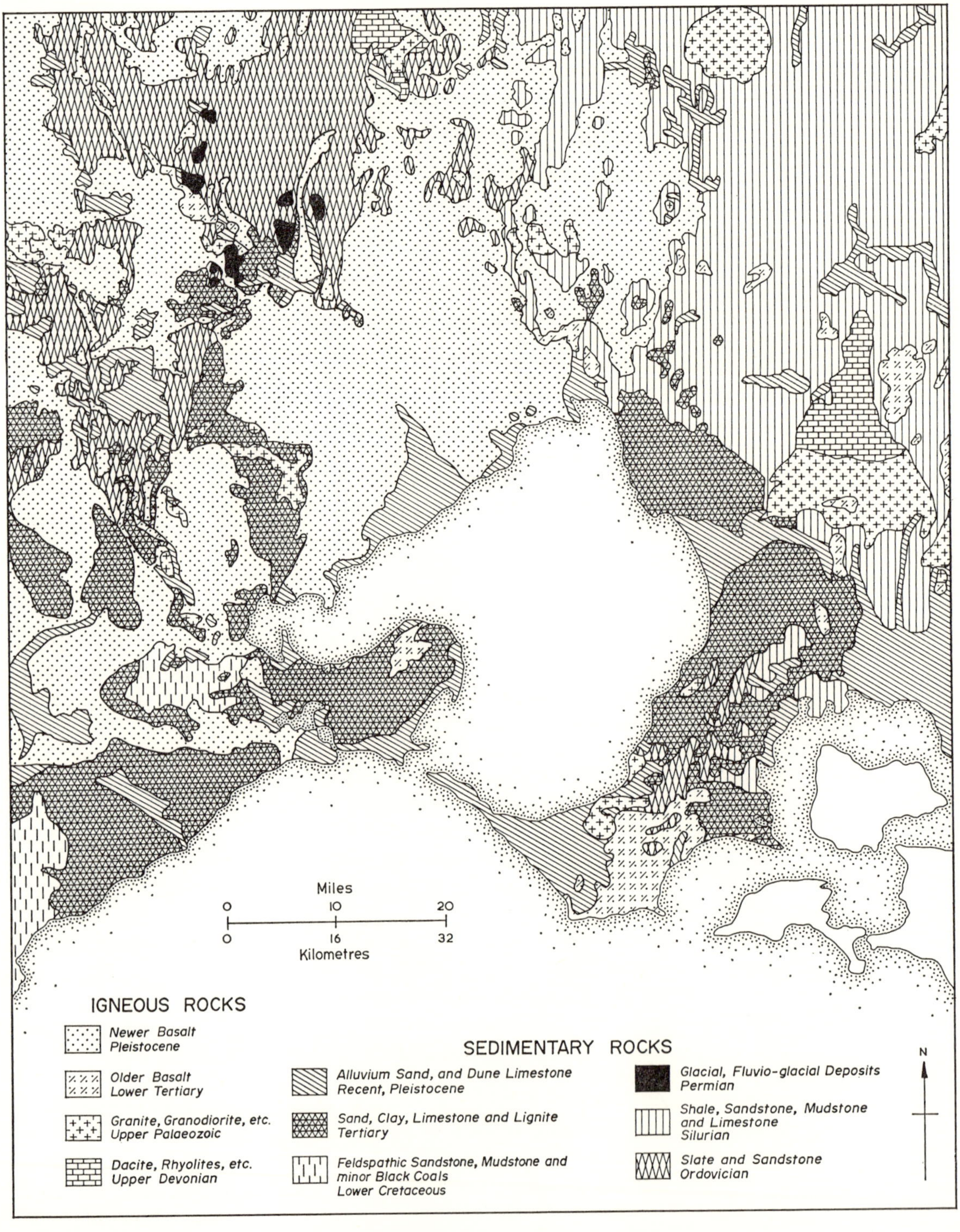

Map 2 Geology

Department of Mines (Victoria), *Geological Map of Victoria*

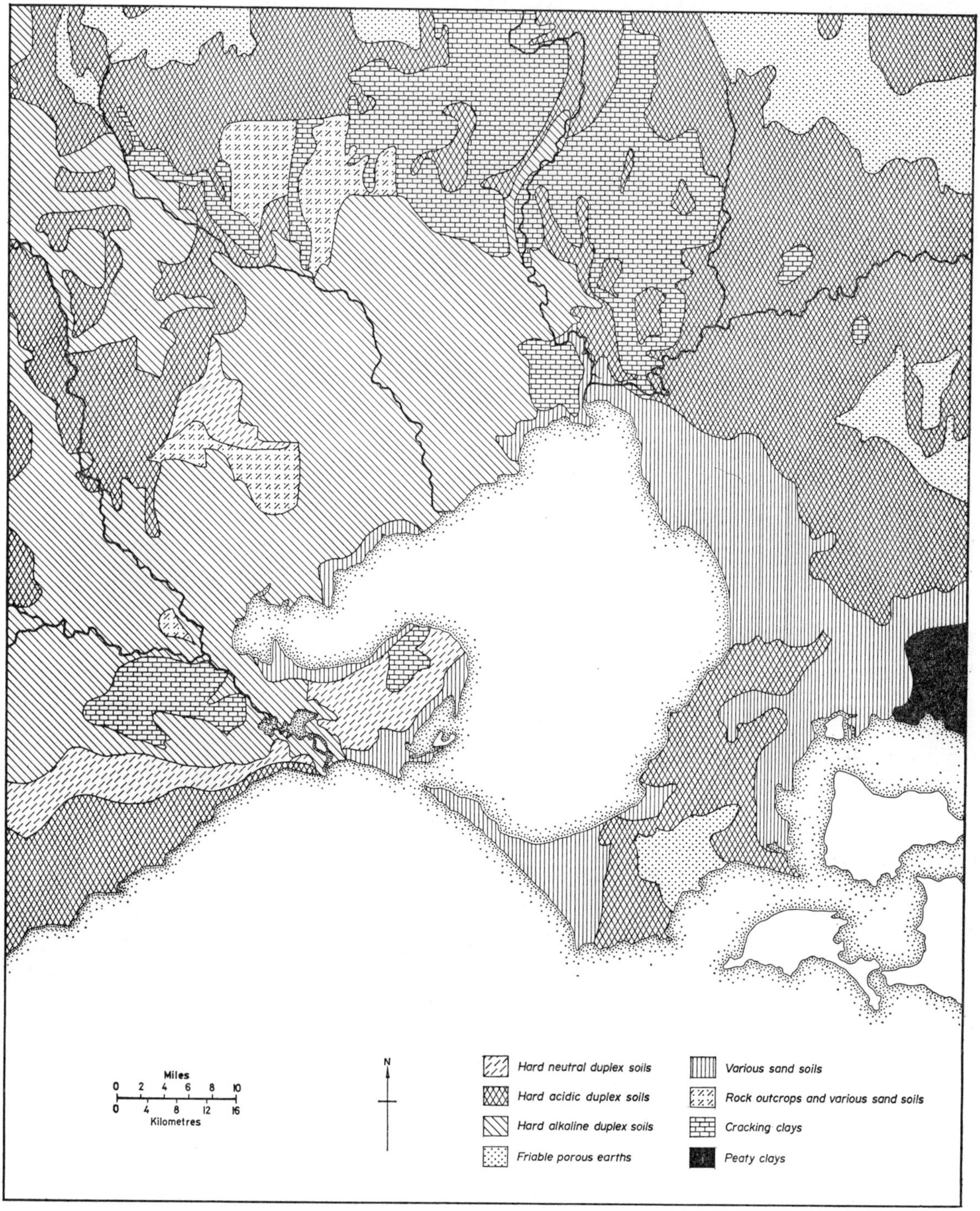

Map 3 Soils

K. H. Northcote, *Atlas of Australian Soils: sheet 2, Melbourne–Tasmania Area*

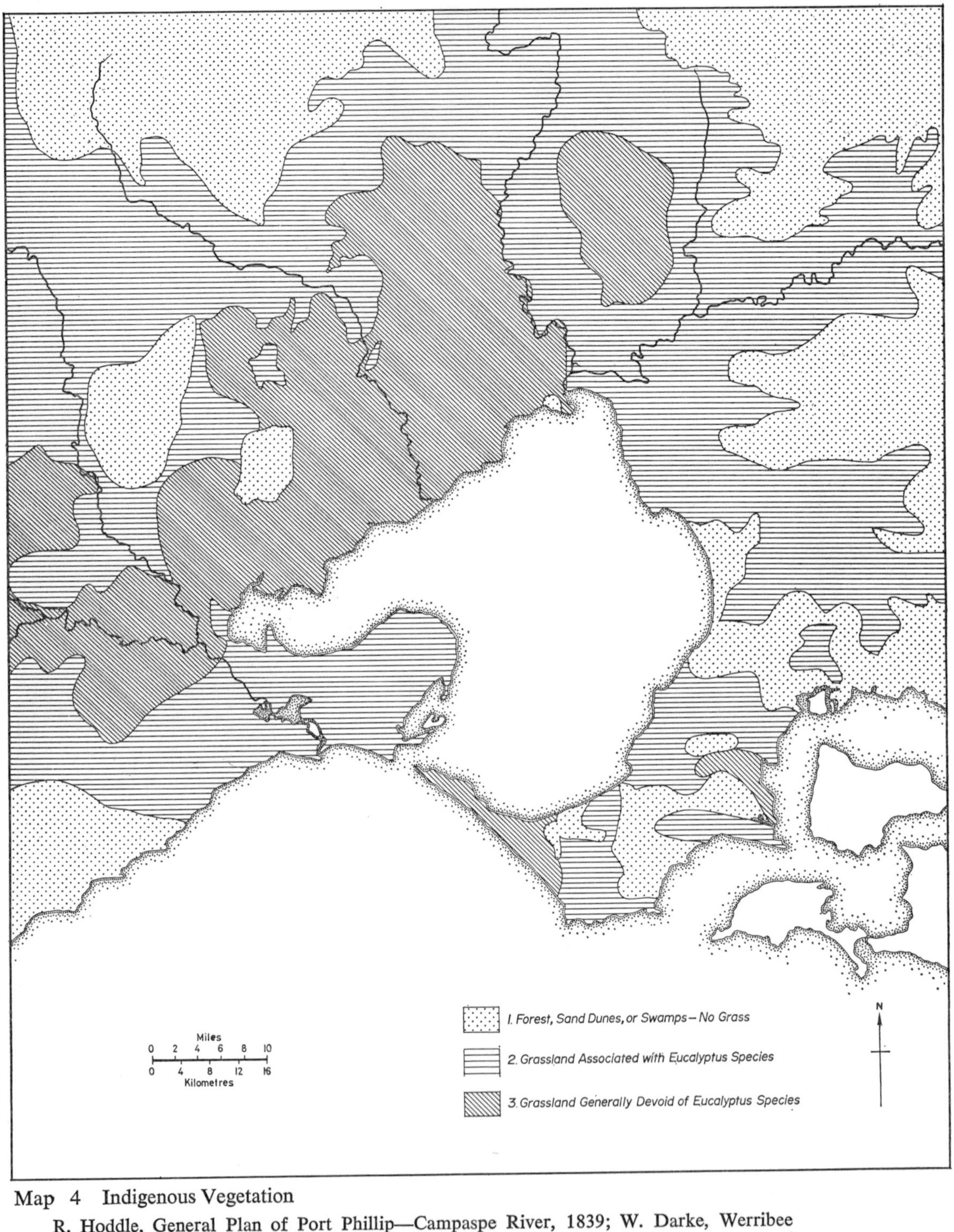

Map 4 Indigenous Vegetation

R. Hoddle, General Plan of Port Phillip—Campaspe River, 1839; W. Darke, Werribee River and Its Tributaries, 1839–40; R. Hoddle, Port Phillip, 1840; W. Darke, Survey of Present and Proposed Lines of Road and the Coast between Melbourne and Geelong, 1841; Settled Districts of Melbourne, 1854(?); First Survey and Settlement of Port Phillip, *V.P.P.*, 1878, vol. 1, no. C15; Skene, map of the Clyde Company's stations, Geelong dis-

During the winter these soils were waterlogged, the subsurface down to the clay became semi-fluid and tunnel erosion occurred easily. The sandy soils consisted mainly of leached sands with compacted layers at varying depths, and much of this land was swampy and of very low fertility. The attempted settlement in 1803 had been upon soils of this nature.

In general the soils of the Port Phillip region had a low phosphorus content, about one-third of the phosphorus content of an ordinary soil in Britain. And since the introduced plants and the farmers who planted them came mainly from that country, the low level of phosphorus soon became a limiting factor in plant growth. Apart from the overall phosphorus deficiency, particular soil associations may also have been deficient in other elements. The loamy and sandy soils on yellow clay were low in potassium and when repeatedly cropped with cereals or cut for hay, could show signs of potassium deficiency. Under these circumstances weeds such as sorrel *Rumex acetosella*, plantain *Plantago lanceolata*, and dandelion *Taraxacum officinale* commonly invaded the area. Molybdenum was also deficient in these soils, particularly on the upper slopes of the highland foot-hills.[4]

During the past 130 years the vegetation of the Port Phillip region has altered considerably and in many areas little trace remains of the plant associations that confronted the early settlers. Any attempt to reconstruct a picture of the vegetative cover as it was in 1835 will yield only approximate results. However, the early surveyors did record sufficient descriptive information on their survey maps to make possible a simple classification of the land according to vegetation.

Using this information, I have drawn map 4 to illustrate the approximate area of land that was immediately available for grazing or cropping purposes and the extent and nature of the tree cover. This map shows three categories of vegetative cover. The first includes the land covered by thick *Eucalyptus* forest, or swamps; in either case extensive clearing of the land or drainage was necessary before the land could be used for agricultural purposes. The second and third categories include those areas where there was at least sufficient native pasture available for sheep to graze, but in category 2 the grassland was associated with *Eucalyptus* trees, together with other tree species, and in category 3 with non-*Eucalyptus* trees. The eucalypts are hardwoods and are more difficult to clear from the land than the smaller and lighter *Casuarina*, *Banksia* and *Acacia* species (category 3). The *Casuarina* species, in particular, were quickly cleared by the settlers since they were easily cut and the timber made excellent firewood.

These three categories of vegetation may be summarized as follows. The comments quoted illustrate the information recorded by the early surveyors on their maps.

1. Forest, sand-dunes or swamps, no grass, e.g. 'Thick forest of stringy bark destitute of grass', 'Scrub—no grass'.

2. Grassland in association with *Eucalyptus* and other tree species, e.g. 'Open country wooded with Gum and Black Wattle producing Good Grass', 'Open Gum Forest good pasture for Sheep'.

---

trict, 1845, in P. L. Brown (ed.), *The Narrative of George Russell of Golf Hill*, p. 239; Military survey maps, series—1 mile = 1 inch, Ballan, Geelong, and Meredith, series—4 miles = 1 inch, Melbourne and Queenscliff; J. D. Lang, *Port-Phillip*, p. 117

3. Grassland in association with *Casuarina, Banksia, Acacia* or other species but generally devoid of *Eucalyptus* species except along the watercourses, e.g. 'Undulating Grassy Hills Timbered with She Oak and Wattle', 'Open Plains, Honeysuckle and Oak', 'Fine Open Country, abundance of good Grass'.

The thick forest of category 1 covered all the higher mountain ranges, and much of this country has remained under permanent forest to the present day. Also in this category was the Great Swamp on the northern shore of Western Port Bay, and the lesser swamps and patches of thick scrub and timber extending across to the Carrum Swamp on the mid-eastern shore of Port Phillip Bay. Farther south on the Mornington Peninsula the two small category 1 areas indicated were swamps, but the larger area was heavily timbered hill country.

The associated grasslands and eucalypts of category 2 extended from the thick forest country across more undulating hills to the shores of the bay in the east and south-west, or to the basalt plain in the north-west. Viewing this country from the top of a tree a few miles upstream from the future site of Melbourne, a member of Grimes's party 'saw it to be gently rising hills, clothed with trees, for ten or fifteen miles . . . The timber in general is gum, oak, and Banksia; the two latter are small; the gum two to four feet diameter, and from ten to thirty feet high; on some of the low ground they are something larger.' But farther south near Arthur's Seat he found 'hills, rocky land, light black sand, fine grass, and the trees low and scrubby.'[5]

The open grassland country north-west of the bay, traversed by Hume and Hovell, was described generally by W. Darke, the assistant surveyor, in 1841 as 'open plains, broken only by very low ridges of trap rock, which are moderately wooded with honey suckle [*Banksia marginata*] and She Oak [*Casuarina* sp.], the plains afford the finest possible sheep pasture, being covered with the richest herbage.'[6] George Russell, who travelled from Melbourne to the Leigh River in April 1836 in search of pasture for his sheep reported that

> the whole of the country we had passed over was very well adapted for sheep grazing, being open plains, stony in parts, and thickly covered with kangaroo-grass [*Themeda australis*] from three to six inches long. The only variation in the quality of the soil was on the banks and the flats of the rivers and creeks: the flats were richer soil, and the grass was mixed with herbs and wild geranium. The Barrabool Hills were the finest part of the country we had seen, and were divided by innumerable valleys and small gullies with rich soil on their banks. These, with smooth rolling hills, gave the country a very rich and pleasing appearance.[7]

Kangaroo-grass, an excellent fodder plant, was the predominant grass throughout the region. It is a tall (1–5 feet) perennial tussock-grass which commences its new season's growth in late spring, flowers in summer and ceases growth before the onset of frosts. Other tall summer-growing perennials associated with this grass were *Poa caespitosa* and *Stipa aristiglumis*. When these grasslands were closely grazed, however, shorter, winter-growing species of *Danthonia* and *Stipa* replaced the tall summer-growing perennials, and introduced species, such as *Medicago polymorpha*, slowly spread through the pastures.

At Port Phillip the summer is hot and dry. A break in the weather comes during autumn and a period of mild weather leads into a cold wet winter. The wettest season of the year is spring and as the weather becomes warmer plant growth is

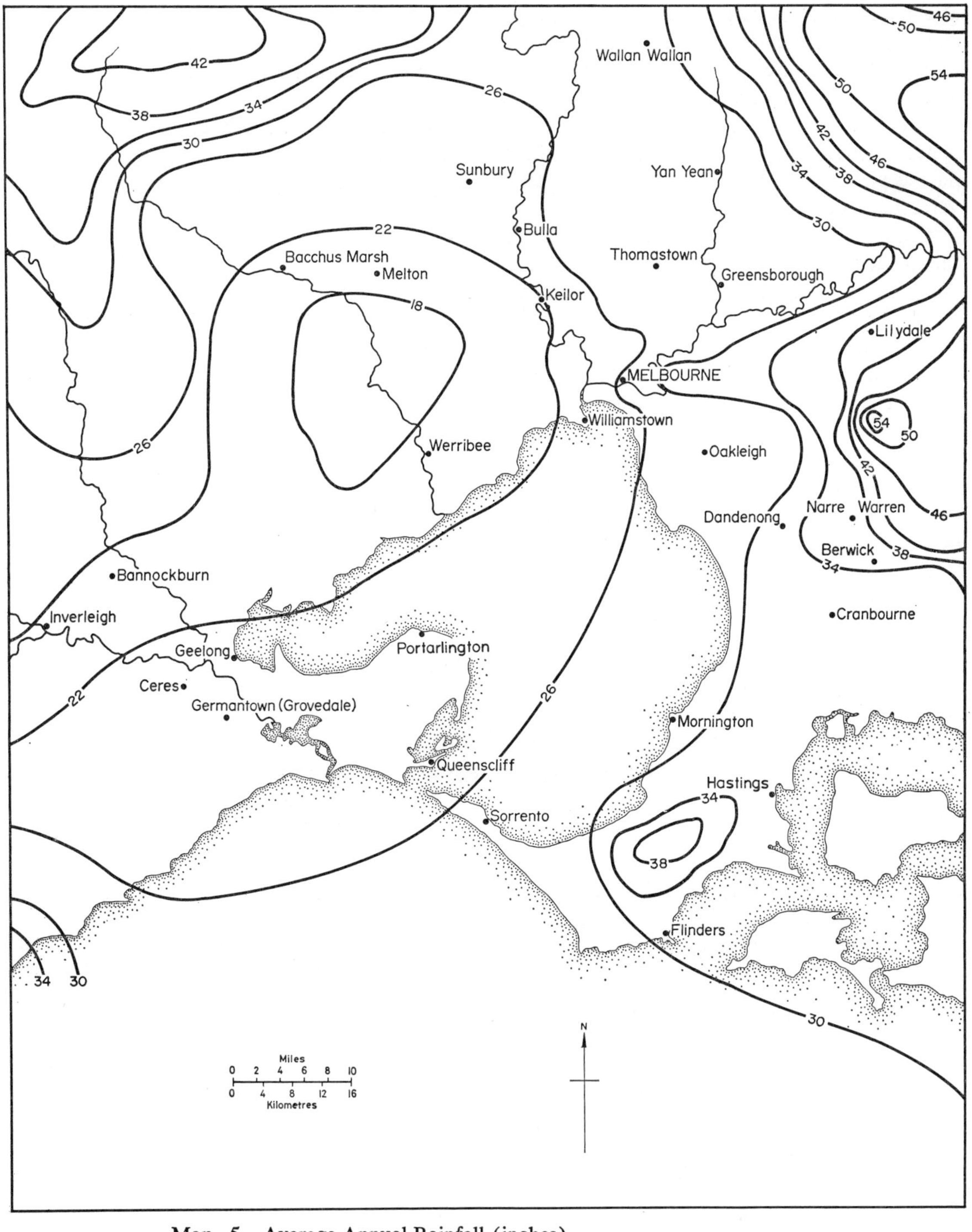

Map 5 Average Annual Rainfall (inches)

Bureau of Meteorology (Australia), *Rainfall Statistics, Victoria,* standard period normals (1931–60) used; Bureau of Meteorology, *Results of Rainfall Observations Made in Victoria* (supplementary volume)

at a maximum, but as summer approaches, plants flower and die off, and by the end of summer the countryside is brown and dry. The limiting factors for agricultural production are the lack of water during the drier months and the low temperatures during winter.

But there is considerable variation in the average climatic conditions. The average annual rainfall varies from over 54 inches in the eastern hill country to 18 inches on the plains on the north-west shores of the bay (see map 5). The year to year variation, too, can be as high as 50 per cent.

Total yearly rainfall figures are only a limited guide to the adequacy of the rainfall for plant growth because of the uneven distribution of the rainfall during the year, and the varying losses from evaporation. A more meaningful guide can be obtained by comparing the rainfall in any one month with the evaporation of water from the soil. Clearly in the hottest months evaporation from the soil will be high, and if there is not sufficient rain to compensate for this, plants will die through lack of water. In any month the effectiveness of the rainfall for plant growth will depend on the amount of rain, the rate of evaporation and the amount of water the plants need for growth. Prescott and Thomas[8] have devised a formula which relates rainfall to evaporation from a free water surface (a quantity more easily measured than evaporation from the soil) to give an index of effective rainfall.

The formula is $P/E^{0\cdot75}$

where P = monthly rainfall

E = monthly evaporation from a free water surface

When $P/E^{0\cdot75} = 0\cdot4$, soil water is sufficient for the break of the season, i.e. the start of growth

When $P/E^{0\cdot75} = 0\cdot8$, soil water is sufficient for the growth of vegetation of low transpiration or for the start of drainage through bare soil

Different plants have different soil water requirements for growth and hence this relationship is an approximate guide only; for example, the minimum value for the growth of present-day wheat varieties in southern Australia is usually accepted as 0·54.

Using this formula the effectiveness of the average monthly rainfall at various stations has been calculated and the results are given in table 1. Also shown are the average periods during which minimum temperatures of 36°F and 32°F occur. As with soil moisture, different plants have different temperature requirements for growth, but in this table it can be assumed that plant growth is retarded and light frosts occur during the periods in which minimum temperatures of 36°F are indicated, and that with temperatures of 32°F there is little or no active growth and heavy frosts occur.

From the information in table 1 it can be seen that for the six stations indicated in the western half of the region, namely Queenscliff, Geelong, Bannockburn, Werribee, Bacchus Marsh and Sunbury, the rainfall is sufficient for plants to grow well for seven months and moderately for a further four months of the year, growth only ceasing through lack of water during January, the middle of summer. For Melbourne, Yan Yean and Mornington, and in general for the country lying

Table 1
Effective Rainfall and Minimum Temperatures at Selected Stations

E.R. = months during which the ratio $\frac{P}{E^{0 \cdot 75}}$ is on the average:

$<0{\cdot}4$ = O (no growth)

$0{\cdot}4 - 0{\cdot}8$ = I (break to moderate growth)

$>0{\cdot}8$ = X (good growth)

36°F = average period during which minimum temperatures of 36°F occur

32°F = average period during which minimum temperatures of 32°F occur

(hatched bar) = no occurrence some years (2–5 in 10)

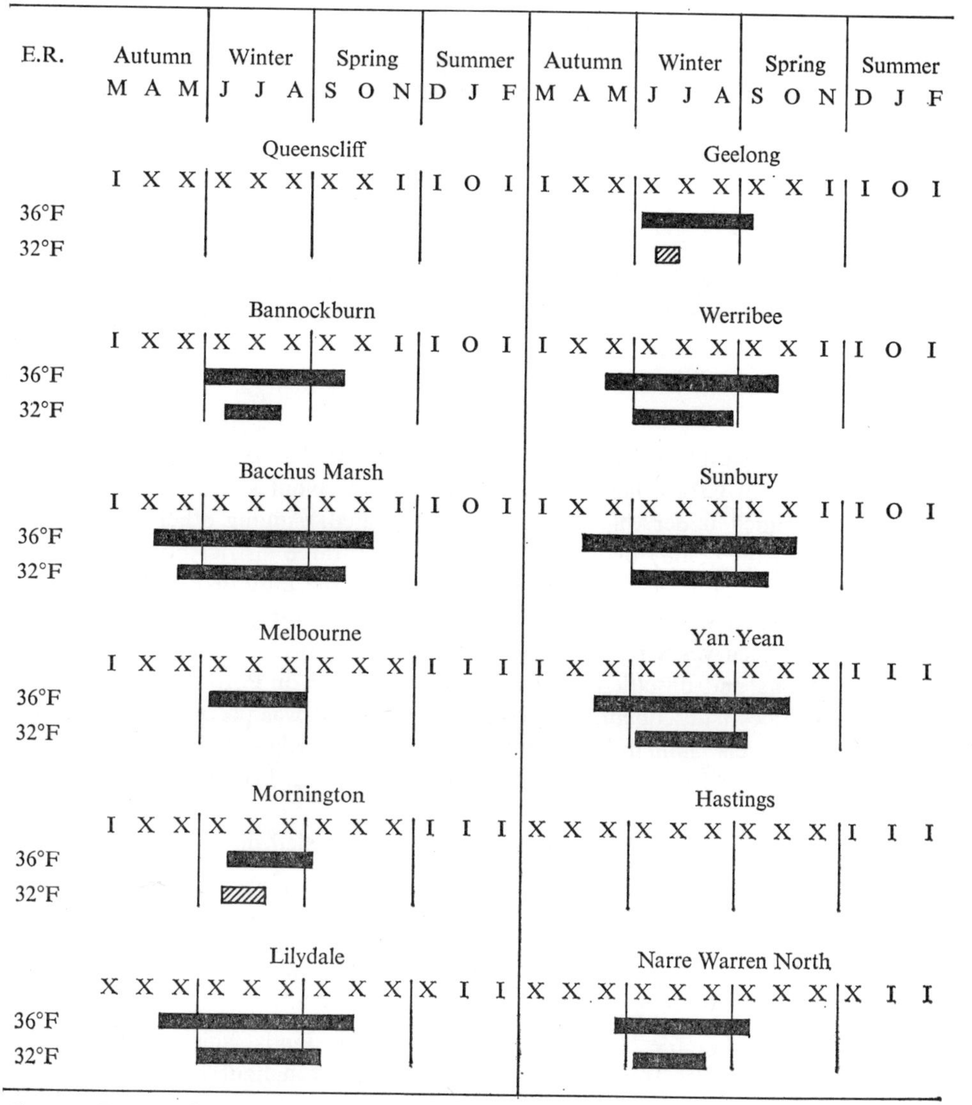

E.R.	Autumn			Winter			Spring			Summer		
	M	A	M	J	J	A	S	O	N	D	J	F
Queenscliff	I	X	X	X	X	X	X	X	I	I	O	I
Geelong	I	X	X	X	X	X	X	X	I	I	O	I
Bannockburn	I	X	X	X	X	X	X	X	I	I	O	I
Werribee	I	X	X	X	X	X	X	X	I	I	O	I
Bacchus Marsh	I	X	X	X	X	X	X	X	I	I	O	I
Sunbury	I	X	X	X	X	X	X	X	I	I	O	I
Melbourne	I	X	X	X	X	X	X	X	X	I	I	I
Yan Yean	I	X	X	X	X	X	X	X	X	I	I	I
Mornington	I	X	X	X	X	X	X	X	X	I	I	I
Hastings	X	X	X	X	X	X	X	X	X	I	I	I
Lilydale	X	X	X	X	X	X	X	X	X	X	I	I
Narre Warren North	X	X	X	X	X	X	X	X	X	X	I	I

Sources: Bureau of Meteorology, *Rainfall Statistics, Victoria*; standard period normals (1931–60) used; C. E. Hounam, *Evaporation in Australia*; Bureau of Meteorology, *Monthly Evaporation in Australia*; J. C. Foley, *Frost in the Australian Region*

between the 26- and 30-inch isohyets,* the rainfall is sufficient for good growth during eight months of the year, and for moderate growth during the remaining four months. Still further to the east, at Lilydale and Narre Warren North, in the foot-hills of the Dandenong Ranges, the rainfall is sufficient for good growth during ten months of the year and for moderate growth during the remaining two months of January and February.

Frost incidence also progressively increases from no frost, on the average, at Queenscliff and Hastings, to over six months of frost at Bacchus Marsh and Sunbury, the stations farthest away from Bass Strait. Therefore during the months when soil water is adequate for good plant growth, growth is nevertheless retarded or halted by low temperatures the farther inland one moves from Bass Strait. This is modified only slightly on the shores of Port Phillip Bay, as indicated by the frost incidence at Melbourne.

Thus the west–east increase in rainfall effectiveness is confounded by a south–north increase in frost incidence and severity, so that the area with the longest growing season is south-east of the bay, the Mornington Peninsula, and the area with the shortest growing season is north-west of the bay, near Bacchus Marsh. The range is from a twelve-month growing season (with nine months for good growth) at Hastings, to just over six months (with one month for good growth) at Bacchus Marsh.

Unfamiliar weather conditions were a major problem for the first settlers, and these variations in growing season within the region were learnt only through trial and error over a number of years, as will be seen in chapter 2.

DEFINITION

In 1846 the imperial parliament in Great Britain passed an Act to regulate the sale and occupation of Crown land within the Australian colonies, and in March 1847 Orders in Council under this Act were promulgated. Among other things these Orders divided the colony of New South Wales into three districts for the purpose of land alienation—the settled, the intermediate and the unsettled districts. Within these districts land was to be made available for lease for periods of up to one, seven and fourteen years respectively. The implementation of these Orders within the intermediate and unsettled districts of the southern or Port Phillip District of New South Wales (subsequently the colony of Victoria) was postponed, but within the settled districts annual leases were granted. Nevertheless all three districts became significant administrative areas for purposes of land occupation and alienation.

Two contiguous areas defined as being within the settled districts were:

> The lands which may be within a distance of twenty-five miles, to be measured or reckoned from any point of the corporate limits of the town of Melbourne in the county of Bourke.
>
> The lands which may be within the distance of fifteen miles from any point of the outward limits of the town of Geelong, in the county of Grant.[9]

Also included within the settled districts were: 'The lands which lie within the distance of three miles from any part of the sea, throughout the extent of the Colony, measured in a straight line.'

* lines drawn on a map through places having equal amounts of rainfall

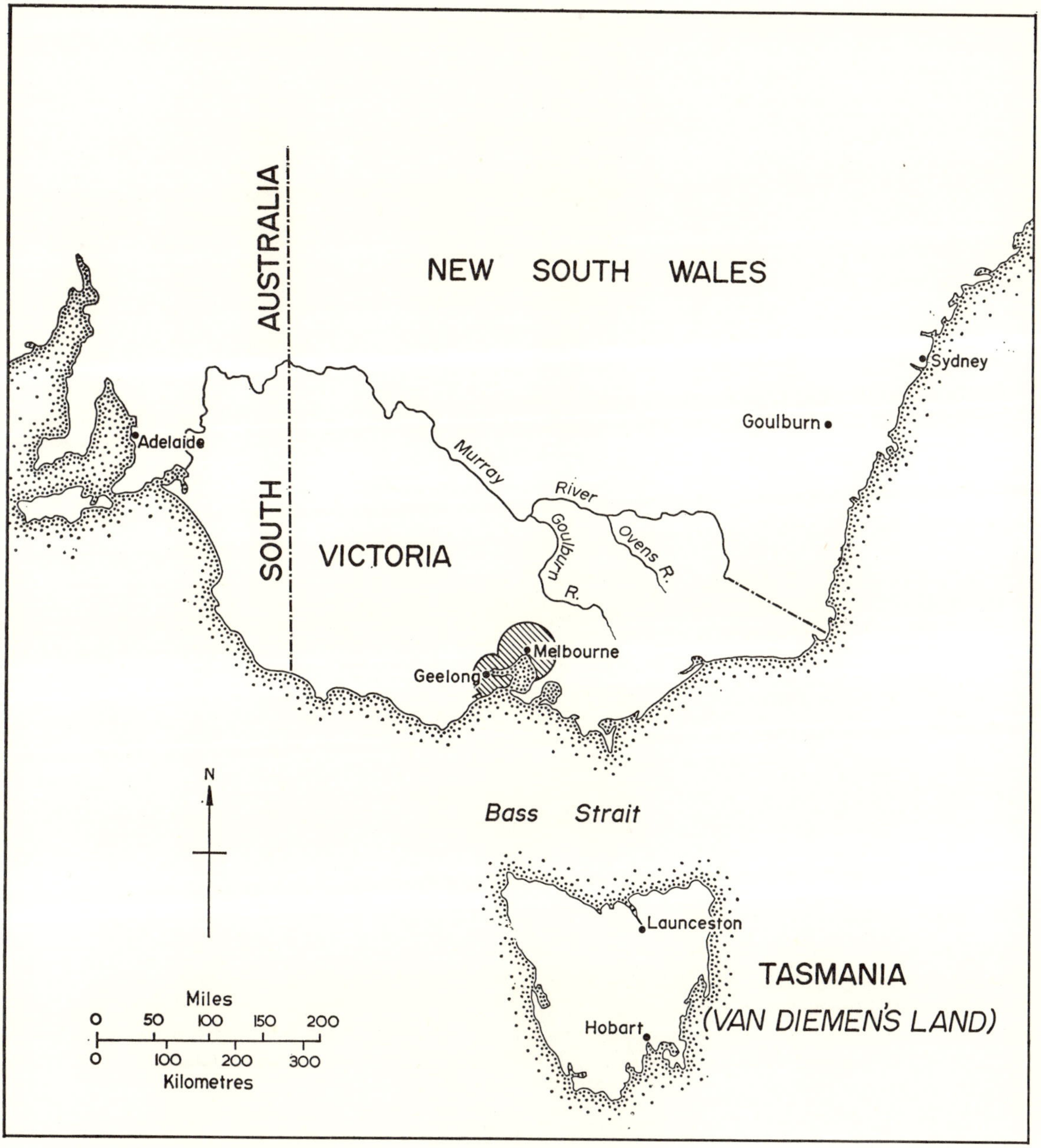

Map 6 Settled Districts of Melbourne and Geelong
H.R.A., ser. 1, vol. 25, p. 431

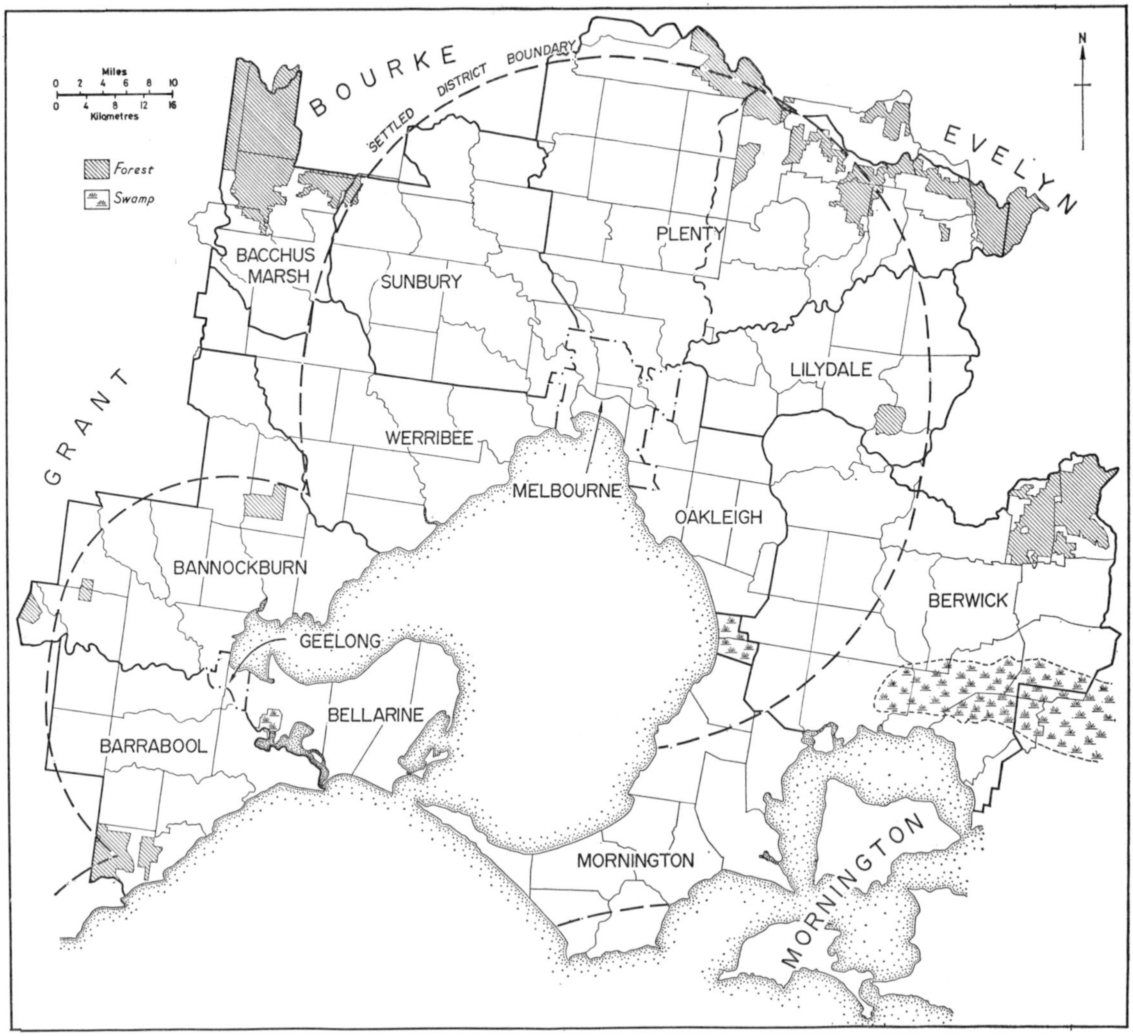

Map 7 Parish Boundaries, and Division Boundaries Based on the Grouping of the 1881 Municipalities

Lands and Survey Department (Victoria), *County Bourke* (Melbourne, 1919), *County Evelyn* (Melbourne, 1928), *County Grant* (Melbourne, 1932), *County Mornington* (Melbourne, 1926); *Port Phillip Government Gazette*, 8 May 1850

These areas constituting the settled districts of Melbourne and Geelong (see map 6), although apparently arbitrarily defined, do cover a natural physiographic region and delimit quite well the region of more intensive agricultural activity around the two main urban centres. This latter point is due in part to the very existence of the boundary only twelve years after the first permanent occupation of the region by European people.

The settled districts' boundary was important in leasing land, but at the same time the parishes (areas of about thirty square miles) remained the basic land units and these were grouped within larger counties bounded by natural features. The parishes were surveyed into square-mile sections and these parish sections formed the basis for land titles and also for census and agricultural statistics until the end of the 1860s. Thereafter the recently defined local government areas assumed increasing importance, and statistics were collected within these areas. The importance of the parish then diminished to its value as a basis for land titles.

In order to obtain a series of comparable statistics and to be able to relate them to land settlement, a compromise of boundaries has been necessary. Therefore I have selected a group of parishes, the boundary of which coincides as far as possible with that of a group of municipalities and both of which approximate to the boundary of the settled districts. The whole region so defined has been subdivided in a similar manner to give eleven rural and two urban divisions, the latter representing the urban areas of Geelong and Melbourne. Although there are boundary discrepancies and these increase in moving from the region as a whole to a single division, they tend to occur in areas of low population density and are not sufficiently important to affect the conclusions arrived at in the following discussion.

For convenience I have called the whole region the Port Phillip region and have named the various divisions thus (see map 7):

Rural Bellarine Barrabool Bannockburn Bacchus Marsh Werribee Sunbury Plenty (Plenty West and Plenty East) Lilydale Oakleigh Berwick Mornington

Urban Geelong Melbourne

2 : Settlement 1835–1848

The existence of Port Phillip Bay had been known in Van Diemen's Land for some years, and following Hume and Hovell's journey interest in the Port Phillip country was reawakened. By the early 1830s the wool market was buoyant and fat sheep and cattle were being exported from New South Wales to the Hobart meat market. Sheep were valuable animals and good sheep pasturage was to be prized. All the readily available land in Van Diemen's Land had been occupied and following the reports of good pasture across Bass Strait various groups of settlers began to consider shipping sheep there. Finally in May 1835 one group of wealthy settlers sent an expedition to Port Phillip Bay to investigate. The group was pleased with what it found and quickly dispatched sheep across the strait. Immediately 'the place became notorious, and all eyes were set towards a country possessing what seemed to the Van Diemen's Land settler the source of unbounded wealth, namely, unlimited pasturage for sheep, and that of the finest kind. Great numbers of sheep were soon sent over . . .'[1] By November 1836 there were at least forty-three settlers' establishments dotted around the bay and along the rivers. The male population was in excess of 178, and already 23 women with about the same number of children had crossed to the new settlement.[2] The following month the first overlanders arrived with stock from New South Wales, and three years later a ship carrying new settlers arrived directly from Leith in Scotland.

In November 1836 John Batman, the leader of the initial expedition, was well established on the Yarra River. He had twenty acres planted to wheat, barley, oats, maize, potatoes and garden, lived in a six-roomed weatherboard house and ran 5300 sheep, 30 head of cattle and 12 horses, although of these 1650 sheep and 5 head of cattle belonged to other people. With Batman were thirteen men, two women and four children. More typical of the group as a whole was John Aitken who had arrived in March 1836. He lived in a tent and with the assistance of three other men looked after a thousand sheep and a horse as agent for himself and a Mr Bryant. Of the twenty-eight people reporting sheep in their possession at this time, twenty-two of them were either partly or wholly acting as agents for other people or were in partnership with one or more other persons.[3] For the time being the principals in these arrangements tended to remain in Van Diemen's Land. As Captain Lonsdale, the Police Magistrate at Port Phillip, noted in February 1837 after about another 180 people had arrived since the census, 'scarcely any of them are persons of respectability . . . The respectable portion of those who have stock in the district have not yet made this their residence.'[4] Port Phillip was still only a grazing annex to Van Diemen's Land, but the settlement was taking shape and growing rapidly.

Batman had noted the site of Melbourne as being 'the place for a Village' when he first visited the area in 1835.[5] After he settled there, others did likewise so that by March 1837 when Governor Bourke visited the settlement from Sydney he found 'on the spot selected for a settlement by Mr. Batman on the banks of the Yarra River at the head of the Inland Sea called Port Phillip, an assembled Population consisting of from sixty to seventy families.' In a letter to Lord Glenelg he continued,

> The situation appearing to be well chosen, I directed a Town to be immediately laid out, which . . . has received the name of Melbourne . . . I directed 100 allotments to be measured and offered for sale at Melbourne on the first of this month [June]. I also directed a few allotments to be put up in Williams Town on the shore of Hobson's Bay, where stores and Commissariat Establishments are likely to be soon formed.[6]

Table 2

Total Population in 1841

Location	Persons
COUNTY BOURKE	
Rural	
West of Sydney Road	
Farming	482
Non-farming	39
Total	521
East of Sydney Road and north of Yarra River	
Farming	1 220
Non-farming	390
Total	1 610
South of Yarra River	
Farming	250
Non-farming	272
Total	522
Urban	
Williamstown	326
South Melbourne	280
Melbourne township	4 479
COUNTY GRANT	
Rural	
Outside Geelong	336
Urban	
Geelong township	454
GRAND TOTAL	8 528

Source: Census, 1841

Rural Industry in the Port Phillip Region

By March 1841 Melbourne had developed into an infant commercial and administrative centre with a population of 4479 in the township of Melbourne itself as then defined. Of these people only 208 claimed to be in any way employed in agriculture. A further 326 and 280 people lived in Williamstown and South Melbourne respectively (none of whom were farming), and the urban population of Geelong at this time was 454. Therefore, within the first six years of settlement, the urban population in the Port Phillip region had reached 5539 and the rural population 2989, a total for the region of 8528 people (see table 2).[7] The trend continued and, despite a depression in the early 1840s, by 1846 the population of Melbourne was 10 954, of Geelong 1370, and of the rural areas of Counties Bourke and Grant 8877.[8]

By 1841 the rural areas had already acquired the characteristic of a hinterland to a major urban centre whose population numerically dominated the region, a feature maintained and emphasized as the population of Melbourne grew continuously for the next forty years. Melbourne became the administrative and commercial centre for the whole of Victoria, and the major link with the rest of the world—the gateway for immigrants and commerce. Here the colonial administration established its headquarters, and from here land alienation was administered. Concurrently stores, banks, agencies and all the commercial ventures catering for the needs of the squatters were established. The squatters, who quickly spread throughout the future colony of Victoria, came to Melbourne to attend to their business with government officials and local businessmen. The presence of one group lent immediacy to the presence of the other, and soon yet more people were able to find employment catering for those already present in the growing town. It was towards satisfying the needs of this population for food and fodder that much of the agriculture of the Port Phillip region was in time to be directed, resulting in diversified rural enterprises which were to displace, in some areas at least, the initial motivating enterprise of sheep grazing.

DIFFERENTIATION OF LAND USE AND LABOUR 1841

From the first year of settlement in the Port Phillip region some attempt had been made to cultivate the land and grow grain and vegetables for the people looking after sheep or living in the infant town of Melbourne. In November 1836 there were ten people without sheep who had land sown to wheat, oats, barley, potatoes and other vegetables, and of the twenty-eight people running sheep, seventeen also had land under cultivation. Nevertheless, cultivation was not extensive and two years later Captain Lonsdale had to report that 'there is scarcely any land under cultivation in this district, a few settlers have put in a small quantity of grain, but . . . in no instance sufficient for the individuals consumption on his station. There is no grain remaining unconsumed as we have as yet obtained our supply of flour either from Sydney or Van Diemen's Land.'[9]

Even so, by 1841 a differentiation of occupation and land use was evident; in the County of Bourke more than twice as many men were employed in forms of agriculture other than sheep grazing, as in sheep grazing. This differentiation, no doubt, was brought about by the proximity of the rapidly growing town of Melbourne with its increasing potential as a market centre for hay, grain and vegetables. The nearby squatters, too, would have benefited from a supply of these commodities.

The household schedules for the rural sector of the County of Bourke, compiled during the 1841 census, give an indication of the activities on the various holdings. For the purposes of table 3 a household whose schedule listed any person as being engaged in any form of agriculture has been classified as a 'farming' household. Where no such person was recorded the household has been classified as 'non-farming'. From the nature of the census this classification was desirable, but it must be emphasized that 'farming' households include, for example, any gentleman's residence where a gardener was employed and conversely a farm will be included in the 'non-farming' group where the farmer worked by himself and listed himself on his household schedule under 'Land Proprietors, Merchants, Bankers and Professional Persons'.

Table 3
Civil Condition and Occupation of Males Aged Fourteen and Older on 'Farming' Holdings, 1841
(indicating the number of holdings on which males in each category were to be found)

Location	'Farming' holdings		Civil condition				Occupation						
	Total holdings	Total males 14+	Ex-convicts, now free		Bond		Shepherds		Stockmen and cultivators		Land proprietors		Other males
			Holdings	Males	Holdings	Males	Holdings	Males	Holdings	Males	Holdings	Males	
West of Sydney Road	47	380	3	6	5	12	39	204	24	50	42	62	64
East of Sydney Road and north of Yarra River	106	644	38	97	27	53	6	11	104	457	56	75	101
South of Yarra River	25	143	4	10	6	23	8	22	22	42	9	9	70
Total	178	1167	45	113	38	88	53	237	150	549	107	146	235

Source: Census, 1841

On the assumption that males aged fourteen and older were the workforce for the farming community, the material for table 3 has been collated from the returns of all the 'farming' households. This table shows that sheep grazing was usually carried on separately from cropping and other forms of agriculture; only 25 of the 178 holdings simultaneously employed different people under the two categories. This does not exclude from the runs a little cultivation or the odd cow for homestead use, but on the majority of runs these activities were so minimal that a man was not employed specifically for them. Similarly some of the cropping farms may have had a few sheep, but this was unusual.

The absence of sheep from the cropping holdings resulted from the nature of the initial settlement. The aim was to graze sheep, and any cultivation on a station was merely a sideline to supplement the rations. As will be discussed below, grazing at this time was a very extensive type of agriculture with about one sheep to every three acres; conversely cropping was intensive and mainly dependent on hand methods. Cropping commenced with the cultivation of small areas of virgin soil to produce a few acres of wheat or potatoes for immediate consumption. A small area of land would be roughly fenced in for the purpose, to protect the crop from wandering animals. Under these circumstances the idea of an integrated agriculture was quite foreign—for the time being it was quite unnecessary. Virgin soil produced reasonable crops, bullocks were used for draught and the butchers' meat was brought out from town or bought from a neighbouring grazier. It was only after land ceased to be so readily available, when farms acquired finite boundaries and the land had to be recropped, that this system of separating livestock from cropping was no longer satisfactory, but by then it had become traditional.

Because of this differentiation, the rural area of the County of Bourke can be divided into three areas according to the predominating type of farming. Most of the cropping was carried on to the north of the Yarra River and east of the Sydney road (i.e. the dray track leading to Sydney), particularly on the cracking clay soils close to Melbourne in the vicinity of the Moonee Ponds, Merri and Darebin Creeks and the Plenty River. To the west of the Sydney road, on the hard red plains, sheep grazing predominated and probably there was some cattle grazing too, rather than cropping. South of the Yarra River the picture is not so clear. In the timbered ranges to the south more emphasis was placed on cattle than sheep, and since stockmen in charge of cattle, and people cropping land were listed together in the census, it is not possible to separate them.

Thus this early differentiation of land use also reflected man's response to the natural environment around Melbourne. The more easily worked of the heavier soils were selected for cropping, the poor sands and the heaviest clays were avoided. The sheep were grazed on the open grasslands with a few flocks penetrating the wetter more timbered areas, but these latter areas were avoided by the sheepmen and were mainly left vacant until cattle were introduced. Following the growth of a market and the identification of the most favourable land for cultivation, the differential location of grazing and cropping was emphasized, and an impetus given to cropping, by the government selling the freehold to the land north of the Yarra, and similarly west of Geelong, while retaining the remaining land and licensing it for grazing purposes only (see map 8).

But the differentiation of land use was only one aspect of a rapidly evolving scene of increasing complexity. The separation between grazing and cropping was further strengthened by the differences between the two groups of people responsible for them. Of all the adult males on the holdings to the north of the Yarra River, 23 per cent were either former convicts or were still bonded, and people in these categories were to be found on 48 per cent of the holdings. The labour requirements for cropping were being met, at least in part, by the employment of convicts and emancipists. By contrast only 5 per cent of the men to the west of the Sydney road on the sheep holdings were or had been convicts, and of the twelve men still bonded, eight were working on the one holding. This is despite the fact that an average of 5·2 men were employed per holding (paid or otherwise) for grazing and only 4·4 per holding for cropping. There were differences, too, in religious adherence. Among the adult males in the cropping area there were proportionately more Roman Catholics and fewer Anglicans and Presbyterians than among the adult males in the grazing area; the respective percentages were 18 per cent Roman Catholics, 56 per cent Anglicans, and 19 per cent Presbyterians in the cropping area, and 15 per cent Roman Catholics, 58 per cent Anglicans and 25 per cent Presbyterians in the grazing area west of the Sydney road. The number of females per 100 males of all ages was also greater in the cropping area where there were 46 females per 100 males as compared with 22 females per 100 males in the grazing area.

In other words, within the first six years of settlement farming communities of different social status and undoubtedly different education and income had developed. It is probably not too much to suggest that here already in the cropping area was the beginning of a relatively depressed sector of the rural community—a future centre of poverty. The persistence of some of these characteristics in this cropping area will be discussed further in subsequent chapters. It remains here to discuss the influences that may account for the differences in the nature of the two communities (the smaller and less differentiated community south of the Yarra River will be ignored).

Scottish men and capital predominated in the initial settlement of the Port Phillip region from Van Diemen's Land. These settlers could bring stock across Bass Strait. Bonded convicts, however, were not allowed to leave the island, so messages were soon sent to the settlers' partners or agents in the United Kingdom to arrange for emigrants to be sent out. Pressure on the government for assistance followed and the first ship with bounty emigrants arrived directly from the United Kingdom in January 1840. Meanwhile the first sales of Port Phillip land were taking place in Sydney, and already numbers of Sydney people had left for Port Phillip. Since the region at that time was part of the colony of New South Wales, convicts bonded in New South Wales could be taken to Port Phillip. Van Diemen's Land, however, was a separate colony and convicts bonded there were not permitted to leave that island. Therefore the Van Diemen's Land settlers were first on the scene and selected the choicest grazing areas; unable to bring convicts with them, their labour force was supplied by free immigrants from England and Scotland. When the Sydney settlers arrived, the best grazing land had been occupied, but they did have the easiest access to the land sales in Sydney and by purchasing at these sales or later at the Melbourne sales they could still obtain land close to the new settlement. Also they could bring their convicts (and former convicts) with them to work this land. It is, therefore, very likely that Sydney people were predominant among the owners of the cropping farms in 1841, although the direct evidence is at present too meagre to allow confirmation of this. If this was the case, the high proportion of convicts and emancipists on the cropping holdings would be a logical result.

Another influence, probably contributing to the differences in the workforce, resulted from the social status ascribed to the farm labourer on the one hand and to the stockman on the other in England and Scotland at this time. The situation tended to vary from county to county but on the whole, despite the possession of considerable practical farming skills, the farm labourer 'was given starvation wages, overlong hours of work, disgraceful housing, little or no education, and was generally treated as of lowly estate and a being of no account, an object of charity, perhaps, but with no prospect of improving his lot.'[10]

By contrast the stockmen—cowmen, shepherds and horsemen—often held responsible positions on the farms and had yearly contracts and steady wages. 'They felt themselves in a much superior position to that of the day labourers . . .'[11] With an English or Scottish background, freemen who had emigrated to the colony in search of better material opportunities would be more likely to seek work associated with livestock than with cropping. Convicts on the other hand would be assigned to the work of lowest status. At Port Phillip, while again allowing for variation, the convention soon developed whereby farm labourers, ploughmen and sheep-washers tended to be employed at a weekly rate, reapers, mowers, threshers and shearers at a piece-work rate, and shepherds, stock-keepers and hut-keepers at an annual rate. To this day, of all the rural activities, grazing is still held in the highest social esteem.

To social pressures of this nature must be added the simple fact that the Australian colonies were known in the United Kingdom for the production of wool, and this type of production would be uppermost in the minds of many immigrants, particularly where the immigrants were adventurous young men unencumbered with family responsibilities and prepared to take risks in pursuing the squatting life. In this they would be encouraged by the squatters who tended to prefer single men since they were less expensive to keep. Those with wives and families would be more likely to stay close to the city with its greater safety and amenities, quite apart from any deterrent from the squatters. Furthermore it was believed that anyone taking up a cropping farm needed to have a large family to assist him. Whatever his former visions, such a life could well have offered an acceptable alternative to the family man on his arrival in the colony.

The basis of the major differences in the rural scene had been laid by 1841. Already by that date numbers of immigrants—some with considerable capital—were arriving directly from the United Kingdom. In time these people were to dominate numerically those who had come from the older colonies. But the early influences persisted for at least the next decade. The squatters continued to cultivate a few acres of land in their 'cultivation paddocks' but their potential wealth lay in their sheep and cattle on the open grasslands or in the wetter gum country, their livestock herded or shepherded and shorn by free, single and adventurous English and Scottish immigrants. At the same time on the more workable soils north of Melbourne and west of Geelong, the less prosperous labourers and families grew grain crops and vegetables to supply the expanding markets in the two towns. Sheep were absent from these farms. To understand the separate development of these two types of agriculture during the 1840s it is necessary to look at the system of land tenure, with its many ramifications, and the grazing and cropping practices of the time. During these years grazing was primarily associated with the licensed occupation of Crown land, and cropping with freehold land.

OCCUPATION OF CROWN LAND

In August 1835, when Batman's activities at Port Phillip were brought to the notice of Governor Bourke in Sydney, the Governor issued a proclamation declaring Batman's party to be trespassers.[12] And when the other settlers, who immediately followed Batman, first sought grants or a legal right of occupancy to the land at Port Phillip, their requests were refused. The standard reply from the Colonial Secretary to private applications in December 1835 and January 1836 was that 'the recent occupation of land [at Port Phillip] has been reported to His Majesty's Government and . . . it is impossible to give . . . permission to occupy land upon any terms whatever.'[13]

But within a year Bourke received permission from London to permit settlement, and an announcement in the *New South Wales Government Gazette*, 9 September 1836, brought the 'vacant Crown Lands, adjacent to the shores of Port Phillip, under the same Regulations as are now in force for the alienation of Crown Lands in other parts of New South Wales . . .' and appointed Captain William Lonsdale to be Police Magistrate for that District.

This announcement meant that as from 1 January 1837 anyone grazing the land at Port Phillip should hold an annual £10 licence, under the provisions of the Act of the New South Wales Council, 7 Wm IV, No. 4, and the regulations of 1 October 1836. But in practice in January 1837 the Colonial Secretary was replying to private enquiries for licences that

> it is not intended to issue Licences for depasturing the Crown Lands at Port Phillip for the present—but the Police Magistrate has been instructed not to interfere with existing occupations until the necessary arrangements have been completed for bringing the lands to sale unless it be necessary for the maintenance of good order in the District.[14]

This continued to be the case so far as the Police Magistrate was concerned until 16 June 1838 when he wrote to the Colonial Secretary, 'I conclude that the direction . . . "that it is not proposed to issue licences for the occupation of land at present" is annulled by the arrival of Mr. Peter Snodgrass as Commissioner of Crown Lands and that squatters are now to obtain licences.'[15] Snodgrass, however, had apparently understood that the squatters should already be licensed, because on 23 June 1838 he wrote from Melbourne to the Colonial Secretary that many people were without licences. This he partly attributed to the great difficulty of making payment for the licences in Sydney, as required under the Act, and suggested that an office for payment be established in Melbourne.[16]

The matter was finally clarified for all by a new Act, 2 Vict., No. 27, of 22 March 1839, and its associated regulations and proclamation of 21 May 1839.[17] This Act stipulated that as from 1 July 1839 all people grazing Crown lands beyond the limits of location were to hold a licence which was to be renewed annually and would cost £10 per annum. On 1 January and 1 July each year the licensee was to make a return of all the livestock he was grazing, which would form the basis for an annual assessment on stock of 1d per sheep, 3d per head of horned cattle, and 6d per horse, to be paid in addition to the licence fee. The commissioners of Crown lands were responsible for the working of the Act. This licence gave the settlers a right to graze a specified area of land but nothing else. Any improvements were at the licensee's own risk and the land could be resumed and sold at any time the government saw fit to extend the limits of location.

The limits of location had been defined in 1829, and consisted of an area in New South Wales centred on Sydney and divided into nineteen counties. Freehold land could be obtained only within these limits, and different regulations related to the occupation (for grazing) of the Crown land there. Grazing land was available annually from 1831 at a fee of £1 per section of 640 acres until 1840 when the fee was raised to £5 per section. By contrast the area beyond the limits, licensed under the £10 fee, was unrestricted until 1844 when a nominal limit of twenty square miles was imposed. For the purposes of administering the 1839 Act the Crown lands beyond the limits of location were divided into districts. The Port Phillip region (as defined in chapter 1) fell within the Port Phillip District which was defined as 'The whole of the Lands comprised in the District lying to the south of the main range, between the River Ovens and Goulburn, and adjacent to Port Phillip.'[18]

In the Port Phillip region, from the first settlement in 1835, to 1839, the settlers were in possession of the land they grazed and did not expect to be evicted from it immediately, but few held even a licence to reassure them of their tenure. From July 1839 their occupation was more regularized but, if anything, more tenuous. During the previous year country land near Melbourne and Geelong, as against suburban blocks, had been sold for the first time. Since all freehold land around Sydney had for many years been strictly within the limits of location, the settlers feared that an area similarly defined would soon be proclaimed around Melbourne and Geelong, thus increasing the cost of occupying this land for grazing from £10 per year for an unlimited area to £1 per square mile (£5 in 1840), or forcing them to purchase the land in order to retain control of it. Early in 1839 this prompted a number of settlers to move their flocks farther inland away from the towns.[19]

On 1 July 1840 the Port Phillip District, as defined in 1839, was divided in two —the Portland Bay District to the west of the Werribee River and the Western Port District to the east of the Werribee River. Still the Crown lands within the Port Phillip region remained under the £10 licence system. But land survey was under way. The system used was the same as that adopted in Sydney, namely division into counties bounded by natural features, the land within the counties being surveyed into a square-mile grid, approximately thirty square miles constituting a parish, which in turn was given a specific name.

As early as February 1838 the term 'County Bourke' was used officially, but another four years were to pass before any attempt was made to declare any Port Phillip land within the limits of location. On 25 December 1842 Governor Gipps noted that

> all county land is elsewhere considered to be *within the Boundaries* of Location and consequently no county land can be held under a squatting licence but must be held under licences of another kind which are offered periodically for sale at auction—the upset price being £5 per section per annum.
>
> As soon as the Boundaries of the three Counties at Port Phillip [Grant, Bourke and Normanby] are definitely settled, it will be necessary to introduce the same system there —and the County lands will then as a matter of course be taken out of the jurisdiction of the Commissioners of Crown Lands who are appointed to act beyond the Borders.[20]

Finally on 13 September 1843 a proclamation further subdivided the Port Phillip District for the purposes of the 1839 Act. In defining the new Portland Bay District as being bounded by County Grant in the east, and the Western Port District as as being bounded by the eastern and northern limits of County Bourke, it effectively excluded these two counties from the operation of the Act, and the regulations applicable to land within the limits of location could be applied to them. However, it must be emphasized that in spite of this land legislation some thousands of acres of grazing land within Counties Bourke and Grant continued to be held under £10 licences by the same people who held them in 1843, or their successors, simply by

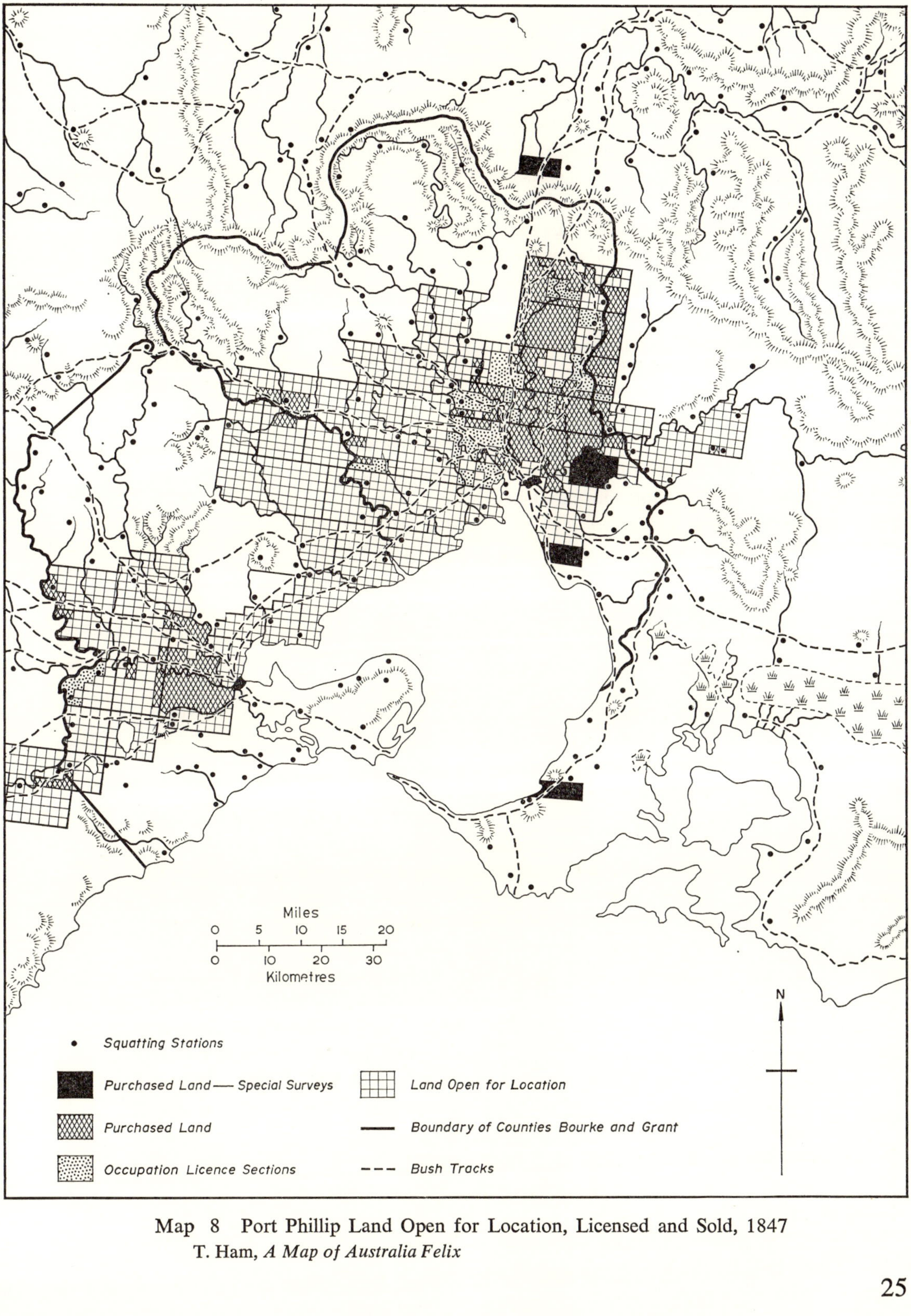

Map 8 Port Phillip Land Open for Location, Licensed and Sold, 1847
T. Ham, *A Map of Australia Felix*

their renewing the licences up until 1849, and despite some of this land being within areas long since surveyed into parishes and pronounced open for location.[21]

After 1843 people wishing to obtain grazing rights to Crown land in the areas surveyed and open for location in Counties Bourke and Grant had to obtain a licence at auction, under the 21 August 1841 regulations. The land was surveyed and advertised by the Crown as it saw fit or at the instigation of a private individual, and then the licence for each 640-acre section was auctioned with a minimum price of £5 per year. The licence conferred the exclusive right of occupancy for the purpose of grazing livestock, but the land could be sold by the Crown at any time and had to be vacated at a month's notice. This system, too, continued in practice until 1849. Meanwhile the land outside Counties Bourke and Grant, but within the Port Phillip region, continued to be held under £10 licences.

In summary the majority of people grazed Crown land in the Port Phillip region without payment of any fee until 1839 when they were obliged to take out a £10 licence for their stations, the boundaries of which were only imprecisely known. Much of the land continued to be held under this system until 1849. But from 1843 onwards new licensees in the areas surveyed and open for location had to obtain their licences at auction and pay a minimum of £5 per 640-acre section annually. This system continued in parallel with the £10 licence system until 1849. The extent of the land held under each system and the land open for location in 1847 is shown in map 8. By far the greater portion of the land was grazed for a fee of £10 per year for 20 000 or more acres plus an assessment on stock.

Before the boundaries of the limits of location around Sydney were even gazetted, the squatters had pushed beyond these bounds in search of fresh pasture for their livestock. With the introduction of the £10 licence system in 1836 the government was simply recognizing what had been fact for some years and conceding that it was unable to confine the free settlers within definite limited bounds when the whole continent waited to be explored and occupied. This system of licensing land occupation had been introduced in response to the exploitative grazing occupation of the land; in turn it was best suited to this form of land use.

By selling land near the towns at Port Phillip, and in 1843 theoretically setting aside further areas from broad-acre squatting, recognition was also given to the growing urban centres and to the potential value these centres could confer on surrounding land. It was for this latter reason that the licensed grazing occupation of the surveyed lands at £5 per square mile was introduced. As will be discussed below, from an agricultural point of view these sections were too small and expensive for large-scale grazing. They could have had a place as grazing land in conjunction with freehold cropping land, but the implied mixed agriculture would have been too advanced for the 1840s. Thus few people made any attempt to obtain £5 licences to the sections, and those who did were probably motivated more by the possibilities of gain from land speculation than from agricultural profit. A few, too, would have taken out these licences to protect more extensive grazing interests.

Therefore throughout the forties the grazing land of the region continued to be occupied under the system of land tenure devised as a token government control during the initial grazing occupancy of virgin country. The short-term licensing of occupation best adapted to the situation in 1835 was still in force in 1848, thirteen years later. During these years some 9000 people settled in the rural areas and a further 12 000 people in the towns. A thriving permanent settlement grew up, experienced a depression in 1841–3, and recovered. The sheep and cattle runs acquired names and finite (if adjustable) boundaries. A licence to a particular run acquired a commercial value, and such licences frequently changed hands as settlers moved farther inland, went bankrupt, died, or decided to seek their fortune in other ways.

The rural situation had changed substantially. Not only in terms of people and livestock, but also in terms of natural vegetation and native fauna. Pastures developed under centuries of kangaroo and emu grazing soon changed under more intensive sheep and cattle grazing. To continue his operations successfully the squatter had to consolidate his position and develop a more viable system of agriculture suited to the changing conditions. Sheds, sheep-washing fixtures and other improvements were needed. And a more permanent place to live was desirable. In short, by 1848 Port Phillip was much more than a grazing annex to Van Diemen's Land, and 'persons of respectability' were making it their home.

The system of land tenure suited to the initial exploitative occupation of the grasslands was not suited to the permanent settlement of thirteen years later. A twelve months' licence with no compensation for improvements was too insecure a tenure on which to establish a viable and permanent station, and was merely serving to prolong the exploitative phase of settlement. On the other hand, purchasing land at £1 per acre was an economically unrealistic way of gaining security on grazing land at this stage of development; furthermore, this was only possible within the areas open for location, with the exception of special surveys. The longer the land was occupied and the closer the station or run was to the towns, the more serious this question of land tenure became for the individual squatter. But this problem was not unique to the Port Phillip squatters; their brothers nearer Sydney faced the same dilemma and had lived with it much longer.

Throughout the 1840s land legislation had been enacted in Sydney (in consultation with London) and events at Port Phillip had had only a very limited effect on the form of the legislation. The details were far more the result of the interplay between conflicting interests of the influential landowners, squatters, emancipists, and government groups in Sydney and in London (where the various groups had their lobbyists). The Port Phillip squatters did contribute to these wrangles[22] but had only a minor voice. Sydney was too far away, and often the squatters had to be represented by proxy. This, however, did not prevent strong feelings arising at times at Port Phillip, and there were various moves for separation from Sydney, though unsuccessful until 1851. It was mainly as a result of the strong feelings aroused in Sydney that effective changes were not implemented in the land tenure system before 1849. The political dissension behind these delays cannot be discussed here, but the importance of the continuing insecurity of tenure in retarding rural development must be stressed since it is an aspect of the land legislation question that is often overlooked.

GRAZING

The Clyde Company's run, Golf Hill, on the Moorabool and Leigh Rivers (partly in the Bannockburn division) was occupied by the resident manager George Russell in 1836 following an exploratory trip from Van Diemen's Land. Russell subsequently acquired a one-eighth interest in this Glasgow-based company founded in 1836 to establish a sheep station at Port Phillip. To stock the station and thereby forestall occupation of the chosen area by other squatters, 3000 recently shorn sheep were purchased in Van Diemen's Land at about 30s per head and shipped across to Port Phillip at a further cost of 5s per head. Later, when John Gardiner arrived overland from New South Wales with the first cattle to reach the settlement, Russell bought ninety-five of his cows at £10 each, together with twenty-two calves. In all, by the end of 1837 the Clyde Company had spent about £7600 establishing its Golf Hill run. The first wool clip, for 1837, consisted of thirty-nine bales (10 023 lb washed) and returned about £750 after deducting shipping and selling costs.[23]

By January 1838 the price of wool was falling and to offset costs the company sold 500 two- to four-tooth ewes to a Hobart Town buyer for 27s 6d each at Geelong. By December 1838 the company's livestock had increased to 5921 sheep and lambs and 208 head of cattle; 12 876 lb of wool were shipped to England for the year 1838 for a net return of about £900, and the expenditures during the year were labour £577, supplies £385, rams £57, miscellaneous £25, totalling £1044.[24]

Thus sheep were shipped from Van Diemen's Land to Port Phillip to grow wool and multiply. The wool was shipped to England for sale and the surplus fat stock back to Van Diemen's Land for the butchers. Most people occupied more land than they needed for their initial flocks, so a rapid natural increase was desirable to stock the land, good young breeding stock being at a premium.

Shepherding was the accepted method of sheep husbandry. One shepherd looked after each flock of 500–1000 sheep by day, keeping them together and protecting them from the attacks of dingoes and from being stolen by Aborigines or unscrupulous Europeans. At night the sheep were yarded into a small enclosure made of brush or rough hurdles and guarded by the hut-keeper, who slept in a watch-box near the sheep, his dog lying close by. During the day the hut-keeper remained in the hut and prepared the meals of mutton, damper and tea for the two shepherds. For this work the shepherds would earn about £30 per annum plus their keep, and the hut-keeper a little less.[25]

The usual months for lambing were April–May and August–September. During the first few years some squatters tried to have three lambings in two years, but one annual lambing proved more successful.[26] Although the squatters wished to increase their flocks rapidly, they could not override nature and ignore the climatic conditions and the breeding seasons of the sheep.

In 1841 Russell expected a lambing percentage in the region of 87 per cent from his older ewes. By January of that year he had a total of 4144 lambs, which represented a 74 per cent survival rate from a combined total of 3981 four-tooth to full-mouth ewes lambed in April and May and 1656 two-tooth ewes lambed in September (excluding ewe deaths). From 72 to 84 rams were kept on the station during this period.[27]

On most stations the main flock was shorn in October, November or December while the lambs were often held over until the following March. Before shearing, the sheep were washed. Miss Anne Drysdale described the scene on her station, Boronggoop, just south-east of Geelong, in 1841.

Tuesday, 12th Octr: . . . All the shearers arrived in the morning, & were engaged the whole day making a washing place, which consists of long logs or spars put out in the river between 2 trees; the spars form 2 pens, into the first of which the sheep are flung & allowed to swim awhile; they are then pushed by a forked stick under the middle spar, & men with flat sticks rub off the dirt, after which they swim out by an approach, & go dripping & exhausted to join their companions . . . Friday, 15th: . . . Yesterday the shearers were idle (had food but no wages), as the sheep cannot be shorn after washing untill the yolk rises, or the wool becomes greasy.[28]

The sheep were left for two full days in this case.

The sheep were shorn with hand shears in the open or in a rough log shed. A tally of 70 sheep in a day was average for an experienced shearer (given the expected inducement of rum), and 20s per 100 could be earned. The regular men were put onto piece rates for the work and extra men would usually be employed. An adult sheep would cut 2–4 lb or more of washed wool depending upon the breed: a Saxony Merino cut about 2 lb per head, while a large-framed, long-woolled Leicester could cut more than double that amount.[29]

During shearing Miss Drysdale noted with some interest that there was no need for the tar brush.

It is a curious thing that when sheep here are cut with the shears, & have many raw places on their bodies, it is not necessary to put tar or any thing else on the sores: at home they would be blown by the flies, but although there are so many here, such a thing never happens . . .[30]

Miss Drysdale attributed this to the dryness of the climate, but in fact the sheep blowfly (*Lucilia cuprina*) was still to reach Australia, in about 1883.

Flies were not a problem but scab was. This parasitic disease, caused by the mite *Psoroptes communis*, is manifested by the sheep becoming restless and rubbing themselves. Scabs then form over the injured areas, the fleece becomes broken and bleached in appearance and finally is shed. Scab was introduced with the sheep from Van Diemen's Land and caused considerable loss among the flocks of the colony. It was a general practice after shearing to dress the sheep with a tobacco and water infusion, possibly with salt and soap added. Common advertisements were 'Tobacco—a few kegs for sheepwash, Colonial Negrohead' or 'Colonial Fig Tobacco, for sheepwash', while some settlers tried growing their own tobacco.[31]

The fleeces from the sheep were folded, sorted and pressed into bales of from 250 lb to just over 300 lb. These bales measured 4 ft by 24–6 in. by 24–6 in. and at Golf Hill the wool was pressed into them in a press worked by a large wooden (later iron) screw from 9–10 ft long.[32] Other presses were operated on the lever principle. The bales of wool were carted by bullock-dray to Melbourne or Geelong and shipped to England. This meant a long wait before the return from the wool was received, so if cash was required urgently the wool could be delivered to one of the agents established in Melbourne almost with the foundation of the colony and either sold outright or an advance obtained on it.[33]

As the flocks increased, fat wethers and aged ewes were sold annually, usually after being shorn, but the regularity of such sales depended on the ruling market prices; if they were low the wethers could well be held over for another year. On the other hand the sale of wethers even at a very low price could provide the necessary money to purchase stores or pay the shearers. Fat sheep and cattle were sold in Melbourne or shipped to Van Diemen's Land where the government made extensive meat purchases for its convict settlement.

The sheep grazed at Port Phillip during the early years were of very mixed breed. They had 'more of the merino type than any other',[34] but there was also a strong infusion of Leicester blood, the latter in response to the demands of the meat industry. The breed of the sheep strongly influenced the weight and quality of wool and the weight of meat produced by the squatter. A wise squatter needed to consider his potential market when selecting his sheep, although with the high demand for breeding stock in 1836 the choice of sheep was probably limited. A less apparent consequence of the breed composition of the flock was its effect on mating. Merino sheep have a longer mating season than Leicesters (the crossbreds in-between) and therefore, when the squatters were trying different mating times or three matings in two years, those with a high proportion of Merino blood in their flocks would have had more success than those with predominantly Leicester-type or other British-breed flocks.

Apart from the generality of mixed-blood flocks, a few very fine pure-bred sheep were also imported into the colony during the first few years of settlement, mainly by people with Van Diemen's Land connections. Andrew Forlonge grazed a flock of pure Saxony Merinos, descendants of some of the finest sheep then available in Saxony, and Mr Simpson, who settled temporarily on the Werribee, was able to sell to Mr Aitken in 1839 'three pure-bred and directly imported Leicester Ewes, and the same number of Rams, for which he paid the enormous price of £80, being at the rate of £13/6/8 per head.'[35]

John Aitken had shipped a flock of carefully selected, pure Merino sheep from Van Diemen's Land to Port Phillip in March 1836 and had occupied his Mt Aitken station in the area of Mt Aitken and the Kororoit Creek (Sunbury division). Aitken was 'a gentleman noted for his experience and judgement in sheep and wool',[36] and during the twenty years following his arrival he bred up one of the leading Merino flocks in the colony. In 1845 he paid £200 for one ram from the Cressy flock in Van Diemen's Land and in 1850 £250 for an imported Silesian ram.[37] 'His aim was to increase the weight of fleece, and to keep up the fineness and density at the same time. This he accomplished by adding to the length of the staple of the wool.'[38] As part of his early breeding plan (*c.* 1840) he crossed Leicesters with Merinos.[39] His success in his overall aim may be judged by market reports such as, 'Advices of wool via Hobart town of a very cheering nature have been received [Oct. 1844]; average about 1/7 p. lb. John Aitken's *averaged all over* 2/4—some of his lambs' as high as 2/5½.'[40]

Cattle at this time were also of mixed breed, animals for meat, milk or draught often being drawn from the one herd. However, as with sheep, some fine animals were also imported and good herds established. George Russell purchased 'two Hereford Bulls imported from V.D. Land for £115'[41] in 1840, and Fifes, Devons and others were also introduced. But the Shorthorn (also known as the Teeswater or Durham) was by far the most favoured breed, and the majority of the cattle in the colony were of predominantly Shorthorn blood.[42]

The first major challenge to the new settlement came in the form of a general economic depression during the years 1841–3. This was an Australia-wide phenomenon, affecting all the colonies to varying degrees. Several interpretations have been put forward regarding the events of this period but, as Professor S. J. Butlin has pointed out, the whole question still awaits competent detailed analysis. This is not the place for such an analysis, but a few comments from the local point of view are in order.

The situation facing Port Phillip squatters was such that in 1839 the right to a licensed station on Jackson's Creek was sold for £95 and the sheep on it averaged 35s per head with prime ewes bringing 43s per head;[43] by 1843 a price of 6s per head for the sheep and no charge for the station was more typical.[44] During the intervening period a number of people had gone bankrupt, merchants suffering particularly, and some banks and businesses had closed their doors. The causes of the crisis seem to have been varied—the financial crisis in England in 1839–42, drought in New South Wales, government financial policies, a labour shortage, speculation, and the slump in wool prices—but at Port Phillip, at least, it would appear that localized factors played the most important part.

From 1835 to the beginning of the 1840s men were able to borrow money relatively easily and invest in sheep. From this investment two gains could be expected given the prices of the day. One was a capital gain in terms of sheep reproduction—sheep capital. George Russell's 74 per cent lamb survival rate could be interpreted as a 74 per cent capital gain (less replacement animals) so long as he had land available to carry these extra animals, as most squatters did, and the price of sheep remained steady. The other gain was from the sale of products, primarily wool. During the late 1830s, if one could occupy a station for a fee of £10, investment in sheep promised considerable riches. However, establishment costs were high, and on the basis of the Golf Hill records annual income would not have exceeded annual running costs until about 1841–2 on a station established in 1836. Therefore during this intervening period the capital in terms of sheep numbers increased, but unless some of this sheep capital was sold there was no money available to pay interest, dividends, or returns on the original capital used to buy the sheep and establish the station—a sum of about £7600 in the case of Golf Hill with its 3000 sheep and 95 head of cattle. Therefore during these establishment years the short-term value of the whole enterprise was closely geared to the price of sheep, for it was here that the largest gains, on paper, were being made. The sale of wool simply covered running costs.

But the value of sheep was dependent on the demand for them. Whereas earlier in the 1830s the demand for meat had played an important part in determining the price of sheep, once the Port Phillip lands were occupied the major demand was for sheep to stock this land. Even to stock the future colony of Victoria sparsely, thousands of sheep were required in a very short space of time, and there is a limit to how quickly sheep can reproduce themselves. Therefore the price of sheep was maintained at a high level as long as good sheep land (on the criteria of the day) was available, but as soon as most of this land was stocked the demand for sheep fell. Once a station was occupied, sheep numbers were most profitably increased to the maximum through natural reproduction, and once the desired stocking rate was reached, there was even less demand for surplus stock. With many more flocks the number of fat sheep produced was greatly increased, but there had been no comparable increase in the demand for meat, and thus that market, too, could no longer sustain high prices for sheep. Inevitably the market price of sheep fell and with it the paper valuation of the stations. Russell had started with 3000 sheep landed at a cost of 35s each. By the end of 1841 he had about 15 000 sheep, a five-fold increase, but soon after, the value of sheep suffered more than a five-fold decrease, and with wool receipts just covering costs up to that period, there was very little return visible on the initial investment. From the long-term point of view prospects were still good, but to see one's assets increase five-fold and then be cut back by the same amount or more must have shaken the confidence of even the steadiest settler. Those who had borrowed heavily to go into sheep grazing might have to face the accumulated interest of up to five or six years, with little hope of paying it except by selling their assets at a greatly reduced price.

But for those who had invested in sheep on a long-term basis, or who could keep their partners, shareholders or creditors at bay, the prospects were still quite good, even at the worst of the depression, for wool prices did not drop drastically.[45] The Golf Hill return for the 1842 clip (sold in 1843 for 14⅛d per lb) was only 4d per lb below the return for the 1837 clip, whereas the return for the 1847 clip (sold in 1848 for 9⅙d per lb) was almost 9d per lb below that for the 1837 clip. The relative equanimity with which the low prices were withstood in 1847–8 bears witness to the stability of the squatters by that time. It also serves to highlight further the instability of the squatters during the earlier period of rapid expansion and establishment, before the costs involved could be absorbed in the increased production of wool.

Another feature of the pre-depression period was the land speculation. Not only did people borrow money and rush to buy sheep and take up land, but investors from Sydney and Van Diemen's Land spent over £330 000 in buying Crown land at Port Phillip up until the end of 1840, and for a while this land changed hands at ever-increasing prices.[46] But this land tended to remain non-productive. Some speculators made a quick profit and left, while those who owned the land at the beginning of the 1840s had little hope of an immediate return from it. Land investment, together with a large investment in imported consumer goods, and the investment in the pastoral occupation meant that a large amount of capital was tied up in the colony for up to five or six years before the depression, with very little real production resulting from it. Much of this capital had originated with British investors, who ultimately would demand a return from it. That investment in grazing was essentially a long-term enterprise, one with high establishment costs but with a promise of good returns, could be a difficult concept to present to investors hungry for dividends; there was a limit to how long people were prepared to go without interest from their investments. And as soon as prices started to fall and confidence began to wane, pressure on borrowers for payment snowballed.[47]

Although this in no way explains the Australia-wide depression of 1841–3, the nature of the rapid expansion of sheep grazing, and the time-lag before net profits were made, particularly when associated with reckless speculation, do go part of the way toward explaining the events at Port Phillip. Here society was still far less complex than in Sydney. Commercial flour milling did not commence in Melbourne until 1841, and so the early distress of the millers at Sydney did not occur in Melbourne. But financially there were close ties between Sydney, Hobart and Melbourne, and events in each town had repercussions in the other two.

In general terms the effects of the depression on the Port Phillip squatters varied according to the indebtedness of the individual squatters. Those who did not have to meet large interest payments were still in a reasonably sound position, particularly as the cost of labour fell, while some who faced large interest commitments went bankrupt. Ultimately, few squatters were able to evade the necessity for adequate capital backing at the time of entering grazing. One group of people who did fare well during the depression were the newcomers who arrived with money in their pockets, since good stations already stocked with sheep could be bought at very low prices. Simon Staughton, who eventually bought large areas of land in the Werribee division, arrived from England at this time. In the Sunbury and Werribee divisions, of the land held under licence in 1848, 20 per cent had changed hands during the depression years; 30 per cent remained in the occupation of those who had held it before the depression; and the fate of the remaining 50 per cent of the land during the depression years is unknown but it did change hands at least once between 1844 and 1848.[48] Therefore in these divisions at least, the occupation of more than 30 per cent of the land was not affected by the depression, and the years immediately following the depression appear to have been equally disruptive with regard to land occupation.

The depression also resulted in more specific changes on the stations. An immediate problem that arose was how low sheep prices would fall. Would the value of sheep fall to the price of their skins and the wool on their backs? For a short while this was a serious concern until in 1843 Henry O'Brien of Yass effectively publicized his results from boiling sheep down for tallow. His trials were repeated and it was quickly demonstrated that good fat sheep, skinned, hind legs removed, and boiled down, could yield 5–8s each from the sale of the skin, the legs of mutton, and the tallow. Bullocks could yield 60–80s each.[49] With the English market providing an outlet for the tallow, as compared with the alternative limited local market for meat, a base value was established for the surplus livestock. Boiling down became an important business and during 1844 in the Port Phillip District, four establishments boiled down 91 000 sheep and 3000 head of cattle.[50] Thereafter boiling down was practised extensively until the gold rushes created a new demand for meat in the early 1850s.

By 1844 the financial situation had begun to improve. With merchants and bankers making advances on tallow as well as on wool, and with the ability to raise credit as a result of the new Act providing for liens on wool and the mortgaging of stock without delivery, the settler could turn his attention to the next pressing problem—the shortage and concomitant high cost of labour. On a sheep station the greatest labour demand was for shepherding and therefore this operation offered the best possibilities of economizing on labour. Economies in labour had already been introduced to some extent. In the districts around Sydney in 1825 the sheep had been divided into flocks of about 300 breeding ewes or 400 wethers each, with a shepherd to each flock, but ten to fifteen years later the flocks had been increased to nearer 800 sheep, and this was a good average flock size when Port Phillip was settled. But under the stresses of the depression, flock sizes were further increased to 1500, 2000 or more sheep, thus halving the number of shepherds required. This practice was aided by both the control of scab and the progressive elimination, through hunting, trapping and poisoning, of the dingo in the Port Phillip region.

There were also some disadvantages to increases in flock size. The sheep received less individual attention; losses increased at lambing time because the shepherds were no longer able to assist the ewes while lambing, or the weaker lambs after birth; and at a time of crisis less control over the flock was possible and again greater losses resulted. With large flocks and the runs still unfenced, once the sheep were stampeded by violent spring storms or summer fires they could run for miles, rivers or forest country forming the only barriers to their progress. During a storm in November 1849 sheep, driven by the wind, stampeded up to twenty miles eastwards across the Werribee plains. Many were drowned or died from exhaustion, but the Pages still found 35 000 sheep on their run, Glencoe, on Jackson's Creek where before they had had only 7000.[51]

The preparation, or getting up, of the wool was another aspect of sheep husbandry adversely affected by the increases in flock size. The colonial wool clips had often invited criticism from the London wool brokers who complained that although the wool was fine, it was often badly washed and full of sand, burrs and grass seeds. This extraneous material was probably more apparent to the English brokers than to the Port Phillip settlers because the British and German sheep were run under a more intensive system of husbandry which ensured greater attention being given to each sheep, particularly during washing. In the wetter climate of these regions, too, the problems with dust and grass seeds were considerably lessened.

In 1841 the inability of the usual cold-water washing to remove the dust from wool was admitted, but at the same time 'the advantages of warm water & soap would probably not cover the additional expenditure which it would create'.[52] John Cotton, a settler on the Goulburn River to the north of the Port Phillip region, was one of the first to introduce a new method of sheep-washing. In October 1845 he wrote his brother explaining the new system:

> It was formerly the custom to wash the sheep in a pool of water or the river, in which men were placed to rub them and squeeze the wool, but a far better plan is now adopted, each sheep being held under a spout of water for about ten minutes, having previously been soaked for about twenty minutes or half an hour. We had, fortunately, the means of erecting a spout at a cost of a few shillings only. The spout only requires two men to stand in the water, whereas on the old plan some six or eight men were standing in the water the whole day, and the sheep were not nearly so well washed.[53]

Cotton claimed 2d a pound improvement in the price of wool washed with the new method as compared with the old. However, not all settlers were able to erect a spout with such facility. George Russell expected to pay about £250 for the construction of a place for spout-washing at Golf Hill in 1848.[54]

As the practice of spout-washing spread in Port Phillip, advocates of warm-water washing publicized their method in Van Diemen's Land, and this practice, too, was soon tried in Port Phillip. A boiler for heating the water was required and W. Lewis, the manager of Golf Hill, had hoped to install one before the 1850 shearing, but installing the boiler and accompanying apparatus took some time and the sheep were not washed in warm water until the following year. These modifications, however, proved worthwhile. 'I am glad to hear', Russell wrote from Scotland to his manager, 'that the wool has been so well got up this season, and that the hot water washing succeeded so well.'[55]

But the time and effort that could profitably be spent in preparing wool for sale was dependent on the value of the wool when sold and the costs of preparation. Just as Russell had considered warm-water washing uneconomical in 1841, so others in 1852 decided to discard washing altogether when labour became extremely difficult to obtain because of the rush to the gold-fields. George Russell, writing from Edinburgh in March 1853, commented,

> A letter from Tom Russell dated end of Octr states that they & many more of the settlers were not washing the sheep; & I am not sure whether this may not be the better plan under the circumstances. It will save the expense of washing; the freights I observe for wool are low, and the present great demand & high price of wool will not probably make that difference in price, which is always the case in a much greater degree when the supply is fully equal to the demand. The sales in London are almost concluded. The demand increased as the sales went on, with a slight advance in price.[56]

As Russell implied, two principles were involved and had to be reconciled: the relation of the costs of production and marketing to the returns from the sale of the wool, and the ability of the market to absorb less well-prepared wool at less discount the greater the demand for the wool. But people soon began returning from the gold-fields, and the labour situation eased. Within the year, Russell, now back at Golf Hill, was telling his Glasgow agents that 'Another article which is much required for sheep washing is an iron boiler—not a steam boiler, but made with plates & rivets . . . it is merely intended to warm the water . . . this article should be sent as soon as possible.'[57]

Removing the dingo and increasing the size of the flocks encouraged other changes. Hurdles were slowly discarded and the sheep, instead of being carefully yarded each night, were quietly camped down in a 'mob' near the shepherd's hut. Gradually even greater signs of stability appeared. By early 1851 William Lewis was trying a new system involving even less supervision of the sheep. At night the sheep were simply left in a brush-fenced sheep paddock at each out-station.

Golf Hill and Mt Aitken were two of the most progressive stations in the Port Phillip region, and whereas boiling down livestock for tallow was an innovation that, through strong pressure of financial circumstances, spread rapidly, other innovations were adopted more slowly or not at all in the region generally. The more capital required to begin such things as spout- or warm-water washing, the less likely were the smaller settlers to adopt them. The Page brothers, John and Edward, who were among the first group of settlers at Port Phillip and had occupied Glencoe, their run of almost 8000 acres, in about 1837, are a case in point. They had little capital—during their first two years at Port Phillip they were unable to afford any extra labour at all—and worked hard at all the station jobs themselves. They washed their sheep in the river by the old method throughout the 1840s but, as so often happened in those days, a flood in 1849 swept away their yards, and the following year when the end of their tenure was in sight, they simply sold their wool in the grease. When their land was sold by the Crown in the early 1850s, they could find sufficient money only to purchase their 640-acre homestead block, and this too they later sold. John for a while carried goods to the diggings and then went to a small farm. He died poor in 1863. Edward became a hotel-keeper in Geelong, but died a ruined man in 1879.[58]

Throughout the 1840s there was continual change on the stations as their managers adapted to changing circumstances. And the underlying features of these changes were the increasing locational stability they demanded, and the continuing capital investment that was necessary in order to maximize profits. Livestock had represented almost the total capital investment at the beginning of the 1840s, and as such was a mobile investment. In leaving one station and occupying another, the squatter would be forced to leave behind little more than a simple bark hut. By the end of the 1840s the more progressive the station, the greater was the commitment in terms of fixed structures—elaborate sheep-washing facilities, fenced paddocks, shearing sheds with their associated press and equipment, more permanent living quarters, and on the larger stations such things as carpenters' and blacksmiths' shops. Clearly to have all this dependent upon an annual £10 licence was becoming a matter for increasing concern and a deterrent to further investment. Once again those with money at their command were in the best position, and George Russell and one or two others did purchase some sections of land in order to protect their investments.

The distance between the two ends of the grazing spectrum was increasing further. The most capable managers and the most financially endowed (and finance alone was certainly not enough) were best able to increase their workforce and control the scab, then dispense with half their shepherds and increase their profits; increase their flocks and risk greater losses; install a spout or warm-water boiler at the opportune time, or shear in the grease as the circumstances dictated; buy a 640-acre section to forestall a competitor, or sell the whole station and buy another further inland. It was moves of this nature that in the long run meant the difference between profit and loss, a successful pastoral future or an impoverished old age.

SALE OF CROWN LAND

From 1838 a system of country land sale was in operation at Port Phillip in addition to the system for licensing land. It was based on the regulations of 1 July 1831 which provided for the sale of land by auction, after survey into parishes, in lots of one section of 640 acres. It was 'not intended to dispose of land in smaller quantities, unless upon special grounds'.[59] The upset price was 5s per acre, but this was increased to 12s per acre on 17 January 1839.[60]

Within the year another change was foreshadowed. Regulations of 5 December 1840 divided New South Wales into three districts for purposes of land sale, the southernmost district being the Southern or Port Phillip District, and within this district all country lands were to be open to purchase, after survey, at the one uniform price fixed at £1 sterling an acre. That is, the auction system was to be replaced by selection. Provision was made for payment for land at the District Land Offices or in the United Kingdom, where a land order could be bought which gave credit for the purchase of land by selection in the colony. Regulations of 21 January 1841 brought this new scheme into effect on 1 March 1841 when any land previously advertised for auction and unsold was made available for selection, and thereafter additional lands were advertised as open for selection from time to time. The 640-acre section was maintained as the basic unit for selection.

Doubt as to the manner of disposal of land immediately around Melbourne, Geelong and Williamstown had existed for some time and on 4 March 1841 all land within five miles of these towns was reserved from sale until instructions were received from England. On the same day regulations for special surveys were announced. These made it possible for any person paying not less than £5120, and thus receiving a land order entitling him to select 5120 acres (or eight square miles), to have a special survey of this land made in an area of his own choosing provided the area so selected was in one block and outside the five-mile limit of the towns. These special survey regulations were rescinded on 28 August 1841, but not before Fred Wright Unwin, Henry Elgar, Henry Dendy, and Hugh Jamieson, or their agents, had taken advantage of the provisions to obtain blocks of 5120 acres each in the Lilydale, Oakleigh, Melbourne and Mornington divisions respectively (the first two surveys adjoined one another; see map 8). William Rutledge also obtained a special survey block just north of the region.[61]

Not only was the special survey system quickly discontinued, but on 10 February 1842 the whole system of land purchase by selection was discarded and the system of selling land by auction, as in force before 5 December 1840, was reintroduced, but with the upset price raised to £1 per acre.[62] At the same time provision was made for people who already held land orders to select the land they were entitled to under the old regulations.

Meanwhile the imperial parliament in London had been considering the question of land sale throughout the Australian colonies and passed 'An Act for Regulating the Sale of Waste Land Belonging to the Crown in the Australian Colonies' (5 & 6 Vict., c. 36) on 22 June 1842. A copy of this Act was received in Sydney on 11 January 1843. It came into force on this date, although regulations for its implementation were not made until 1 March 1843. Land within the (at least provisionally) proclaimed counties was now divided into three classes: first, lots within the actual boundaries of towns; second, suburban lots within five miles of towns of at least 1000 people; and third, country lots. All land was to be sold by auction, after survey, with a minimum upset price of £1 per acre, but a higher upset price could be set for first- or second-class land. Country land that was auctioned but not sold became available for purchase by private contract.

Suburban land could be sold in lots of 2–640 acres and country land in lots of up to 640 acres. But special country lands, defined as 'Lands suited for cultivation, or likely to be purchased for small farms', were to be auctioned in lots of 20–320 acres. Up to one-tenth of all country land could be sold in this way and with a higher upset price than the minimum of £1 per acre set for ordinary country land.

A quite separate provision in the Act allowed for the purchase of unsurveyed land in blocks of not less than 20 000 acres. Purchase was by private contract with the government at a price of not less than £1 per acre, and the land was to be surveyed at the time of sale.

This legislation continued in operation until 1849 and remained substantially unaltered until replaced by the Victorian Land Act of 1860.[63] Therefore from 1838 to 1843 country land could be purchased in sections of 640 acres within the parishes that had been surveyed by the government. After 1843 smaller lots in particular localities were made available. The minimum price for this land was increased from 5s to 12s per acre, and then in 1841 to £1 per acre, at which level it was kept, although a higher minimum price was stipulated for particular lots of better land or for land close to the towns. For six months during 1841 special provisions allowed for the purchase of unsurveyed land in blocks of 5120 acres and similar provisions allowed for the purchase of unsurveyed land in blocks of 20 000 acres or more after 1843.

Despite the multiplicity of regulations only a small area of land was sold by

1849 in the Port Phillip region and this was concentrated in the Barrabool Hills (Barrabool division), between the Moorabool and Barwon Rivers (Bannockburn division), and along the Plenty River and Merri Creek (Plenty division). Land was often passed in at auction without a bid. The location of the land sold and the parishes surveyed by 1847 are shown in map 8. Much of this land had been purchased, during a brief period before the depression, in isolated blocks for speculative profit rather than for farming.

There was an extensive sale of land took place about three weeks ago [5 February 1840], about 20,000 ac. in the district of Geelong and an equal quantity in the Melbourne district: it averaged about thirty shillings per acre, and realized the Government upwards of £59,000. One or two of the sections situated nearest to the Townships brought £4 p. acre; that portion of it which was in the Geelong district was situated about three to twelve miles from the Township. It was purchased principally by Capitalists from V.D. Land & Sydney, and I believe most of it bought on speculation. One party sold his purchase two days afterwards for upwards of £2,000 profit by giving a credit of six Years, the money mortgaged on the land at 12½ p. cent. p. ann. It was purchased by small settlers . . .[64]

Because the land was sold in square-mile sections until 1843, and the price was often forced up by speculators, immigrants of limited means who wished to crop their own land faced considerable difficulties. Not only was a large outlay necessary to purchase the land but, having purchased it, more money was then needed to clear it, fence it against marauding animals, erect a hut and provide the necessities of life until the first crops were sold.

After 1843, when more consideration was given to the prospective cultivator and land was sold in smaller lots, the prospective cultivator could commence with an area more suited to his ability and finance. But in practice, relatively little Crown land was bought in small lots by small farmers. The predominating influence of the man with capital, who had already bought the best land, remained. During the years 1837–42, 227 000 acres of Crown land were sold in the Port Phillip District, in 1843–6, 16 000 acres, and in 1847–8, 45 000 acres.[65] In other words the great bulk of the land sold up until 1849 had been sold before 1843 in lots of 640 acres or more.

CROPPING

Since the government showed no intention of leasing or licensing Crown land for commercial cultivation, it is not surprising that most cultivators obtained their land either under lease or by purchase on terms from private individuals. The owner of an isolated block of about 640 acres could graze it, crop it or divide it into smaller lots and lease it or sell it, probably on terms. Grazing sheep on 640 acres at a rate of about one sheep to three acres yielded a flock of about two hundred sheep, or a herd of about twenty-seven head of cattle, and even with higher stocking rates on the better land of up to one sheep to the acre, the flock was still too small for economic wool and tallow production under the sheep husbandry methods of the day. And this was even more so if there was no water frontage for stock watering and wool washing. So unless the purchased section could be used in conjunction with licensed grazing country, this form of land use was impracticable for a 640-acre section during the 1840s.

Where freehold land was held in conjunction with licensed grazing land there was the option of using it for grazing with the licensed land or of cropping it. Since squatters were generally agreed that it was cheaper to let a tenant grow crops (usually wheat) rather than crop the land themselves, this became a question of either grazing the land or leasing it for tenant farming.[66] But at no time during the forties was there a marked advantage in leasing freehold land for cultivation if the land could be used in conjunction with licensed grazing land. From the depression until about 1846 the proposition was quite unattractive and for the remainder of the decade became marginally so when wool prices slumped in 1848.[67]

Cropping the land was also an unattractive undertaking for absentee landowners. For a short time during the years 1839–40 cropping had promised quite reasonable returns. The population in Melbourne was growing rapidly and most of the food was still being imported from Van Diemen's Land. There was a heavy demand for flour, hay and other produce, and Van Diemen's Land potatoes were selling in Melbourne for about £16 per ton during 1839, with prices rising as high as £24 per ton in June. Although the small supply of locally grown potatoes sold for less, £12–16 per ton, there nevertheless appeared to be good opportunities in growing and selling food.[68] But almost immediately the depression came. In Sydney the cropping farmers suffered greatly, prices fell in Melbourne, and the likely returns did not warrant an absentee owner incurring the trouble and expense of cropping land near Melbourne. Furthermore, very few would have bought the land with this intention, despite the previous high prices for cropping produce.

Dividing the land into small farm units was more feasible, and was also consistent with the agricultural traditions of the British people likely to farm them. It was generally accepted that a farmer working for himself on a small farm could operate at a lower cost per unit of produce than a larger landowner employing men to do the same type of work. Thus in 1845 it was maintained that it would pay the larger landowners to produce wheat if the price was 5s per bushel, but at a price of 4s per bushel it would still be profitable for a small farmer working his own land. The reason for this was that the farmer working his own land would work harder and be satisfied with less material reward, in return for the freedom and social standing he enjoyed as an independent farmer. Furthermore it was assumed that the cultivator would have his own family's labour to assist him.[69]

Current farming practices also tended to result in small farms. As previously noted, sheep were for the shepherds and squatters, not for cultivators, during the 1840s. Instead the cultivator would have his dairy cows, his draught animals (bullocks) and his crops. But cropping methods were expensive in labour; one man, for example, could reap only about half an acre of cereal crop in a day.[70] Therefore when the returns from the crop made it unprofitable to employ outside labour, even if the farmer could find the money to do so, the number of hands the family was able to muster at harvest time could well determine the area cropped. In other words, quite apart from tradition, the area of land a cultivator wanted for his farm was influenced by the farming techniques of the time and by his physical ability to farm it. Without capital to employ extra labour the cultivator was restricted by his hand methods to small areas of land.

Not only was it more practicable for the speculators to divide their land into small farms and sell it on terms or lease it, but an impetus was also given to these practices by the demands of people who came to Port Phillip with limited means.

As the diary of one of these immigrants shows, it is quite wrong to assume that these people made a series of sound agricultural and economic decisions in embarking on the life of a farmer. Their optimism and irrational decisions, usually through ignorance of the local situation, undoubtedly did much to fan the flames of rural land speculation before the depression.

William Greig, an occupant of one of the cropping farms listed in the 1841 census, left a diary covering a five-month period.[71] Short as this diary is, it presents well the hopes and frustrations of this young man of twenty-four who, together with his wife of two years, had recently arrived from Britain. This was Greig's first attempt at farming, and his diary opens optimistically on 1 October 1840. He had just bought a Van Diemen's Land plough for 8 guineas and hired a team of six bullocks at £1 per day of seven working hours, the driver to provide his own food. In preparation for ploughing he and his two married workmen were busy clearing stumps from 'a nicely lying Flat & two Banks [on the Plenty River] in all about an acre & a half of as good soil as any in the Colony and to be surpassed by none in richness in any Country whatever—from which I fully expect an abundant Crop of Potatoes.' Already his original six chickens had multiplied to fifteen, and more eggs were hatching. A garden had been started and during the next few months Greig planted, apart from the potatoes, a wide range of vegetable seeds many varieties of which he had brought with him from Britain. These included mustard, cress, cabbages, turnips, peas, carrots, spinach, melons, lettuce, radishes, cucumbers, cauliflower, broccoli and onions. Apart from the chickens, the animals on the farm were dogs and a pony. The pony played a vital role in providing transport to and from Melbourne for both people and supplies. Fresh meat, in particular, only kept a day or two and so a man had to go to Melbourne on the pony several times a week to fetch it. The seed potatoes and other heavier items, however, had to be sent out by cart.

The ploughing took longer than expected. The bullocks kept straying (a common occurrence at this time of few fences) and the coulter on the plough broke and had to be sent to a nearby station for repair. The work was rough and where the plough missed the men dug with spades. The bullocks then went over the ground again with harrows borrowed from a neighbour. It took the bullock team ten days to accomplish six-and-a-half days' work. On the day this work was finished, 'Owing to Jerry again giving me impudence', Greig asked this workman and his wife to leave. The potatoes were planted by 23 October and Greig now waited 'in expectation for a good crop'. Meanwhile he and his men busied themselves preparing, fencing and planting a vegetable garden, the work punctuated by frequent trips to town for meat. A replacement, too, was needed for Jerry at the end of October.

But William Greig was waiting in expectation of more than a good crop of potatoes. With every trip to town there was also a vain search for mail. Despite being a landowner employing two workmen (the area of the farm is unknown), he had purchased his land on terms and did not have the money to meet his first payment which came due early in January. He was in fact a very anxious young man whose whole hope was based on an expected remittance of money from an uncle in Britain, and some months had now passed since he had last heard from home.

In November work continued on the garden while in town prices started to fall, a foreshadowing of the depression. With persistent optimism Greig decided to broaden his activities and arranged for his man to inspect some cows belonging to

Mr Watson of Watson & Hunter: 'as I intend starting a dairy if possible and he is inclined to be liberal as to receiving payment it will be always able to bring in something and would with proper management pay itself off in the first year, so I shall make the attempt.' But Greig's man only found twenty cows in the herd of two to three hundred likely to be suited to a dairy, and since neither Mr Watson nor anyone else was inclined to be particularly liberal and prices were falling rapidly, Greig's enthusiasm for dairying waned, although not before he had made some preparations for the cows and bought dairying utensils. On 4 December he noted, 'I am now very dubious as to trying the dairy at all as I am afraid the expense & trouble at this distance from Town is too great to be worth it. I think I'll get a Bullock team which will bring as much & more money in than 20 cows wd independently of there being no trouble.' The memory of straying bullocks had faded. Meanwhile his potential source of income, the potato crop, was under attack: 'the rats are playing havoc among the potatoes, going down the drills regularly and eating them up by the very roots, I'll have to tie the dogs up all night beside them.'

During December he worked on the garden and potatoes; workmen were hard to find and no replacement had been found for Jerry. His enquiries about a bullock-dray had also been unfruitful. By mid-December the hot weather, too, was taking its toll: it made him feel weak, he was losing great quantities of meat through spoilage, and it now appeared that his potatoes had been sown too late to do well. By Christmas and New Year the rosy veil of optimism had fallen and the festive season was passed under a gloom of intense anxiety. Greig wrote in his diary, 'I am far from being enviably placed now and the great anxiety I am in completely unfits me for everything . . . With assistance from friends at Home I think I could ensure success, but without that I have nothing left for it but to make the best of my way home. There to begin a world of troubles . . .' Still no letters had arrived from home, and the only horse had gone lame. Trips to town were now dependent upon borrowing a horse from a neighbour. At the same time a reluctant creditor was persuaded to renew his bill for three months.

Early in January a young lad who had deserted from a ship was engaged for three months as a cook and to be generally useful at £4 a month, and work continued on fencing and the garden. Towards the end of the month Greig and his men started to clear twenty-five acres for cropping at a rate of about five acres per week. At last, after five months, some more letters arrived from London (they had been delayed two months in Adelaide), but still no money, and early in February Greig went to Melbourne in search of a cottage to rent. As the diary closes, on 24 February 1841, he is arranging to rent a cottage in Melbourne for £150 per year: 'I want to try & get a stable & Hen House & cow shed put up—and is [sic] so am to be charged 20 per cent. on the additional outlay added to the rent.' Apart from these comments we know nothing of Greig's purpose in taking this cottage or what happened to him after the end of February.

How typical Greig was of the other cropping farmers at this time, we also do not know, but there is no reason to believe that he was atypical. He had been able to raise finance and including himself there were three men working on his farm as compared with the average of 4·4 on the cropping holdings recorded in the

1841 census. His attitudes and management probably reflect quite well those then prevalent, particularly among the immigrants arriving directly from Britain. Greig in his determination to maintain his station in life, his status as an employer and independent landowner, was prepared to run deeply into debt. In this he was not alone, but simply acting as many of his fellow-countrymen might have acted, nurtured as they were in the social climate of status-conscious nineteenth-century Britain. Similarly, new to farming, Greig foresaw no problems in raising crops or producing milk. Providing there was 'proper management', abundant returns might be expected. But unfortunately the complexities of farming were all too easily overlooked by those ignorant that such complexities even existed.

Then there was the question of capital. Up to the time the diary closes, two and often three men had been working on Greig's farm for five months to produce a one-and-a-half acre crop of potatoes, most of the produce of which was going to be needed for seed for the coming year and for home consumption. Apart from this, some fences had been built, a garden planted (the produce of which seems to have been used on the farm), and six chickens had increased to thirty. In addition, meat and other provisions had been bought to feed the four to six adults on the farm, and wages had been paid to the employees. Obviously some time would have had to pass before this farm could have become economically viable. But the inability, through lack of finance, of its occupant to buy bullocks, kill his own meat, and otherwise broaden his activities, meant that much more time would have been needed for the farm to have become viable, if ever. In other words, during this time when cropping was so dependent on hand labour, there was a high monetary cost in establishing a farm on virgin land, and this cost had to be met before the natural soil fertility could be exploited. Thereafter, as with grazing, the more easily the cropping farmer was able to adapt to changing circumstances the greater were his chances of economic success. But reasonable financial liquidity was essential for flexibility in farming operations.

The willingness of people to take on small farms, for a variety of reasons, therefore made it possible for speculators to utilize their land and pass on much of the financial burden to those small farmers prepared to accept it either as lessees or as buyers on terms. This financial burden, however, varied considerably with the people involved. Stringent as some terms were, other landowners appreciated the plight of the small man, particularly after the depression, and for some years rent in kind, or improvements in lieu of rent, became common in leasing arrangements. For instance, George Russell let forty-one acres at 10s per acre for seven years in 1846, the rent for the first four years to be taken as value for all improvements in the form of buildings and fencing.[72] Throughout the 1840s leasing land for tenant farms provided a means of utilizing land purchased for other reasons, and at the same time satisfied a demand by people of limited means for small cropping farms.

After the depression small farming was mainly carried on by former local employees who had saved a little capital while at the same time, intentionally or otherwise, gaining valuable local experience. John Aitken, for instance, had employed a father and his fifteen-year-old son on his sheep station for five years by which time they had saved £290 and were able to go out on their own.[73] With wheat prices so consistently low, it was a hard life for these people. But with prudence, local experience, hard work and reasonable terms in their leases, they could succeed in establishing themselves, and eventually buy farms of their own.

Table 4
Area (acres) under Crop near Melbourne, 1845

Location	Wheat	Barley	Oats	Potatoes	Maize	Garden	Vines	Turnips	Lucerne	Peas	Tares
Darebin Creek	926	66	187	45	9	—	—	—	—	—	—
Plenty River	855	66	266	75	23	5	5	5	6	—	—
Yarra River	1286	193	771	244	4	41	5	—	9	—	1
Merri Creek	2067	227	765	150	—	57	—	—	—	16	—
Moonee Ponds	1183	280	1556	173	10	48	6	—	—	—	—
Brighton	110	40	100	40	—	10	—	—	—	—	—
Total	6427	872	3645	727	46	161	16	5	15	16	1

Source: J. D. Lang, *Port-Phillip*, p. 102

Throughout the 1840s the major crop on the small farms was wheat (see table 4). Initially in the new settlement at Port Phillip flour, rather than wheat, had been the main commodity imported and marketed for bread-stuffs.[74] In 1841 the first steam flour mill was erected in Melbourne, and other water-driven mills were built soon afterwards, but for some time the millers were heavily dependent on Van Diemen's Land and other imported wheat. Flour, too, continued to be imported in large quantities. The few people who grew wheat ground it themselves with small hand mills; a surplus only gradually became available for sale. In February 1843 one miller estimated that about 60 000 bushels of wheat from the new harvest could be spared for the Melbourne market.[75] But in time, mills were built in all the main wheat-growing areas to cater for the needs of the local people, and by December 1850 there were two steam mills in the city of Melbourne proper, one water and three steam mills in the town of Geelong, and five water and three steam mills in the adjacent cropping areas.[76] Facilities thus became available for milling the farmers' wheat. The city millers, however, were not dependent upon the local supply of wheat. In general the local market price for wheat was governed by the supply of wheat from Van Diemen's Land and South Australia augmented by periodic shipments from South America. Of these wheats and the locally grown wheat, the South Australian wheat had the best milling quality and therefore was the most readily sold in Melbourne.[77] Also the increasing use of the stripper, invented in South Australia in 1843, gave the South Australian growers an advantage over the Port Phillip growers in production costs (see chapter 6).

In the Australian colonies Sydney had always been the main market for wheat, and until 1839 wheat prices had been high. Following the failure of the 1838 harvest, however, large quantities of wheat, particularly from South America, were shipped to Sydney. This import trade continued because the relatively cheap overseas wheat could compete with the previously highly priced local product.[78] As a result the domestic price was forced down, and with the relatively cheap sea transport around the Australian coast (compared with land transport over rough bush tracks from potential wheat-growing areas farther inland), the wheat prices throughout the Australian colonies remained uniformly low until the gold-rush period in the 1850s, although widespread crop failures and losses through fire did force the price up early in 1851 before the gold-rush demand set in.[79] During the 1840s South Australia and Van Diemen's Land had both developed wheat surpluses which

Table 5
Average Prices for Local Wheat in Melbourne 1840–1854

Year	Price per bushel
1840	0 to 21s*
1841	15s* to 15s 9d*
1842	8s* to 10s*
1843	3s 6d to 5s
1844	3s to 4s 6d
1845	2s 6d to 5s
1846	3s to 6s 9d
1847	3s to 5s
1848	3s 6d to 5s 3d
1849	3s to 4s 2d
1850	3s to 5s
1851	5s to 11s
1852	5s to 12s 6d
1853	7s to 13s 6d
1854	12s to 16s

* Seed wheat

Sources: *Port Phillip Herald*, 1840–8; *Melbourne Morning Herald and General Daily Advertiser*, 1849–54; *Argus*, 1850–4

contributed to the lower prices as colonial exporters encountered considerable shipping and duty problems in establishing an export trade.

The average prices for local wheat in Melbourne are given in table 5. When these are compared with the figures of 4s per bushel (farmers' own labour) and 5s per bushel (employed labour) suggested in 1845 as being necessary for profitable wheat cultivation, the difficulties facing the wheat grower, up until the 1850s, become evident—quite apart from any problems resulting from the vagaries of the weather, or from disease. The higher wheat prices, it should be noted, coincided with the period when speculation in land was high. High interest rates or rents were agreed to by some small farmers at this time and this further increased the farmers' economic difficulties in subsequent years.

At Port Phillip wheat and meat were the staple foods. From the years of the depression onwards meat was in such excess that the graziers were boiling down livestock for tallow and it was pointless for a small farmer to produce mutton or beef. The markets for small farming produce were therefore very limited and after the depression small farming lost its allure.

DETERMINANTS OF DEVELOPMENT

In broad terms the settlement at Port Phillip was prompted by the apparent opportunities for economic gain from sheep grazing, and the rapidity with which the settlement developed, once the initial move was made, bears witness to the strength of this economic motivation. At this time the eastern Australian colonies were going through a period of prosperity, with high prices for local rural produce and good returns from exported wool. This prosperity, associated with a natural environment admirably suited to sheep grazing, made the rapid expansion at Port Phillip possible.

But the rush of investment associated with the initial grazing expansion engendered a pervasive excitement among people in the colonies and in Britain which led to considerable irrational investment. At this point a number of influences jointly resulted in a bifurcated agriculture of livestock grazing and cropping. These influences initially were the growth of an urban centre to service the pastoral expansion; the inflated demand for food by the people in this centre—at first all food had to be imported; the land tenure system, imposed by a distant colonial administration and confining cropping to freehold land; and the irrational investment (particularly in land speculation) prompted by these other factors. Together these influences then gave rise to a system of land ownership and land occupation which, when combined with the contemporary farming practices, left little alternative for anything but a separation between grazing and cropping, and strongly influenced the form in which these two branches of agriculture developed. This separate development was then further reinforced by the personal decisions to enter into cropping of British people possessing little capital but strongly influenced by the peculiar social significance attached to land, and by the contemporary British attitudes towards small farms and farming. The impetus these decisions gave to the speculator interest led to further opportunities being created for cropping, but at a price commensurate with the prevailing optimism and apparent prosperity.

However, this whole edifice had been built up on the basis of the grazing expansion and when this expansion was curtailed through a lack of suitable land for newcomers to expand into, and by the far-reaching effects of the depression, the whole settlement was forced to readjust. More particularly, sheep lost their value as agents of expansion, and also, as a result of their multiplication during the period of expansion, much of their value as a scarce source of food. Thereafter sheep were valued primarily for their wool and tallow. The marked economic repercussions of the 1841–3 depression period were further magnified by a psychological reaction to the change of events; but by then total abandonment was unthinkable because too many resources, both human and otherwise, had been committed to the new settlement. Instead a rationalization of investment followed with considerable financial loss to those people who had not used their money productively. The essential economic nature of the original expansion was further emphasized as people who had not allowed sufficient funds for the costs of establishment, in either cropping or grazing, now found themselves unable to meet their commitments.

After the depression and to the end of 1848 rural development was gradual, changing in detail rather than in form. Developments in the grazing industry were largely in response to fluctuations in the London wool market. Downturns in wool prices emphasized the difficulties and costs of obtaining labour and these in turn led to changes in sheep husbandry methods to reduce the amount of labour needed. However, disturbing one element in the sheep husbandry system—previously evolved in the older colonies—tended to disturb other elements and thus a chain reaction resulted which gradually changed washing, lambing, camping and other practices, some inherited from Britain and centuries old. These pressures also led, in time, to further (often sponsored) immigration from Britain to supply more labour. In 1848 and 1849 11 662 people received assisted passages to Port Phillip, as compared with a total of only 2499 during the preceding five years.[80] By December 1848 there were about 51000 people in the Port Phillip District, and on the basis of the March 1851 census figures, 60–70 per cent of these people were within the Port Phillip region (of the males 3–5 per cent were of convict origin).[81] However, throughout this period, besides the labour shortage and other difficulties, there was a retarding influence in the form of uncertain land tenure, which acted against any trends towards investment in fixed improvements and therefore helped to maintain the status quo.

There was even less change in cropping. There had been a withdrawal of small investors from cropping and an increasing emphasis on family production by former employees trying to improve their lot, but cropping was dependent on a wheat market dominated by imported wheat. Flour, together with mutton, was the traditional and basic food-stuff and therefore both cultural and economic pressures indicated the production of wheat, but the demand for it when compared with the augmented supply was insufficient to raise the price above the very minimum for a profitable return under the prevailing system of production. The market for the other types of produce was also limited to the immediate demands of the local population, and was still shared with imports from Van Diemen's Land where farm establishment costs, with the assistance of convict labour, had long since been recouped. As a result there was little money available for improvements on the cropping farms, and limited incentive. The traditional cropping techniques of Britain were, on the whole, maintained, and in contrast to the grazing industry there was little practical acknowledgement of the new environment. The factors leading to the inventiveness prevalent during this period in South Australia were not present at Port Phillip. The reasons for this possibly lay in the limited leasehold tenure under which many of the Port Phillip cropping farms were held, in the uncertain nature of the market, and in the relatively low social and economic status of the cropping community.

From the foregoing it is evident that no single factor determined the form rural development took at Port Phillip. It was largely a laissez-faire development, since even the land tenure system resulted more from a holding operation than from anything else, despite the influences of E. G. Wakefield and others who sought to create settlements along predetermined lines. However, as far as the people at Port Phillip were concerned it was probably fortunate for them that there was a minimum of premeditated interference in the region's development. For the factors that influenced development were so diverse and some, for instance traditional and cultural factors, so all-pervading and powerful in effect, that it would have defied the wit of any official to accommodate them all in a workable plan and at the same time make allowance for the unforeseen external factors, such as movements in vital markets, over which there was no local control.

3 : Transition 1849–1854

The regulations concerning Crown land that came into force in 1849 were first outlined in 1846 in the United Kingdom Act (9 & 10 Vict., c. 104) which regulated the occupation of Crown lands in the Australian colonies. Under this Act an Order in Council was passed on 9 March 1847 which divided the lands of the colony of New South Wales into three districts—settled, intermediate and unsettled. The settled districts included the land within twenty-five miles of the corporate limits of the town of Melbourne, within fifteen miles of the limits of the town of Geelong and within three miles of the sea. The intermediate districts included all other lands in Counties Bourke and Grant (and Counties Evelyn and Mornington when defined administratively in 1849), and the unsettled districts included the remaining land of the Port Phillip region (until the above counties were defined). As described in chapter 1, the settled districts of Melbourne and Geelong together with some land around Bacchus Marsh and the Mornington Peninsula constitute the Port Phillip region. Within the settled districts Crown land was to be made available for pastoral purposes under yearly leases. Leases of up to eight years were to be available for the intermediate districts and of up to fourteen years for the unsettled districts. However, for the settled districts implementation of this Order was deferred until 1849, and other provisions were never implemented.

Before looking, almost exclusively, at events in the settled districts of Melbourne and Geelong it is pertinent to point out that this legislation was enacted with the expansive unsettled districts of the colony in mind. The debate on how these lands should be made available had waxed and waned in New South Wales and in England for some years and it was to resolve this debate that the British parliament passed the 1846 Act; the provisions for the settled districts that followed were merely a corollary to the main purpose. It was vaguely appreciated that land on the edges of the main cities was put to different uses and, because of its location, had a higher value than that fifty or a hundred miles distant and should not therefore be made available in large tracts on long-term lease; hence the provision for the settled and intermediate districts.

Another point of interest, on which subsequent events within the settled districts possibly show some light, is the concept of locking the lands. Many people in the Australian colonies at the time thought that the Crown lands had been irrevocably handed over to the squatting interests, and subsequent historians have in general supported them. S. H. Roberts in *The Squatting Age in Australia* summed up the position as follows:

Rural Industry in the Port Phillip Region

That day of October 7, 1847, which saw the proclamation of the *Order-in-Council* in the colony, was the last occasion when Australia's land-problems could have been attacked with something like justice to all sections. But once the *Order* was in force in every colony in Australia, it was impossible to put the clock back—monopoly had entered, and could not be banished at notice, or indeed, at all. Earl Grey and those who had departed from Gipps had saddled Australia with an incubus that could not be shaken off, a problem that could not be solved—and the country has been paying ever since.[1]

The whole theme of unlocking the land, and its implied result of settling the landless on small areas of land so that in time they might become contented farmers with a newly found pride and confidence in their ownership of land and independence of employment, would appear to stem not only from a sincere concern that 'the poorer classes' should be given the opportunity to achieve such independence, but also from a lamentable lack of knowledge and understanding of agricultural reality. Throughout this period any form of rural production other than wool, tallow and hides was dependent on the local population for the greater part of the consumption of its produce. With a small population, growing only slowly, the extent of land that could be utilized for purposes other than grazing sheep was very limited. The only other alternative was to create a subsistence economy—a highly impracticable step within the already commercialized economy. Therefore for farming to be economically profitable, either wool had to be exported or other produce sold to the local market. The unprofitability of the latter on a large scale and the difficulty of profitably utilizing small areas of land have been shown in the last chapter. Pundits seeking a more intensive use of the land and a less secure tenure for the grazier were seeking an agricultural system suited to a more improved technology and greater home-market consumption which just did not exist in the late 1840s—and the gold-rush population, of course, was not foreseen in 1847—or else they sought a subsistence economy within the confines of a highy commercialized economy.

The virtues of the rural way of life dominated the thinking of all those who sought the betterment of their (less prosperous) fellow-citizens. Whether politicians or clergymen, it went without saying that the best way to help those with limited means was to make small farms available to them (see chapter 4). The association of social prestige with land ownership by the urban middle class, and the tendency of this class to invest in land for this reason further confounded the issue. The tragedy of nineteenth-century Australian land legislation, however, was that the flood of fine rhetoric and eloquent writing on this theme was taken not only as the theoretical but also as the practical basis for action. For the aura of rural land as an ennobling possession conflicted at times with the land's role as a raw material for the production of food and clothing. Once schemes of settlement per se and one group's notions of the farming way of life were given priority over the concept of land as a raw material for agriculture (or for recreation and other public uses), and without regard to the finer points of rural living and agricultural production, the agricultural industry tended to suffer. Large and powerful concerns were tempted to exert their influence to obtain control over large areas in order to protect their interests. Small, less well-endowed people were forced out in the struggle. And more often than not, those people artificially settled on predetermined acreages with little or no capital at their disposal ended up as poor citizens encased in a rigid system from which only gradually they and their descendants were able to escape, and the land was slowly once more returned to its role as a resource for agriculture; a resource which needed to be available within a sufficiently flexible system to allow the form of its usage to be varied over time with changing technical, economic and national circumstances. When this was not the case human poverty and misery tended to result.

That long leases with optional purchase were the most practical solution to the land tenure question in 1847, and would have allowed the land to remain in a greater number of hands and with sounder development than short leases or enforced purchase, is a case that could well be put, although an investigation of this proposition is beyond the scope of the present work. Nevertheless, if the landless poor of the city were to be settled on the land as independent farmers, those settled closest to the Melbourne market would have been in one of the best positions to succeed. But here as elsewhere the need for capital and acumen was all too apparent.

In this chapter it will be shown how the sale of the land in the Port Phillip region forced smaller graziers off the land and allowed land in the localities best suited to grazing to be accumulated in large areas by a few people with a lot of capital at their disposal. The enforced outlay of capital for grazing land was just not possible for many poorer settlers. In short, rather than 'protect' the small man and the land closer to the city, the result of the new legislation was to deprive some smaller men of land while those with extensive capital obtained control of much larger areas. What this did provide for, in the long run, was a flexible land system wherein a rational development of land utilization became possible. Shortly after the changed legislation began taking effect, gold was discovered and the influx of people created an explosion in the demand for farm produce other than wool. This in turn led to an increased demand for land to produce these commodities throughout the colony, and also for land as an investment opportunity for the newly found wealth, and the whole agricultural system had to readapt to the changed circumstances. During the same period, abnormally severe fires and floods further added to the upheaval.

CROWN LAND AFTER 1849

The regulations of 29 March 1848 and 1 October 1849, made under the 1847 Order in Council, announced that within the settled districts holders of purchased land could use any adjacent Crown land for commonage and had first option in obtaining exclusive occupation of it by taking out leases, without competition, for an extent of three times the amount of freehold land held. This area was commonly termed a 'grass right' (and will be hereafter), although the government referred to it as a 'pre-emptive right'.[2] The rent was fixed at 10s per 640-acre section per year. The remaining Crown land not leased in this way could be leased to anyone in 640-acre sections, the leases to be purchased at auction with a minimum price of 10s per section. The leases were for one year only but could be renewed. However, the land could be sold at any time with only one month's notice to the lessee.

But people who were already in actual occupation of this land under the 21 August 1841 regulations and who applied to purchase not less than thirty acres, could rent the remainder of that section and occupy it under the same terms as before, until the section was offered for sale. This land could not then be leased by people owning adjoining land in fee simple.

All other land already in licensed occupation, whether under the 1841 regulations or under the £10 annual licensing system, was to be let to the present licensed occupant on a yearly lease at a fixed rent of £1 per section for so long as it was not required for sale, or by the holders of purchased land for a grass right. These licensees were, however, allowed one concession: no section containing valuable improvements was for the present to be open to lease to other than the present licensed occupant.

These new regulations meant an increase in the rent for Crown land depending upon the size of the station—15 000 acres now cost nearer £24 than £10 as under the old £10 annual licensing system (but with no assessment on stock to pay). And they also encouraged the purchasing of land—adjoining land could be leased for 10s per section per year instead of £1 (if already occupied) or whatever the auction might bring where no freehold land was held, and first option to this land went to the owner of adjacent freehold land. However, in all cases, lessees were specifically restricted to using the land for grazing purposes only, and land within five miles of Melbourne or two miles of a town of 1000 or more inhabitants (e.g. Geelong) was excluded from these provisions.

The leases under these regulations commenced on 1 January 1849, but there was some confusion as to the rights of people who had previously occupied their land under the £10 licensing system and did not wish to purchase part of it (or could not afford to?) and certainly had no desire to pass their land over to a neighbouring owner of purchased land. Superintendent La Trobe acknowledged the former vagaries and possible future hardships of the land system and instituted a transitional period for Port Phillip. A notice in the *Port Phillip Government Gazette*, dated 1 October 1849, outlined his plan for the people previously in licensed occupation of the land:

> Nevertheless under the actual circumstances of the case, seeing the impossibility of clearly defining what the term 'boundary of location' in this district may mean; and further, that many, in consequence of a misconstruction of the intentions of the notice of November last, have been led to consider that their continued occupation of the land was admissable, it may be just to extend to these classes certain consideration.
>
> It is, therefore, directed that within 10 miles of the 5 mile boundary around Melbourne, for instance, such claims for the present and ensuing year only, shall now be admitted in the face of the pre-emptive [i.e. grass right] claims, to the extent of the occupation of the section containing the homestead or other improvements; and any two sections adjoining, previously held under license, viz., 3 in all:—from 10 to 20 miles from the above limit, to the occupation of an area if previously held under license, not exceeding 6 sections in all—and, beyond that distance only, to the occupation of the full number, namely nine sections, in cases clearly justifying the admission of such claims.

The same general rules were to apply to the land around Geelong. Despite the concession, the notice closed with a strict injunction.

> It must be born in mind by all who, although within the Settled District may be thus protected, for the present, in the occupation of a certain area of Crown Land previously held under £10 license for depasturing purposes, notwithstanding claims urged by the

owners of adjacent lands in fee simple, under the 16th clause [regulations, 29 March 1848]—that such protection is but temporary:—that this occupation must give place to the pre-emptive right [grass right] of occupancy claimed by such holders of adjacent purchased land, in strict accordance with the real intentions of Her Majesty's Government, as set forth in the Orders in Council.[3]

As foreshadowed, the reprieve for the former licensees was short; a new notice appeared in the *Port Phillip Government Gazette* dated 27 July 1850 and was frequently reprinted. It stated in part:

Referring to the Government Notice . . . dated 1st October, 1849; the attention of both classes of occupants therein alluded to [i.e. previous licensees of Crown land under 21 August 1841 regulations who did not apply to purchase, and under £10 licensing system], is called to the change, which in many instances may be operated, in their position after the close of the present year; and they are reminded that unless sufficient cause be shown for their continued temporary occupation of any section or sections, notwithstanding the claims of neighbouring holders of purchased lands, such occupation will after the 31st December give place to the pre-emptive right [grass right] of occupation conveyed to the latter by the 16th clause of the regulations (29 March, 1848) wherever exercised.[4]

By this time the settlers, to whom all these notices had been directed, were most confused. George Russell was prompted to write,

Certain previleges have been allowed to holders of purchased land; but the Regulations are so intricate & contradictory, and have been amended & added to, so that I have had great difficulty in obtaining the leases of such sections as I was entitled to claim, & have had a lengthy correspondence with some of the Government Officials for some time past.[5]

The words 'the change, which in many instances may be operated, in their position after the close of the present year' were prophetic—far more so than even La Trobe could have imagined before the gold-rush population prompted extensive land purchases. The implications of this will be discussed below with reference to the actions of W. J. T. Clarke and others. But one further point must first be clarified.

The still outstanding question of the fate of the former licensees' homestead sections was finally resolved by the regulations of 8 December 1851 which followed from the 19 June 1850 Order in Council. These regulations allowed for the issue of new leases in 1852, allowing the lessees to purchase at a fixed price 'such portions of such Crown Lands containing valuable improvements as they have hitherto retained under the special provisions made in their favour in the 24th clause of the Settled Land Regulations of the 29 March, 1848.'[6] This pre-emptive right of purchase was limited to the section on which the homestead had already been built, and was for one section only (see map 9). Hereafter the term pre-emptive right will be used to refer to this homestead section as distinct from the aforementioned grass right, which was also called a pre-emptive right in official correspondence.

These various regulations remained in force throughout the 1850s and had far-reaching effects which are best illustrated by the experiences of the extraordinary man William John Turner Clarke with his land purchases. Although exceptional, Clarke's activities stand out more for their magnitude than for their difference in kind. Events similar to those involving Clarke were to be repeated on a smaller

E

scale throughout the region during the 1850s as freehold title was obtained for former leasehold Crown land.

W. J. T. Clarke, 'Big Clarke' or 'Long Clarke', as he was variously known in the colonies, was a heavily built man of reddish complexion. His friends called him frugal, a far-sighted man of few words. Ultimately a millionaire, there were others who described him in far stronger terms, and newcomers were warned against dealing with him in livestock.[7] A farmer's son from Somerset, in 1829 he emigrated to Van Diemen's Land where he obtained a free grant of a thousand acres and became particularly active in supplying mutton under contract to the government.[8] In 1837 Clarke shipped two thousand ewes to Port Phillip and occupied land in the You Yangs and Little River area. He remained there for about two years and then moved farther out and away from the settlers near him, leaving his first run to anyone who cared to settle on it. During the next fifteen years he occupied large areas of land to the north-west of the Port Phillip region and concentrated particularly on the increase of his sheep, cattle and horses; he also dealt extensively in livestock.[9]

Clarke placed particular emphasis on grazing well-bred Leicester sheep for mutton. Fat wethers shipped to Hobart in 1846, he claimed, averaged 140 lb with 7 lb of wool. The essence of his success was noted by the Reverend John Dunmore Lang, after sharing a voyage across Bass Strait with him in 1846.

> Mr. Clarke appeared to me to be one of those long-headed men who occasionally succeed in making a fortune by dealing in an inferior article which other people undervalue; for, although I did not pretend to offer any opinion on the subject, there did appear to me to be some reason in the observation of a respectable colonist, who had taken no part in the controversy, but who, I understood, had succeeded very well with Saxon sheep, that if every person were following Mr. Clarke's example, the colony would lose its character for raising fine wool, while its produce of that description would be unsaleable in England, except at the lowest price, and the fat sheep would find no market in the colony.[10]

There was undoubtedly much truth in these observations. If all the colonists had concentrated on producing mutton instead of wool, the meat market would have been glutted earlier than it was. But, on the other hand, for an astute businessman well versed in the butchery trade, the government establishment did provide an outlet for good-quality mutton. The depression was a leaner period, but even then some mutton was still needed, and sheep especially bred for the trade, rather than for wool, had a better chance of competing in the limited market. Furthermore, towards the end of the depression Clarke was able to purchase another station cheaply, and by concentrating on building up large flocks was able to sell sheep at a very good price during the gold-rush period. It should be noted, though, that Clarke came to Port Phillip with considerable capital. In 1837 the sheep he shipped to Port Phillip were worth £4000 and in 1840 he paid £4000 for four hundred head of cattle; other dealings were unrecorded. He was prepared to work hard, plan ahead and bide his time until he could reap his profits, and these he immediately reinvested. In no way was he a man given to luxury or ostentation.[11]

The land purchase regulations of 1 March 1843, made under the 1842 Land Act, had continued substantially unaltered throughout the 1840s and were not replaced until the Land Act of 1860. Little notice was taken of the special provision for purchasing unsurveyed land in blocks of not less than 20 000 acres until August 1850, when Clarke submitted an offer to purchase an unsurveyed area near Sunbury as a special survey. Clarke's first offer was accepted by the Executive Council and Governor in Sydney. Following further negotiations it was agreed that an area of 28 000 acres should be surveyed for which Clarke would pay £1 per acre to the Crown, and compensation to the present lessees for any improvements. The transaction was to be completed on 1 May 1851. (The area of this survey as finally shown on the Survey Department maps was 31 375 acres.)[12]

Before the end of 1850 Clarke submitted an offer for this special survey to be increased to 40 000 acres. However, the Executive Council did not treat it with the same equanimity as the previous offer and on 15 January 1851 Superintendent La Trobe reported to Clarke that the 'Executive Council . . . have not been able to advise His Excellency to accede to your request, but they have recommended agreeably to my suggestion, that the lands adjoining your authorised selection, which you may be desirous of purchasing, should be brought forward for early sale by Auction, upon your application to that effect.'[13]

After receipt of this letter, and following personal consultation with La Trobe, Clarke made an offer on 21 January for a second and separate special survey in the County of Bourke. Again the offer went to the Executive Council in Sydney (separation from New South Wales was not effective until 1 July) and this time La Trobe informed Clarke that the special survey provisions were to be referred back to the home government in England and that no further offers could be accepted.[14] Here was a quandary. Within the letter of the law Clarke was correct. He was simply offering to purchase land under a clause laid down in the 1842 Land Act. But in practice no one had purchased land under this clause before in the Port Phillip District, and most people had forgotten that it even existed. More importantly, since this legislation had been passed, other quite distinct legislation in the form of the 1846 Act and the 1847 Order in Council had been passed which did, however, give advantages, in the form of the grass right, in leasing land to holders of freehold land. When the effects of these two ostensibly separate pieces of legislation were brought together, the situation arose whereby if someone purchased the minimum of 20 000 acres, they could obtain the exclusive right of lease to a further 60 000 acres (if sufficient adjacent Crown land was available) and thereby effective control over 80 000 acres within the settled districts. It was this probably unforeseen potential land monopoly that disturbed the Executive Council in Sydney and prompted them to refer the whole matter back to the original lawmakers for clarification.

Clarke was not easily dissuaded, however, and in April he applied for a 20 000-acre special survey near Belfast in a settled district area in the Western District of Victoria. In May, upon receipt of a negative reply to this application, he immediately applied for another special survey in the County of Mornington, but again to no avail.[15] No instructions were received from the government in London until early in 1853.[16] By that time, with the influx of people searching for gold, the local circumstances affecting the land market had altered so much that to sell 20 000 acres in the settled districts in one block had become inconceivable.

While Clarke, La Trobe and the Governor in Sydney were exchanging dispatches, the local press saw fit to comment from time to time. A certain amount of anger and cynicism was expressed which varied in intensity according to the interests of the parties concerned. Much of the comment, however, was misinformed —perhaps not surprisingly so considering the complexities of the situation. For instance, one incorrect report in the *Melbourne Morning Herald* of 15 February 1851 maintained that Clarke's second offer had been accepted, which in fact it had not been:

> Great Land Purchase.—Mr. Clarke's second application for 20,000 acres has been allowed by the Government, and it is his intention to apply for another 20,000 acres, and then stop for awhile. This will give him the pre-emptive right [grass right] to 204,000 acres more. A comfortable little property this?[17]

In the light of the criticisms of the so-called squatter monopoly of the grazing land it is surprising that there was not far more opposition to Clarke's purchase. Apparently those people most directly affected were a non-vocal minority,[18] and to the population at large, practical land monopoly by purchase was not as reprehensible as potential monopoly under lease or licence. Perhaps the notion of the landed gentry—the local squire—was still sufficiently strong to lend respectability to the former proposition while condemning the latter. After all, the large landowner could make land available to the landless in the form of tenant farms. The Crown licensee or lessee, of course, could not.

As indicated above, Clarke's freehold purchase entitled him to a grass right over three times the area of his freehold land if sufficient adjacent Crown land was available. For a short time this resulted in a considerable advantage. Early in 1854 Clarke was leasing 59 378 acres in the County of Bourke, under the grass right system, for an annual rent of £46 6s. This bonanza, however, was relatively short-lived because this land was rapidly auctioned, over 21 000 acres of it being sold by October 1854.[19]

With regard to the former lessees of this land, a long chain of events was set in motion when Clarke's first special survey application was granted. Under the terms of agreement all improvements on the land had to be valued and paid for by Clarke. One lessee, George Evans, had already applied for his homestead section before Clarke had applied for his special survey, and therefore Evans's application took precedence and he was able to complete his purchase. Since he did not accept Clarke's offer for this section, it subsequently appeared as an island within Clarke's special survey and Clarke simply surveyed around it (see map 9).[20] Once Clarke had completed his purchase, those lessees whose land would come under his grass right had the option of purchasing their pre-emptive right sections first. These purchases entitled them to select their grass rights appropriate to these purchases (in practice only from land they had previously leased) before Clarke selected his grass right from the remaining land available[21]—the regulations of 8 December 1851 had been foreshadowed and then promulgated while negotiations were still proceeding.

On the land Clarke purchased under his special survey, six settlers had previously occupied 44 square miles (approximately 28 000 acres) and grazed 21 930 sheep, 574 head of cattle and 99 horses between them. The runs of fifteen settlers (including four of the above settlers and Clarke himself) were wholly or partly taken up by Clarke under his grass right. These runs had previously covered in all 139 square miles (approximately 89 000 acres) and run 51 454 sheep, 107 head of cattle and 123 horses. Before Clarke's purchase, seventy-nine people were living on these stations. There was a human element in this purchase, quite apart from land, money and livestock.[22]

The people displaced from their leaseholds (all former licensees by now held leases) by Clarke's purchase had varying fortunes thereafter. The majority had previously leased 5000–10 000 acres each. John Aitken lost the southern portion of his Mt Aitken run but was not affected too seriously because he held other runs. The Page brothers purchased their 640-acre homestead section and leased their 1920-acre grass right but did not prosper.[23] George Evans found his 640-acre homestead section was an island within Clarke's purchased land and therefore could not claim any grass right. Although he purchased this section, at the same time he invested in an hotel in Melbourne and eventually moved there to live. He may have lost his leasehold land but he did have livestock to sell. Evans remained in Melbourne for the rest of his life and invested successfully in a number of city properties. Neither the Jacksons nor W. Headlam took up their pre-emptive right sections, the Jacksons preferring to move to their other stations at Casterton in the Western District, while Headlam apparently was not able to purchase his land.[24]

Martin Batey, although only able to obtain a grass right to about eight hundred acres, survived the crisis partly by renting nearly two thousand acres (of leasehold land under grass right) from the Page brothers and also by entering the butchery business. J. Pinkerton was less successful. Much of his run was absorbed by Clarke's grass right, and so he in turn leased grazing country from Clarke during the 1850s at 10s per acre. But, with an outbreak of scab, and falling prices as the gold-rush boom eased towards the end of the 1850s, he was unable to afford such a high rental and eventually was ruined.[25]

The essential difference between Clarke's purchase and the extensive land sales that soon followed was that Clarke paid the minimum price of £1 per acre and could select his land, whereas other buyers had to compete for the land at auction where the minimum price was the same. Apart from their homestead sections (if they had applied for them to be auctioned or after the pre-emptive right regulations came into force), the former lessees of the land had no opportunity to bid against Clarke for their land. Once Clarke had selected the location of his special survey, these people had no option but to quit this land. By contrast, when land was auctioned in the usual manner, the former lessees at least could make their bid. However, as will be shown below, the overall result of displacing former lessees was similar whichever way the land was sold.

Although ordinary country Crown land continued to be offered for sale in sections of 640 acres throughout the 1840s, by 1852 it was being temporarily withheld from sale so that the square-mile sections could be further subdivided into four or six lots which were then auctioned individually.[26] An increasing emphasis on purposely providing land for cultivation is evident here. Whereas during the 1840s the land system had been adapted to a grazing occupation, by 1852 the influence of the gold-rush population and its new demands for food was forcing the land administrators to consider more carefully the requirements of the cultivator. Furthermore the speculators were again active.

I am informed that the land purchased at the Moorrabool in April 1852 is now worth double what was paid for it: this will give you some idea of the great increase in the value of property, particularly land if situated near the principal towns, country townships, or bordering on the roads leading to the diggings. Money appears so plentiful in the country that many descriptions of property have attained an unprecedented increase in value: whether such a state of things will continue, or how long, it is impossible to say, but there is no doubt that much of the money recently invested in land yields little or no annual return; its value is kept by the demand for it & the abundance of money.[27]

In 1854 the Crown land in the parish of Derrimut was auctioned in sections of approximately a hundred acres. Previously, in 1849, and probably until it was sold, the land of this parish had been divided between three lessees—J. Pinkerton, F. Anderson and the trustees of a Mr Scales. Each had occupied 6000–9000 acres. A fourth lessee, the partnership of McLachland and Yuille, had held one section. All of these lessees except Anderson had also leased land in adjoining parishes.[28]

When the land was sold, Anderson bought 23 lots which together with his pre-emptive right homestead section represented 2817 acres, and Pinkerton, the only other former lessee to purchase land, bought his 640-acre pre-emptive right homestead section. Of the remaining land, Clarke bought 47 lots comprising 4210 acres, and the other 105 lots were bought by fifty-nine different buyers.[29] The actual increase in occupants was not so dramatic; from 1856 to 1865 only 27–31 separate holdings were listed in the agricultural statistics for this parish.

Thus the subsequent Crown land sales (see map 10) had a similar effect on the former lessees to Clarke's purchase of his special survey—both served to displace the graziers from the land. In both cases the operation of the grass right clause hastened the rate of this dispossession. But Clarke's purchase also brought to light several anomalies in the letter and administration of the land law. At the time of Clarke's purchase, Crown land could only be bought, under the 1842 Act, within the limits of location.[30] These limits were never as clearly defined at Port Phillip as they were around Sydney, and administrative decision rather than official proclamation appears to have been the main determinant of actions in many cases. However, the settled district boundary was the limit at Port Phillip in 1850. Consequently the very boundary which had been created to set apart the land close to the centres of population, in order to protect this potentially valuable land from monopoly, also became the boundary within which the greatest possible monopoly, in the form of the special survey, was restricted. Furthermore, by buying 20 000 acres or more, Clarke was able to buy at the minimum price by negotiation with the government, whereas, it was considered a hard-won concession when the squatters within the settled districts were finally granted the right to buy their 640-acre homestead sections at a fixed price, rather than competing for them at auction. This latter concession, too, was strictly administered and the full 640 acres was not always allowed.

Of the thirty-four settlers who leased runs of 1000 acres or more in the Werribee and Sunbury divisions in 1849, eighteen purchased the pre-emptive right to their homestead sections during the 1850s, and the succeeding lessees to five more runs did likewise, while six other settlers already owned a portion of their land or purchased a portion at auction.[31] On the above criteria, this suggests a success rate of the order of 70 per cent. But such figures, based on this very small sample, overlook men like the Jacksons, who withdrew to their leasehold properties in other parts of the colony, and Pinkerton, who, although he purchased his pre-emptive right section, had to depend on privately leased land and ultimately went broke.

A more long-term estimate of the viability of the lessees in this period can be obtained from a comparison of the leasing and pre-emptive right records of 1854 and the Land Tax Register for 1880. With reference to land rented from the Crown and that purchased under pre-emptive right (that is, excluding land purchased at auction) it can be shown from the records that of the seventy-six families and partnerships each, in 1854, occupying more than 2500 acres, twenty occupied as freeholders at least this acreage in 1880 while fifty-six did not.[32] The major test for these 1854 lessees undoubtedly would have come when the land they occupied was auctioned in small sections.[33] Depending upon location, this may have occurred any time between 1854 and 1880, although the bulk of the land would have been sold by 1860. For this particular group, just over one-quarter of the families or partnerships consolidated their occupation and subsequent ownership of a holding in excess of 2500 acres for about a generation. Anderson, in the parish of Derrimut, and Clarke belong to this group. That the other three-quarters did not, may have been due as much to a lack of inclination to further invest in the Port Phillip region as to a lack of ability to do so.

GOLD

In July 1851 gold was discovered in the colony of Victoria. At the beginning of that month separation of the Port Phillip District from the colony of New South Wales and its erection into the colony of Victoria had taken effect. Immediately a totally new factor emerged in the new colony, which was to have a profound effect upon the population.

At the census of 1851, taken in March just before the gold discoveries, there were fewer than 23 000 people in the rural divisions of the Port Phillip region, 23 000 in the city of Melbourne proper and 8000 in the town of Geelong.[34] By 1854, less than three years after gold was discovered, the rural population in the Port Phillip region had increased by about 5000, although some of these people were undoubtedly just en route to the gold-fields at the time the census was taken. The population in Melbourne had increased to 82 000 and in Geelong to 19 000. A total of 54 000 people had expanded to 129 000.[35]

As the gold-fields were opened up in the ranges, particularly to the north-west, 50–150 miles from Melbourne, gold seekers were initially attracted from the local population in the second year from abroad, most coming from the United Kingdom.[36] The lure of gold enticed workers and employers alike. Martin Batey, a leaseholder at Sunbury, left his wife and two young sons, together with a seventy-four-year-old shepherd, to look after his run while he went to the Ballarat and then on to the Bendigo gold-fields with neighbouring settlers.[37] While near the mouth of the Werribee River, the Chirnside's manager was forced to ride to Geelong in search of labour. He finally persuaded some sailors to come and tackle the shearing: 'an unhandy lot they were, but the clip was saved.'[38]

The main concern of all landholders during this period was expenses. High wages had to be offered to compete with the lure of the gold-fields, and food prices soared with each shipload of new people to feed. On the sheep stations shearers were paid 30s per 100 sheep, with provisions; shepherds and their wives about £60 per annum, with provisions; and flour sold for about £30 per 2000 lb in 1853. Increases in local transport costs also added to the problem. A shipment of hardware and harness sent to Golf Hill in 1853 cost £27 7s 2d in freight from Glasgow to Melbourne, and £8 12s from Melbourne to Geelong. Since this shipment went to

Melbourne, although intended for Geelong, it incurred further expenses of £21 10s 6d in Melbourne.[39]

But the graziers had their compensations. Fat sheep were selling for 15–20s each during the winter of 1853.[40] The Batey family, for example, had prospered in Martin's absence because one of the routes to the gold-fields passed through his station. His sons sold sheep 'rapidly in lots of from six to a dozen at a time to various people who had set up in business. Some of the sheep cost 5/–d. each, they were being sold at 15/–d. per head.' One of their customers was the proprietor of a new refreshment tent in Sunbury, where 'camp oven bread, mutton chops, hashed ditto, pickles, tea and coffee' could be had for 3s.[41]

The high cost of labour, the difficulties of obtaining it, and the resultant decrease in attention given to the sheep did, however, have further effects. By 1853 scab was spreading rapidly again throughout the colony, and it was feared that 'from the great numbers of sheep on the runs [it would] be a serious matter eradicating the disease'.[42] And post-and-rail fencing became so expensive that wire fencing was quickly introduced. Details of a boundary fence (in the Bannockburn division) completed at about the end of 1852 illustrate the increased costs of post-and-rail fencing.

> There are 62 chains in all of pretty good fencing: of this, 26 chains only are the regular post and rail split stuff, and these are charged only £1–5–0 the chain, as it was done chiefly in the cheap times. The 36 chains that remain have good posts, but merely saplings for rails; but these are better than usual, and he charges for them £2–18–0 the chain . . .[43]

Until this time the more substantial fences had usually been built of posts and rails of split timber, but they often needed renewing after about ten years. Wire, therefore, now appeared to have several advantages, as James Riley explained when arranging to erect his boundary fences in July 1853: 'As there is great difficulty in getting timber split & carted, I propose doing it with Iron wire, which can be put up at about one half the cost and makes a more lasting fence.'[44] By November 1853 Dennistoun Brothers and Company of Melbourne were arranging for a trial shipment of twenty-five miles of wire fencing from their parent firm in Glasgow.[45]

Thereafter fencing spread rapidly throughout the region. The major impetus to this was the sale of Crown land. Once a freehold title to the land was held, investment in a substantial boundary fence became worthwhile in terms of both ease of operation and security for crops and livestock. But other factors were also important. On the grazing properties the difficulties in obtaining shepherds, and the costs involved, prompted the use of fences rather than shepherds to control the sheep. And with the renewed spread of scab, and the threat of catarrh from farther north and west (although catarrh did not become a problem in the region), a fence became an important means of preventing other people's diseased animals from infecting a grazier's flocks. Furthermore the greatly increased movement of both people and livestock through the countryside made a substantial boundary fence almost an essential protection for any type of farm.

The effects of the gold rushes were felt no less on the cropping than on the grazing holdings. One of the most immediate results was that people left the farms, and the cereal crops, mainly wheat, were not planted. The 1851 crops were already in before the rush gained momentum, but the acreages planted in 1852, 1853 and 1854 were greatly reduced. Thereafter the high prices and demand for food reversed the trend and the acreage planted to wheat expanded rapidly. No statistics are available for the Port Phillip region, and those for Victoria are unreliable though they do indicate the general trend of events—the region became the main wheat-growing area in Victoria. In round figures the recorded area sown to wheat during these years was as follows:[46]

Year	1849	1850	1851	1852	1853	1854	1855	1856
Acres	24 000	29 000	30 000	17 000	8 000	13 000	43 000	80 000

The increase in 1856 is partly due to an improved collection of the statistics following the appointment of local collectors in each district.

Not only did wheat growing suddenly become more profitable, but providing the miners with any type of food was worthwhile. The farmers west of Geelong soon discovered the profitability of growing fruit and vegetables, making jam and butter, and taking this, and other produce that came to hand, in covered wagons to the Ballarat gold-fields. With 75 000 more people within the Port Phillip region alone, small farming was suddenly given a new lease of life. Those farmers already on small farms who remained and cropped their land, now had an excellent opportunity to pay off past debts and to establish themselves soundly. But by the same token many more people were attracted into farming by the high prices for produce. A new clamour for land was created, and high prices were paid for it and contracts for high rents were entered into. Soon, as disappointed miners drifted back from the fields, ideological and political overtones further stimulated the clamour for land as the miners saw the possession of a farm as one of the hallmarks of the truly free man.

Above all else the discovery of gold led to an entirely new demographic situation both within the Port Phillip region and immediately beyond. In the short term this disrupted both livestock and crop production and created an unprecedented demand for food and manpower. A new demand for freehold land and farms followed and in the longer term a large proportion of the land in the Port Phillip region was brought under freehold. Food production was gradually increased to feed the miners and the permanently increased populations of Melbourne and Geelong. For people farming before the rush started there were now excellent opportunities to profit if they continued in their vocation. For those who entered farming after the prices of land and farms had risen, success was less likely, as will be shown in chapter 6. Some innovations were introduced on the farms, and fencing especially spread rapidly on freehold land. But the old dichotomy of grazing and cropping continued very much as before.

THE EMERGING PATTERN

Gradually from this turmoil of land sales and the gold rush a new pattern of agriculture emerged. Events in the Sunbury and Werribee divisions will again serve as an illustration. In these two divisions three men—W. J. T. Clarke, Simon Staughton and Thomas Chirnside—purchased from a third to half of all the land. The land which each purchased directly from the Crown is shown in map 9. But it must be emphasized that Clarke in particular and Chirnside to a lesser extent continued

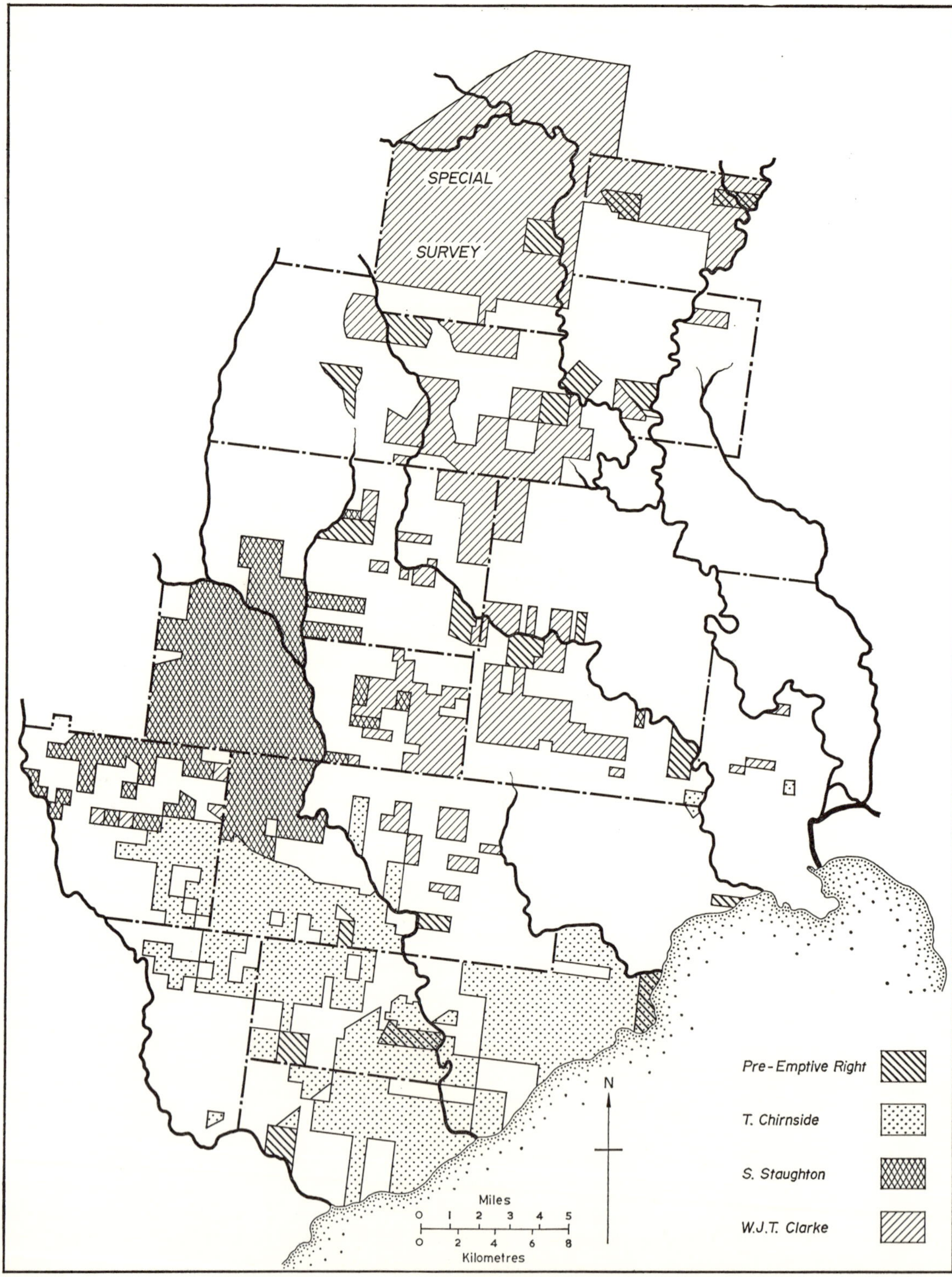
SPECIAL
SURVEY
Pre-Emptive Right
T. Chirnside
S. Staughton
W.J.T. Clarke
N
Miles
0 1 2 3 4 5
0 2 4 6 8
Kilometres

to purchase further lots of land from private individuals for the next twenty years.

Simon Staughton came to Port Phillip from England and took up his Brisbane Ranges and Exford runs around the junction of the Toolern Creek and Werribee River and to the west during the depression in the early 1840s. Staughton, buying his licence and livestock at a favourable time, prospered and started purchasing his land as soon as it became available. By the time of his death in 1863 his Exford estate covered approximately 100 000 acres and was carried on by his sons.[47]

Thomas Chirnside, a native of Berwick, on the border of England and Scotland, landed in Adelaide in 1839 and from there went to Sydney. During the next few years he overlanded cattle to Adelaide and sheep to the Loddon River where he occupied a run in 1840 and was joined by his younger brother Andrew. In 1842 he took up the licence of Mt William in the Grampians in western Victoria and thereafter continued to purchase the rights to other runs either alone or jointly with Andrew and others. By 1860 the two brothers held interests in at least eleven properties in Victoria. In 1849 or 1850 Thomas first purchased a lease to land on the lower Werribee River and in May 1851 made his first purchase in that district of freehold land from the Crown. Between 1851 and his death in 1887 he purchased an area of approximately 85 000 acres and this constituted his Werribee Park estate. Here he made his home. Before his death he transferred half his property to his brother Andrew, the property then being run under joint ownership.[48]

Much of the land that Clarke, Chirnside and Staughton did not buy from the Crown was purchased in small areas by many different people. But, as shown in the parish of Derrimut, many of the sections were resold again or leased fairly quickly and a number of people acquired estates of reasonable size. Francis Anderson from Derrimut, for example, eventually acquired about 4000 acres.[49]

With regard to the small holdings, George Russell's decision in relation to freehold land he wished to sell in 1853 is illuminating: 'I have engaged a surveyor to divide the land in lots of 100 to 150 acres, wh. I think will be small enough for agricultural or dairy farms, The land being most suitable for that purpose.'[50] This was Russell's considered opinion as a former tenant farmer himself (in Van Diemen's Land). But when the surveyor finally arrived, Russell was persuaded, considering the exceptional circumstances of the time, to divide the land into smaller lots of two to about fifty acres, no doubt to promote greater competition at the sale.[51]

But the clamour for land for small farms, and the government's provision of land in lots of about a hundred acres had only limited effect on the pattern of farm holdings that emerged. In practice a viable holding was the important factor and here soil fertility, farming methods and economic factors outweighed selling expediency, politics and ideology. If a lot of 640 acres was put up for sale, fewer people could hope to purchase it at the initial sale than if it were in lots of thirty

---

Map 9 Crown Land Purchases by T. Chirnside, S. Staughton and W. J. T. Clarke in the Werribee and Sunbury Divisions

Manuscript and published parish maps in Counties Bourke and Grant, various dates, Lands and Survey Department (Victoria) and La Trobe Library; Crown Lands' Sale and Leases, *V. & P.*, L.C. Vic., 1854–5, vol. 3, no. C8a; Valuation of Crown Lands under Pre-emptive Right, *V. & P.*, L.C. Vic., 1854–5, vol. 3, no. C26a

acres. But, overall, the new owners soon amalgamated or divided the lots into areas of land most suited for viable holdings under the prevailing conditions. In the parish of Derrimut the 100-acre sections were soon grouped into larger units, whereas in the parish of Tullamarine (also in the Sunbury division), where the land had been sold in sections of 640 acres or more to nineteen buyers, it had been subdivided into about sixty small farms.[52] Although about equidistant from the city, the land in Tullamarine was bounded or cut by three creeks or rivers and was generally more fertile and easily worked than the land in Derrimut where there was only one creek along the boundary of the parish and otherwise very little water.

The progressive spread of the land sales is shown in map 10. Most of the readily accessible land had been brought under freehold by 1860 and only small inroads were made into the more heavily timbered mountainous areas during the next two decades, and even then mainly only during the seventies. Very little land was alienated during the sixties, and from about the beginning of that decade onwards land legislation ceased to be a major factor in the agricultural development of the Port Phillip region.

Thus a pattern emerged of several very large holdings covering tens of thousands of acres each. Interspersed between these were smaller holdings ranging from about 1000–10 000 acres, and then between these again were the small properties, the majority of which were between 30 and 350 acres. The lack of holdings of about 640 acres, at least until the sixties, further emphasizes the difficulties of profitably utilizing the land in a holding of this size under the prevailing farming methods.

During this period, then, to the mid-fifties the two major factors determining rural development were the land system and the gold rush. Natural disasters simply served to set back progress and to produce considerable human misery. The average squatter on his 5000–15 000 acres of leasehold land only got the security he so badly needed at a very high price—greatly inflated by the gold boom. As a result, this type of enterprise gradually ended. Some people moved farther up country where they could continue grazing Crown land, others consolidated their operations on smaller areas of freehold land, and still others went into other occupations. Grazing was practised on a series of freehold properties, several much larger than before, but most smaller. On these properties, with tenure now assured, capital improvements in terms of fencing, sheds, sheep-washing facilities and comfortable homesteads were slowly built according to the availability of finance. By now the major investment was in land and improvements and no longer in livestock, and the total investment in a grazing property had greatly increased, though even fewer people could now afford a grazing property within the region.

The gold rush had brought a market for produce other than wool, and many people took up small farms to profit by it. Although it is notable that the large landowners still did not turn to cropping on a large scale on their own account. Instead they sold livestock to the butchers and otherwise relied on wool. The sudden demographic change had long-lasting consequences and the resulting permanently increased demand for food in Melbourne formed the foundation upon which the future development of the region was based. But the events in the early 1850s were only the beginning, cropping was still separate from grazing, and many people taking up small farms during this period knew little about farming. In other words, while the grazing farms were becoming soundly established under a viable

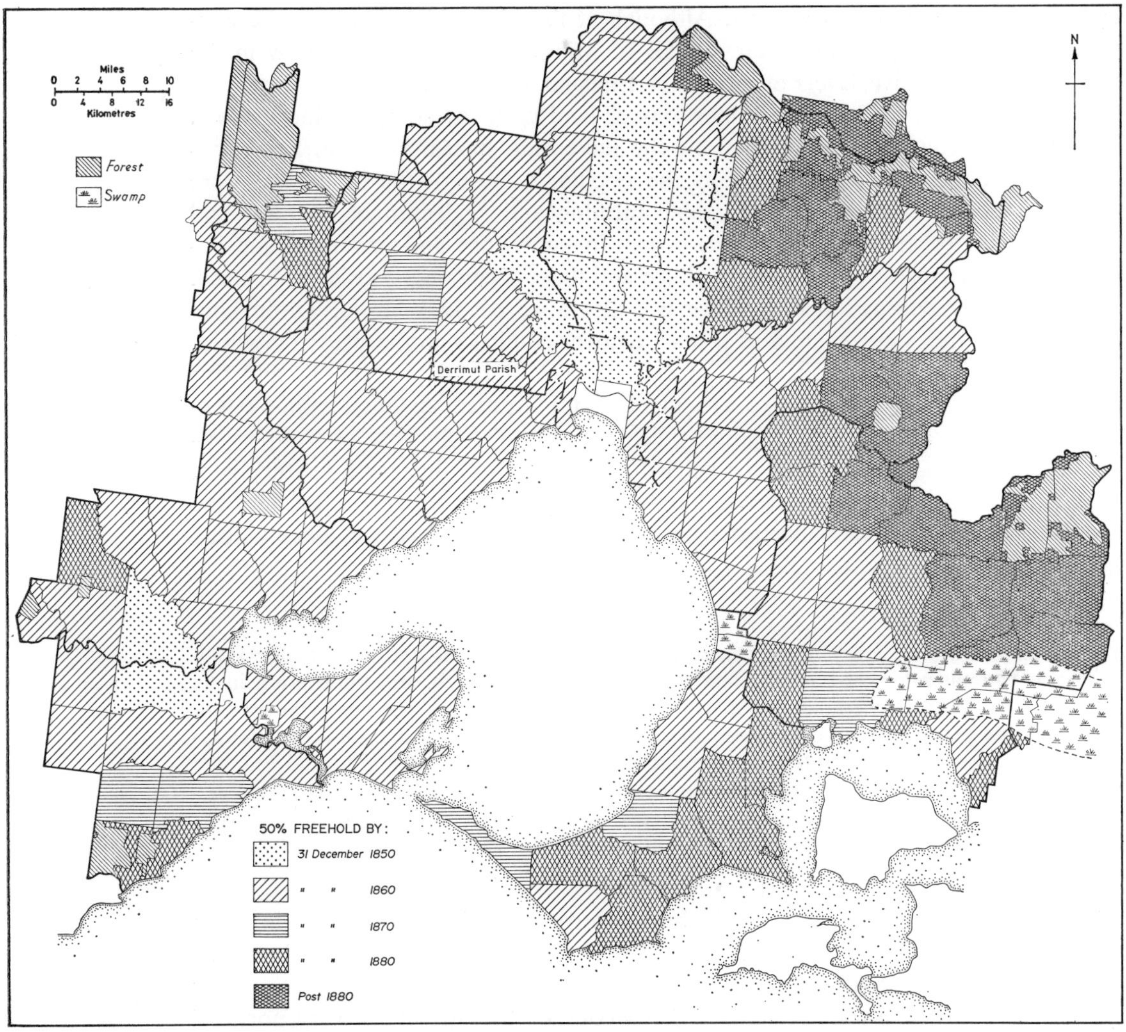

Map 10 Freehold Purchase of Land

Manuscript and published parish maps in Counties Bourke, Evelyn, Grant and Mornington, various dates, Lands and Survey Department (Victoria) and La Trobe Library; Land Sale by Public Auction, Country and Suburban Land, 1849–1880, Manuscript Registers, Lands and Survey Department (Victoria); Crown Lands' Sale and Leases, *V. & P.*, L.C. Vic., 1854–5, vol. 3, no. C8a; Valuation of Crown Lands under Pre-emptive Right, *V. & P.*, L.C. Vic., 1854–5, vol. 3, no. C26a; Proclamations of Farmers' Commons, *V.P.P.*, various dates

agricultural system, the cropping farms were still in the exploitative phase, with the emphasis on wheat cultivation, and were yet to develop a long-term, viable system of farming.

In the last chapter it was suggested that there was a socially and economically inspired preference among rural workers coming from England and Scotland for livestock rather than cropping, while in this chapter it has been implied that the community in general favoured any actions that might have led to an extension of cropping at the expense of grazing. Although at first sight this appears to be contradictory, it actually is not. Professor G. E. Mingay has pointed out how in the long term the relative levels of prices in England during the nineteenth century largely determined the relative proportions of land used for cropping and grazing. However, the consequences of this and the increasing specialization in rural production were not fully appreciated by the popular writers of the time, who were overly concerned with wheat and arable farming and neglectful of pastures and livestock.[53] In other words, there was a gap in knowledge and understanding between those actively engaged in agriculture and those commenting from a distance.

This same preoccupation with wheat was also apparent in Victoria. Throughout the period of this study there was a marked over-emphasis in the press on wheat, compared with the importance of the crop in overall rural production, and this appears to be a fair reflection of articulate, if uninformed, colonial opinion (excluding, of course, the minor squatter voice). Despite the diversity of fruit, vegetables, meat, fish and dairy produce needed to feed a large nineteenth-century city, production of these commodities was barely mentioned by comparison. Perhaps the thought behind this is best illustrated by an editorial in the *Weekly Times* written in 1879.

Farmers to the Rescue!

The sheep-farmers we grant, are likewise creators of wealth; but not at all in the same degree as the cultivators of the soil. The wool on the sheep's back, and the mutton in its carcase, stand both of them second in value to the bread which is the very staff of life. Wheat comes before even wool. Then, moreover, the squatter's is a transitory occupation. He lives only so long as the soil remains unbroken. But the time is bound to come when the soil must be broken up, and then the farmer steps in and takes the squatter's place. This is the natural order of things all the world over, and in all ages of history. Pastoral occupation comes first, and agriculture follows it as certainly as day follows night.[54]

These views on wheat had probably been strengthened by the poverty in early nineteenth-century England, where there had been great dependence on bread as the major component of diet, and almost as the sole component for the poorer people, particularly in southern England. By contrast the diet in the very north of England and parts of Scotland was more adequate and consisted mainly of oatmeal, milk, and vegetable broths. Despite the predominance of meat in the Port Phillip diet, this difference in the background of the various groups of immigrants would have further emphasized the Scottish-born graziers' lack of interest in commercial wheat growing and further highlighted the seemingly opposing interests of wheat and wool.[55]

In the light of the views expressed in the *Weekly Times* and the preponderance of English-born in the population, the contradictions between the preferences of workers in the rural community and ideas fostered largely in the city become more understandable. And so too does a land system whereby wheat growing was fostered in preference to grazing, and land purchases such as Clarke's could take place in the most 'protected' areas.

4 : Community Development

The next in natural rotation after the squatter, should have come the *farming grazier*; but somehow—whether owing to the land laws, or the want of them, I don't know—we skipped entirely over him, and passed at one bound from the squatter to the farmer pure and simple, with his ploughs and harrows.

Josiah Mitchell, 1866

The immigrant farmers of Port Phillip had come to the colony from various regions and social classes. There was the Scottish farmer from the Lowlands, the agricultural labourer from Essex, the Swiss baron from Neuchâtel, the bricklayer from Grantham, and the merchant's son from Dublin. Bond or free, rich or poor, each had brought with him his own particular outlook on life and his own attitudes which reflected his culture and social background. These people came together at Port Phillip to form a new society and culture based on a mixture of diverse segments from the old interacting with a new environment.

The immigrants had left behind an intricate rural society with its small farms and various well-defined classes of workers, and various members of the Port Phillip community showed a strong desire to re-create it. In his book *Phillipsland*, published in 1847 and again in 1853, the Rev. Dr John Dunmore Lang strongly advocated the division of large sections of the Western District of Victoria into 160-acre farms for people 'above the class of mere labourers or farm-servants, and possessed of moderate capital. . . Farms of this size, according to Mr. Story, would afford a sufficient extent of land for cultivation, and leave pasture enough besides for the draught cattle.'[1] A plea for this type of settlement was not new. As early as 1838, when the colony had been less than fully stocked with sheep and cattle and there had been little possibility of marketing any other commodities on a large scale, the editor of the *Port Phillip Gazette* in the first edition of the newspaper had written, 'We trust, therefore, to see this an agricultural country; everything ought to be done, every inducement held out, every facility afforded to the class of small farmers who can and will turn every foot of land to account, every acre to the production of "corn".'[2] But in practice idealism and tradition were tempered by economic and practical possibility, and pastoral land use progressed unabated until the population increased sufficiently to create a demand for the small farmers' produce. The depression of the early forties, in particular, had tended to put an end to these small-farming notions in so far as the farmers themselves were concerned, and the difficulties of the small farmers thereafter continued to deter the cultivators and encourage the graziers.

These lessons of experience, however, were restricted to those who had been directly affected by them; among the newer immigrants of the fifties and the urban population, idealism persisted. Under the quotation from Adam Smith 'The plenty and cheapness of good land will always promote the prosperity of new colonies' the *Melbourne Morning Herald* spelt out the popular concerns of the emigrating Englishman in the early 1850s:

There are two considerations, one moral and one material, which exercise great influence on the mind of every working man. He is anxious to know with what associates he and his family will be brought into contact if they leave their native land, and what facilities he will find for that which is to an Englishman, whether rich or poor, the ultimate object of labour and ambition—the acquisition of an independent landed property, to be enjoyed by himself, and to be bequeathed to his descendants.[3]

This desire for an independence based on landed property was strengthened and encouraged as the 1850s progressed. New democratic leaders emerged from the ranks of the recent immigrants and fired the gold diggers' enthusiasm for holdings of their own. The urban middle class, too, added to the clamour as wealthy businessmen sought to increase both their wealth and social standing by investing in land. Since all the land was now occupied, the only way to satisfy these desires on a large scale was to make the grazing leasehold (or licensed) land of the colony available for cultivation and small farming. This of course brought the new democrats into conflict with the grazing interests, and despite the fact that the former were new to the colony and conversant only with city life, they interpreted opposition to their plans as opposition to the will of the majority and as tacit support for the graziers' 'privileged' interest. They could not see that there might be sound agricultural reasons why an independent landed property was not immediately feasible for the thousands.

The new surge of political activity resulted in the selection legislation of the 1860s which mainly concerned the Crown lands of the colony beyond the Port Phillip region and had only limited relevance to events within the region, although Melbourne did form the main venue for the arguments revolving around the question of land settlement, and the opportunities offered in the land settlement legislation did enable some people to leave the region and take up farms in the new selection areas. The new democrats eventually 'were to suffer defeat and disillusionment before they admitted that many of the squatters' arguments were simple truth and not special pleading'.[4] Small farmers had to have a market for their produce if they were not to be subsistence farmers, and the major markets continued to be centred in Melbourne and Geelong.

With so many newcomers seeking social and psychological security as well as material security during the 1850s and 1860s, 'tenure' and the notion of the small family cropping farm reigned supreme, while the details of agricultural activity were simply left to fall into line. Throughout the period of the immigrant generation, memories and ambitions of the Old World, whether factual or idealized, played a very important part in rural development. There was a continual conflict between what people thought rural life and activity should be and what it actually was. This conflict permeated in varying degrees both urban and rural existence, and is probably seen in its most obvious form when the ideas and actions of the popular urban orators are contrasted with the daily activities and economic situations of the farmers in the nearby rural areas. As a result, many of the government's legislative and administrative actions concerning rural affairs showed a decided lack of knowledge and a misconception of what was actually happening in the countryside (see chapters 7 and 8).

However, at the practical farming level, too, Old World experience was no less influential. The realization that what was good farming practice in England could be the reverse in Victoria, undoubtedly came only slowly and painfully. To plough to a good depth turning up the subsoil or only to break up the first few inches of topsoil, to sow the wheat early with the first autumn rains or to sow late, to house the dairy cattle and horses during winter or to leave them continually out to graze, to shepherd the sheep closely or to graze them in large mobs—the initial decisions on these matters and many others were influenced by past European experience. It was only in time that this influence slowly faded and local colonial experience supplanted it. This, of course, posed further questions and prompted different decisions which will be discussed in a subsequent chapter on farming methods.

Detailed backgrounds of the miscellaneous group of people who came together at Port Phillip and created a new community have not been recorded but an indication of their countries of origin and their religions is available. In this period of strong religious feeling these two factors tended to act as the nuclei about which social groupings formed, for the assertion that the prospective emigrant is 'anxious to know with what associates he and his family will be brought into contact if they leave their native land . . .' was no idle comment. Even within an area as small as the Port Phillip region, differences between the various localities became evident and can in many instances be traced to the origins of the people. As will be shown, the new rural society reflected but did not duplicate these origins.

COUNTRY OF ORIGIN

English, Scottish and Irish

The people who settled in the rural areas of the Port Phillip region were nearly all born in England, Scotland or Ireland; other nationals were numerically insignificant although their concentration within a few particular localities is noteworthy. The English were by far the most numerous; they outnumbered the Irish and both groups outnumbered the Scottish. (Few Welsh settled in the region, and those who did have been included with the 'Other Europeans' in table 1 in the appendix.)

In 1841 the Scottish had outnumbered the Irish except in the cropping area north of the Yarra River where there had been a slight difference in favour of the Irish, and in urban Melbourne and Williamstown where there had been approximately twice as many Irish as Scottish.[5]

By 1851 the relative numerical position of the Irish and Scottish had changed and the Irish outnumbered the Scottish in both the rural and the urban parts of the region. Despite this, control of the land remained in the hands of the English and the Scottish. The majority of the Irish who were in the colony in the early years from 1835 to 1841 were relatively poor and unskilled, and preferred to stay in the urban centre of Melbourne, but thereafter their numbers in the rural areas increased as employment possibilities increased with the development and consolidation of rural settlement. Their advent formed almost a second phase of settlement. They became the workers who followed in the wake of the front-line settlers, who claimed the 'right to the land'.

The proportionately rapid increase in the number of Irish-born in the population continued and between 1854 and 1861 the number in the rural population increased by 117 per cent while the numbers of English- and Scottish-born increased by only 78 and 73 per cent respectively (see table 6).

Neil Coughlan has recently studied the emigration of the Irish to Victoria during the 1850s and 1860s, basing much of his work on an analysis of the marriage certificates of three Roman Catholic church parishes—St Mary's of West Melbourne, old St Francis's, and St Monica's of Moonee Ponds. The first two are in urban Melbourne but the third includes the Shire of Keilor, one of the four shires comprising the Sunbury division. Coughlan also used the passenger lists from the emigrant ships, among other sources, and found that of the Irish who came to Victoria during the fifties and sixties,

> two-thirds of them came from [Munster], from Galway in Connacht, and from Kilkenny on the southwestern edge of Leinster. One in five came from Tipperary alone.
>
> eighty-nine per cent were unskilled . . . Of the English and Scottish men, an even fifty per cent were unskilled . . . One Irish male adult in ten was married; of the English and Scottish, one in four . . . Seventy-nine per cent of the Irish males . . . were between the ages of 17 and 31; of the English and Scottish only fifty-four per cent . . .

As Coughlan quite rightly points out,

> these figures make no allowance for Irish Protestants. Consequently Ulster is minimized in the proportions derived from them. All external evidence, however, indicates that the migration of northern Presbyterians to Australia in this period was quite small. Likewise it was the Catholic peasant who was leaving the South in large numbers, not the Protestant gentry.[6]

A comparison of the totals of Irish nationals and Roman Catholics in the various divisions in 1861 supports this contention for the Bacchus Marsh, Sunbury and Berwick divisions, which have the same proportions, and also for the Bellarine, Barrabool and Bannockburn divisions, but there is some indication that there were more Protestants among the Irish in the Oakleigh division than in these other divisions.

Quite apart from any lure of gold, this emigration was induced by the aftermath of the potato famine in Ireland. Many evictions had occurred and those who remained on the land took a much sterner attitude towards commercial farming. Primogeniture spread quickly. Meanwhile things had improved sufficiently for the labourers to save a few pounds and it was the young and unmarried landless rural labourers who began fleeing the country. Many who settled in Australia were soon able to send money back to relatives to enable them, in turn, to emigrate. Religion and cultural background tended to keep these Irish people together on the emigrant ships coming to Victoria, and on their arrival these people gravitated to areas such as that just north of Melbourne where, proportionately, large numbers of poor labourers and Irish had been living since 1841, thus further strengthening the tendency to form subgroups within the larger community.

The young and single Irish farm labourers and farmers who settled in large numbers in the Sunbury division during the latter half of the 1850s, found employment as labourers either on the farms (which by now formed part of the extended cropping area), where the ratio of farm employees to farmers of 2·3 to 1 was the second highest of any division in 1861, or in the quarrying industry. Their importance in terms of agricultural development was more as a labour force working under the direction of other people, contributing physical manpower but having little influence on the farm management decisions. Their background of peasant life based on the cultivation of the potato had less impact on agriculture in this area than their numerical strength might indicate.

For the year 1861 the rural divisions of the Port Phillip region fall into two groups, those in which the English had an absolute majority numerically over the Scottish and Irish together, and those in which they did not. As shown in map 11, the English had an absolute majority in the southern part of the region (Bellarine, Barrabool and Mornington divisions) and in the north-eastern part (Plenty East

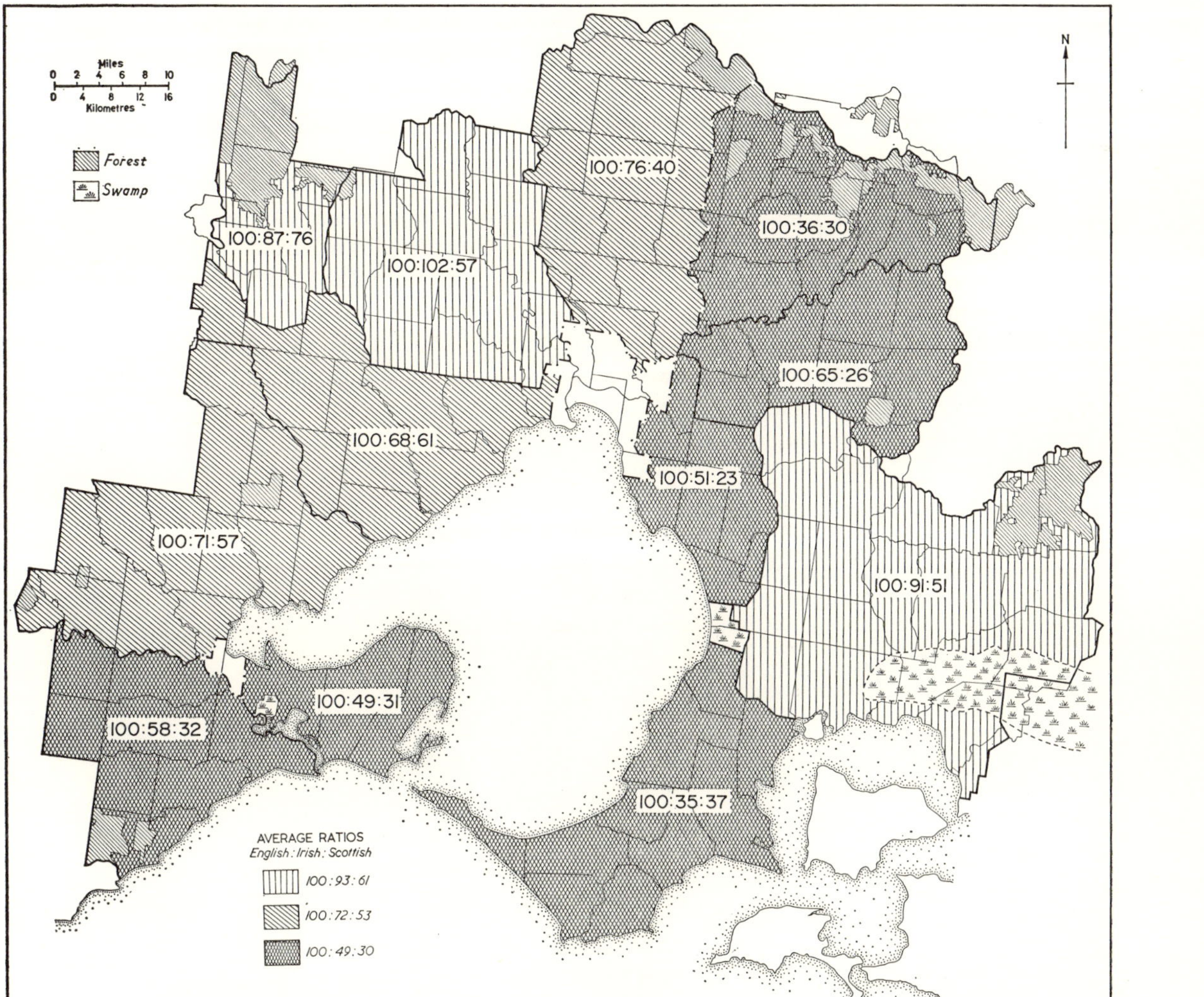

Map 11 Population in 1861—the Ratios of English to Irish to Scottish
Census, 1861, Birth-places

and Lilydale and Oakleigh divisions). In all of these divisions the Scottish formed minority groups which were numerically only 23–37 per cent as strong as the English. The Irish total varied 35–65 per cent of the English. In the Lilydale division the Irish formed quite a substantial group while the Scottish were few in number, but in the Mornington division the Scottish outnumbered the Irish by 37 to 35. This was the only division in which this occurred, but the number of people involved was small—only 231 Scottish and 221 Irish—and certainly not a significant difference considering the numbers involved and the reliability of the census.

In general it may be said that the southern and north-eastern parts of the region were settled by English-born people together with small groups of Scottish and small to quite substantial groups of Irish. In the remaining divisions, where the English did not have an absolute majority, there were higher proportions of both Irish and Scottish to English; the range being from 40 per cent to 76 per cent of the English total for the Scottish, and from 68 per cent to 102 per cent for the Irish. In particular in the Bacchus Marsh and Berwick divisions the Irish were approaching the English in numerical strength (330–381 and 446–488 respectively) and in the Sunbury division they outnumbered the English in the proportion of 102 to 100 (1880 to 1841).

In the succeeding decade, 1861–71, when there was a net loss of people from the region as a whole, the greatest loss was among the Scottish-born—a net loss of 27 per cent of the 1861 total by 1871—next were the English with a 23 per cent loss, and lastly the Irish with a loss of 18 per cent. From 1871 to 1881 the losses continued with the Scottish decreasing by a further 24 per cent, again the highest rate of decline although lower than the previous decade. The English rate of loss had also declined—to 18 per cent; however, the Irish depopulation rate had increased to 22 per cent (see table 6).

Table 6
Intercensal Changes in the Numbers of English- , Scottish- and Irish-born (rural divisions)

Period	English	Scottish	Irish
1854–61 net gain (excluding Sunbury and Oakleigh divisions)			
1854 total	6 904	2 811	3 626
Change (no.)	+5 350	+2 058	+4 239
Percentage change on 1854 total	+77·5	+73·2	+116·9
1861-71 net loss			
1861 total	16 753	6 537	11 095
Change (no.)	−3 769	−1 765	− 1 982
Percentage change on 1861 total	−22·5	−27·0	−17·9
1871-81 net loss			
1871 total	12 984	4 772	9 113
Change (no.)	−2 271	−1 133	−2 033
Percentage change on 1871 total	−17·5	−23·7	−22·3

Sources: Censuses, 1854, 1861, 1871, 1881, Birth-places

In other words, from 1854 to 1881, when the total population was increasing, the numbers of Scottish-born increased at the slowest rate, and then declined at the fastest rate when the total population was declining, so that during the whole period the numerical strength of the Scottish relative to both the English and the Irish was steadily declining. Similarly from 1854 to 1871 the English were losing ground to the Irish, but from 1871 to 1881 the positions of the English and Irish were reversed and the Irish declined in numbers at a faster rate than the English.

It is tempting to determine the significance of the differences between these figures and to interpret them in terms of relative settler stability. But this would be an over-simplification, because the changes in the net totals of the nationals reflect the composite result of differential birth- and death-rates, immigration into and emigration from the region, and this implicates the various 'push' factors in the source countries and the relative 'pull' of the region.

The most likely explanation is that of a largely English and Scottish farming community occupying Crown land at a nominal rate under licence, with some freehold ownership and tenant farming. These people predominated and remained in control until the early fifties when sale of the land forced many of them to move, and the gold-fields attracted others. This movement was complicated during the fifties by the arrival of new settlers who bought land at the auctions for new farms, leased farms, or just worked on the land. At this point the Irish arrived in considerable numbers, but as employees rather than employers. By the sixties crops were failing and prices for produce, inflated by the gold rushes, were returning to a lower level. Many of the English and Scottish who had been in the area for some years decided it was time to leave. The Irish, however, had not been in the area quite so long and, being relatively impoverished and less skilled, many could not afford to leave. They persevered, even if only as labourers. By the seventies many among the Scottish and English, particularly the proprietors of farms, would have moved if they were going to, and those who now remained were well established. The death-rate among these people was increasing by this stage. The Irish people, however, had now had time to improve their financial position, were a little younger than the English and Scottish, and increasingly were able to leave the somewhat depressed region for other areas.

During the years 1835–81 the Scottish tended to be the most mobile, and this was evident in almost every division. Margaret Kiddle found that at least two-thirds of the settlers who took up land in the Western District were Scottish, and nearly all of them were Lowlands farmers.[7] People from the same group settled the Port Phillip region (part of which is in Margaret Kiddle's Western District). These people were enterprising and had come from one of the most advanced farming areas in the United Kingdom; many had some capital and had been in the colony early enough to prosper from leasing Crown land and grazing sheep. Such people followed the opportunities across the colony, as did some of their English counterparts. Not, however, the urban unskilled and the Irish crofter. They had neither the experience nor the capital to help them to prosper in a competitive rural economy already dominated by the more skilled and affluent English and Scottish people; they remained the less mobile labourers.

Thus the major overseas influences on agricultural development came from England and Scotland. It was from these countries that the majority of farm occupants came and it was to these countries, and in particular to the Royal Agricultural

Society of England and the Highland and Agricultural Society of Scotland, that the leading farmers turned to learn of the latest developments in agriculture.

Germans, Swiss and other minority national groups

Small groups of Germans settled in the Barrabool division at Germantown (now Grovedale) and surrounding areas, in the Plenty division at Thomastown and nearby parishes and in the east at Greensborough, in the Lilydale division around Doncaster, Bulleen and Nunawading, in the Oakleigh division particularly in the parish of Boroondara, and in the Berwick division.

These groups of German settlers were farming people who normally settled in the rural areas outside the townships. They occupied undulating to hilly land, often quite heavily timbered and in the higher rainfall areas of the region. They were hard-working farmers who characteristically owned their own small farms and farmed them intensively. Their location on the outer extremities of the then cultivated areas, pushing the boundaries of these areas farther back into the timbered country yet still remaining within a day's journey of the city market, probably reflects a strong desire for farms of their own and a willingness to work very hard to achieve this.

At about the same time that Germans were coming to Victoria, either directly or via South Australia, they were also emigrating in larger numbers to other parts of the world including Texas, another region where virgin land was being occupied. In Texas in the pre-war period from the 1840s to the 1860s the German settlers tended to own smaller properties and in general to farm on a smaller scale than their Anglo-American neighbours, but they farmed their land more intensively, were more commercialized in their undertakings, and had a higher degree of freehold ownership, apparently shunning tenancy where possible. The Germans were also less mobile than the Anglo-Americans; having acquired their land they preferred to remain on it.[8] The Germans in the Port Phillip region showed similar tendencies; like their Texas counterparts, they grew similar crops to their neighbours though they did show a preference in some divisions for viticulture.

In 1861, in the parish of Berwick, the Germans were primarily engaged in clearing their land and growing wheat, oats and potatoes;[9] they were also very active in dairying. These people were mostly Silesians and probably had no knowledge of viticulture; similarly many of the Doncaster Germans were from Silesia, and a number of the Thomastown settlers were from Mecklenburg, Saxony and Silesia[10] (a similar origin to many of the Texas Germans). However, sufficient Germans did have an interest in viticulture for them to plant many small vineyards, particularly around Germantown in the Barrabool division but also around Melbourne. Nevertheless they tended to remain among the lesser of the entrepreneurs, the Swiss being the leaders in this field.

Individual Germans may have pioneered the way for, and lent impetus to, orcharding, market gardening and other forms of intensive land use, such as dairying, located reasonably close to the city and supplying the growing population. In Texas the Germans showed an affinity for this type of enterprise, which was consistent with their rural background. It is perhaps significant that there is a correlation between the location of these enterprises and the location of the German settlers. In this field the German settlers in the Doncaster area were probably the most important because it was in the Lilydale and Oakleigh divisions that orchards, and to a lesser extent market gardens, were most extensively planted. But the extent to which the German and British settlers influenced each other, or in turn were influenced by other factors, in developing the orchards remains a question as yet unresolved.

Few other Europeans settled in the Port Phillip region. Of those who did, the Swiss were the most numerous. The emigration from Switzerland, mainly from Canton Neuchâtel, is an example of chain migration which in this case was initiated by Charles La Trobe, Superintendent of the Port Phillip District from 1839 and Lieutenant-Governor of Victoria from 1851 to 1854. La Trobe, although an Englishman, had lived in Neuchâtel from 1824 to 1827 and later married the daughter of one of the leading aristocratic families of the Canton. Shortly after he and his wife came to Port Phillip, there was considerable political unrest in the Swiss cantons as a result of which the aristocracy lost much of its power. With encouragement from La Trobe to come to Victoria, a number of Swiss people emigrated to the colony and, in turn, induced more of their countrymen to emigrate.

These Swiss people settled near Lilydale, in the Barrabool Hills and in the Bannockburn division around Batesford and along the Moorabool River. Their major contribution to the agriculture of the region was in viticulture, in which they were the acknowledged leaders, and the wines from such vineyards as Yering, Yeringburg and St Hubert's near Lilydale, or Paradise and Victoria near Geelong, were successfully exhibited at a number of international exhibitions.[11]

The influence of the Swiss in the field of viticulture was out of all proportion to their numbers; they do not appear, however, to have influenced any other sector of agriculture, and the greatest influence in viticulture was due to the activities of only a very few men, in particular Hubert and Paul de Castella, and Baron Guillaume de Pury near Lilydale, and Louis Pettavel, John Belperroud and James Dardel near Geelong.

The de Castellas and de Purys brought capital with them when emigrating and subsequently developed the three large vineyards near Lilydale—Yering, Yeringburg, and St Hubert's—vineyards which overshadowed all others in the neighbourhood both for the scale of the undertakings (the largest was 260 acres) and the enterprise with which they were conducted. They sold on the London as well as Australian and New Zealand markets and imported much of their equipment from France and Switzerland.

Other much smaller vineyards were planted near Lilydale but they tended to be (with a few exceptions such as that belonging to the Deschamps, another Swiss family) only a minor part of a mixed farm, or else their owners were partly involved in outside work. The de Castellas brought out a number of Swiss from Neuchâtel to establish their vineyards, and subsequently some of these people moved to the Barrabool Hills and joined countrymen already there.

A few Frenchmen were associated with the Swiss people and played their part in establishing viticulture near Lilydale and in the Barrabool Hills. But they, like many of the Swiss and Germans, had emigrated as single men and therefore the necessity for intermarriage prevented the creation of any strong national community groups.

Of the non-Europeans the only group requiring comment is the Chinese. They usually were represented only by single men, and few were living in the Port Phillip region at the time of any of the censuses. In 1861, 73 Chinese (all males) were recorded in the Bellarine division living in tents in and around the Queenscliff township, and at the next census, in 1871, 23 Chinese were recorded as living under similar conditions. These people may have been engaged in fishing and more particularly in buying and drying fish for the use of their fellow-countrymen in the colony.[12]

Throughout Victoria wherever gold-fields were established, Chinese were to be found, and the gold-fields at Queenstown and the surrounding hill country in the Plenty East division were no exception. In 1861, 74 Chinese were recorded in this division, with a total of 104 in the whole of the Plenty division, and this total rose to 140 by 1871. As on other gold-fields, the Chinese formed a separate group and occupied themselves fossicking among the mullock heaps in search of gold missed by the other diggers, and growing vegetables to sell to the diggers on the fields, an undertaking which waxed and waned with the shifts of the gold-fields population.

Although these minority groups of Germans, Swiss, Chinese and others did not influence the agriculture practised by their neighbours to any great degree, the native culture of these people was important in determining the agriculture of the Port Phillip region as a whole in that vineyards, orchards, market gardens and small intensively cultivated farms flourished in situations where they probably would never have existed if the settlers had been of entirely British origin. Economic factors are often important in determining the location of an agricultural enterprise, and wherever there is a large number of people grouped together in a city someone will exploit the possibilities of economic gain in supplying the food needs of these people. The presence of the cities of Melbourne and Geelong undoubtedly attracted the minority groups but it was their native heritage, more than the market demand for any particular type of produce, which determined the type of farming they practised. For example, while the vineyards lasted, the owners had difficulties finding a remunerative market for their wines.[13] The Germans laboured hard and long to clear and intensively farm small areas of land at a time when more extensive and less arduous farming was the common practice. The Chinese on the gold-fields were often prepared to work under conditions and for rewards that their British neighbours would not have accepted—again as a result of the contrasting cultural frameworks with differing value concepts of labour, money, standard of living, etc.

The agriculture typical of these minority groups mainly lasted only for the lifetimes of the immigrants. As noted previously, no national communities developed, and as the individuals died, so did their characteristic type of farming wherever it diverged markedly from the common practice of the area. This was particularly true in the case of viticulture, where considerable enthusiasm had often been necessary to continue in the industry in the face of poor markets, pests and diseases, and often more profitable alternative land uses. By 1881, 60 per cent of the population in the rural divisions was Victorian-born and it was from about this time that the influence of the people who had immigrated during the 1850s started to decline; thereafter their numbers and their influence declined at an ever-increasing rate.

COMMUNITY FORMATION

Despite the turbulence of the times and the seemingly ever-changing population, some families settled permanently, community groups formed and townships developed throughout the countryside.

As individuals and families became more permanently established in their new locations, the single-roomed tents, wattle-and-dab huts, sod huts, and so on, of the 1836 and 1841 censuses gave way to larger more permanent buildings. With each influx of new settlers the pattern was the same—a rough one- or two-roomed hut was erected from the materials most readily to hand and this sufficed until the owner either moved on or was in a position to build a more substantial house of brick, stone or wood.

The number of dwellings rose and fell with the fluctuations in population, at least from 1861 onwards and presumably for the twenty-five years before that date (see table 7). The fluctuations were mainly accounted for by variations in the number of dwellings of two rooms or less. For example, in the Sunbury division between 1861 and 1871 the population fell sharply and this was accompanied by a fall in the number of dwellings from 1517 to 880. If these numbers are broken down into size of dwellings it will be seen that the dwellings of two rooms or less fell in number from 894 to 240, while the houses of three to six rooms increased from 403 to 493 and of seven or more rooms fell slightly from 125 to 120.

At times, however, the housing situation was complicated by contrasting trends. New people settling in an area, particularly if they had little capital or were uncertain of their future, initially erected a one- or two-roomed hut. As the years passed the settlers who had been in the area for a long time built more comfortable homes and this usually implied houses with more rooms. Therefore the longer an area had been settled, the larger the average number of rooms per house (up to an optimal level). But many of the longest-settled divisions received new influxes of settlers from time to time who had to live under pioneering-type conditions because they did not have the resources to improve their lot immediately or possibly the inclination for permanency, and the resources of the division available to them were limited. In this way a new group of one- and two-roomed dwellings was erected against the background of the more permanent homes of the earlier settlers. Part of this new population went on to establish itself and build larger houses; the other part left and the huts soon fell to pieces.

Some areas after initial occupation were settled at a slower but steadier rate than others, and more particularly at a rate within the capacity of the division to absorb more people while at the same time increasing the overall standard of housing, and presumably of living, within the division. This was the case in the Lilydale and Oakleigh divisions from 1871 to 1881 when a decrease in the number of one- and two-roomed houses was associated with a more than compensatory increase in the number of larger houses.

The Berwick division is an example of the pioneering situation continuing up until 1881. This division consisted of lightly to heavily timbered country and swampland. After the initial occupation of the timbered grassland, settlement was gradually extended back into the more heavily timbered country and swamps. This is reflected in the overall number of houses increasing steadily from 1861 to 1881, and also the number of houses in each category.

A prior requisite for the formation of community groupings is a population with some degree of locational stability. The extent to which this was achieved at Port Phillip is reflected in the type of housing erected by the settlers in the various divisions and at different times. Once some of the settlers had become permanent residents and had made contact with their neighbours, the building of a church or

Table 7
Number and Types of Dwellings
1861, 1871 and 1881

Division	Year	Total no. of dwellings	No. of dwellings having 1–2 rooms	3–6 rooms	7+ rooms	Rooms not specified
Bellarine	1861	982	420	435	77	50
	71	954	264	547	128	15
	81	1062	165	642	205	50
Barrabool	1861	1205	502	548	75	80
	71	1075	256	672	122	25
	81	841	109	572	129	31
Bannockburn	1861	1140	625	407	64	44
	71	970	219	597	123	31
	81	813	86	531	155	41
Bacchus Marsh	1861	347	161	142	34	10
	71	461	143	269	43	6
	81	412	71	242	73	26
Werribee	1861	175	90	64	12	9
	71	299	109	148	28	14
	81	296	72	174	37	13
Sunbury	1861	1517	894	403	125	95
	71	880	240	493	120	27
	81	855	144	527	160	24
Plenty	1861	3016	1243	1290	288	195
	71	3282	1019	1750	448	65
	81	3050	460	1937	567	86
Lilydale	1861	656	354	222	33	47
	71	891	342	455	60	34
	81	1192	285	735	122	50
Oakleigh	1861	1734	674	728	166	166
	71	1817	429	1121	257	10
	81	2383	282	1520	518	63
Berwick	1861	443	205	178	39	21
	71	678	228	336	91	23
	81	1092	307	559	163	63
Mornington	1861	366	183	113	30	40
	71	647	265	287	73	22
	81	847	206	455	131	55

Sources: Censuses, 1861, 1871, 1881, Inhabitants

the establishment of a post office became a tangible sign that a local community was forming. In 1879 Narre Warren was a postal centre serving a small scattered population in what was still a pioneering area in the Berwick division. Besides the post office, there was only an Anglican church and Wesleyan chapel. Ceres, on the other hand, which was one of the oldest townships in a long-settled part of the Barrabool division, in 1879 boasted a post office, blacksmiths, wheelwrights, stone quarries, boot and shoe manufactories, two stores, an electoral registry, a deputy registrar of births and deaths, a state school, a large temperance hall, and places of worship for Catholics, Anglicans, Bible-Christians, Wesleyans and Presbyterians.[14] As was often the case, some of the churches were in or near the township, but others were scattered in isolated splendour throughout the surrounding countryside. Solid edifices of local stone, as befitted a religious people, they were the finest and most permanent structures in the neighbourhood. Several of these churches, now over a century old, are still in regular use.

As nuclei for group formation, the churches were important. As K. S. Inglis noted with reference to the rural people around Bathurst, New South Wales, 'when attendance at worship is counted, they score low; but their lives are affected by religion in ways that are visible only if a denomination is seen as a sort of large family'.[15] Within these 'religious families' much of the entertainment and social life of the community was to be found. Not only was it natural for the members of a 'religious family' to fraternize together, but this was decidedly to be encouraged to prevent inadvertently encouraging a courtship between perhaps a young Roman Catholic lady and a Presbyterian gentleman—a situation to be avoided at all costs by the families of both parties. Divisions of this nature became stronger as the population increased and became more settled, and are still strong in the rural communities of the Port Phillip region today, particularly between the Protestants and Roman Catholics.[16]

These attitudes were in no way unique to rural Australia. As an old English yeoman farmer from Somerset commented after recounting an exploit of his boyhood years—he was born in 1859—'[Father] expected us to respect every denomination, for in those old days, the differences were extremely marked by bigoted bloated Churchmen and the most intolerant nonconformity. Consequently there existed too often a great gulf between these Christian bodies which made Church and Chapel life somewhat intolerable in any village.'[17]

The extent of the religious controversy and unrest at Port Phillip is illustrated by the decision in 1861 of the statistician to list thirty-two categories on the census sheets designed to show the religions of the people of Victoria. Despite this multiplicity of creeds, the overall groupings of Anglican, Presbyterian, Methodist, Roman Catholic and minority groupings remained. Furthermore there is a highly significant correlation between the numbers of Irish-born and Catholics and between the numbers of Scottish-born and Presbyterians recorded in the divisions in 1861, and 98 per cent of the variation between the divisions in the numbers of Presbyterians and Catholics can be accounted for by the variations in the numbers of Irish-born and Scottish-born, respectively. National and religious differences thus reinforced each other.[18]

As the community developed, various secular groups also developed. Agricultural societies were formed, various benefit and friendly societies were established, people organized themselves into local government areas and petitioned the government to proclaim roads board areas and subsequently shires. The mechanics' institutes and the hotels, the latter particularly for the poorer farmers and men, were important places of contact, and from time to time strong political feeling brought people together in support of one cause or other. All provided important opportunities for communication, though they were mainly the trappings of the maturing communities.

The underlying pressures during community formation emanated from the religious, national, social and economic differences, all of which tended to reinforce one another. These pressures were less important during the pioneering days of initial settlement when it was indeed the struggle of 'man against nature', but the Port Phillip region passed through this phase fairly quickly. As people felt themselves to be more secure in their new environment, and the embryonic community groupings took shape, the old differences slowly came to the surface. The resulting pressures then gave form to the community groupings which, through the mutual influence of the individuals, in turn helped to shape the agriculture of the region.

5 : The Farmers

POPULATION 1854–1881

Throughout the 1850s the gold fever raged in the colony of Victoria as new finds enticed diggers to new fields. Meanwhile in the Port Phillip region the population grew rapidly. Melbourne, the centre of commerce, the gateway to the gold-fields on one side and to the world on the other, continued to expand. People disembarked there and some stayed; many others returned there from the gold-fields and also stayed. Likewise newcomers and ex-diggers moved out into the rural divisions seeking work and land. Between 1854 and 1861 the population of the rural divisions more than doubled from 27 986 to 57 981, and in Melbourne the population rose from 82 430 to 124 861. In Geelong, however, the changes were slight and the population only rose from 19 079 to about 21 000.

During the first three years of this period the greatest influx of people was to the Bellarine, Barrabool and Bannockburn divisions around Geelong, and to the area between the Plenty River and Deep Creek in the Plenty division north of Melbourne. Of these divisions, the largest gains were in the oldest agricultural areas in the Barrabool and Plenty West divisions where the increases were of the order of 1111 and 1120 people per year respectively (see table 8).

During the following four years the overall rate of population growth in the rural divisions fell and the centres of settlement shifted from the Geelong area, except for Bannockburn where the increase was still about 462 people per year, to the Oakleigh division, south-east of Melbourne, and to Sunbury, north-west of Melbourne, where the average rates were 647 and 598 people per year respectively. Both these areas had been farmed for some time and, as with the previously mentioned divisions, were major centres of population before 1854.

These long-settled areas attracted the ex-diggers (many of whom had little money)[1] because a tenant farm could only be obtained where the land was already under freehold, and rural work was to be found only where farms were already established. With thousands more mouths to feed, farm produce of all types had a ready market and many landowners were happy to lease their land for high rentals. When prices were at their peak in 1854 and 1855 annual rentals of 35s per acre and upwards were agreed to for land on the Bellarine Peninsula and Barrabool Hills.[2] Small farming boomed around Geelong and in the established cropping areas, and many cartloads of produce were dispatched each week to the diggings. But the gold-fields were not the only market; burgeoning Melbourne needed ever-greater quantities of food, and as the gold-fields populations moved farther away

Table 8
Average Population Gain (persons per year) in Each Division

Division	Population in 1854 (persons)	1854–57	1857–61	1861–71	1871–81
Bellarine	2 287	598	184	− 6	56
Barrabool	2 212	1 111	203	−70	−138
Bannockburn	1 178	849	462	−18	−98
Bacchus Marsh	1 157*	72	106	64	−19
Werribee	321	161	14	62	− 2
Sunbury	4 116	252	598	−190	−55
Plenty West	9 303	1 120	298	70	−117
Plenty East	996	328	135	119	−16
Lilydale	829	415	271	138	114
Oakleigh	4 677	147	647	177	317
Berwick	496	318	215	123	136
Mornington	414	198	192	114	88
Geelong	19 079	661	−36	−114	−57
Melbourne	82 430	7 186	5 218	6 659	7 094

* Includes Gorong parish to the west

from Geelong and more food was grown closer to the diggings, an increasing emphasis was given to feeding Melbourne. Settlers moved into the Oakleigh division in particular, opening up market gardens and small farms, while timely sales of Crown land in this area also lent impetus to this migration.

A decline in many areas followed the rapid growth of population in the 1850s. The exodus was considerable in some divisions, for despite a high birth-rate there was still a net loss (see table 8). The three divisions around Geelong—Bellarine, Barrabool, and Bannockburn—had average net losses of 6, 70, and 18 people per year respectively during the decade 1861–71. The trend was the same in Geelong where the population fell at a rate of 114 people per year. However, the decline in the country divisions cannot be solely attributed to the decline in Geelong, because the Sunbury division, too, was losing population at a rate of 190 people per year in the same decade and in an area which was at most only twenty-five miles from Melbourne where the population was increasing at a rate of 6659 people per year and by 1871 had reached a total of 191 449 people.

The contrasting population trends in Sunbury and Melbourne continued during the next decade, 1871–81, with the population of Melbourne reaching 262 389 people by 1881. The Barrabool and Bannockburn divisions, together with Geelong, continued to lose population, and in fact the population fell in all the rural divisions from Lake Connewarre north and east around the bay to the Yarra River. The only division to reverse the trend was Bellarine where the population had declined from 1861 to 1871, but increased from 1871 to 1881, despite a declining population in Geelong and adjacent areas. This exodus of people was mainly due to the collapse of the unstable cropping enterprises which had been built on the demands of the transient gold-fields populations and the excess optimism of the earlier period. The subsequent reversal of the trend in Bellarine was mainly due to the increased activity in onion, potato and pea growing, and stripping wattle bark, for which there was a good market in the 1870s. Such produce was easily shipped to Melbourne and Geelong, sea transport providing a considerable advantage over alternative forms of transport.

The areas that maintained a continual growth in population from 1854 to 1881 were the four divisions south of the Yarra River and east of Melbourne, namely Lilydale, Oakleigh, Berwick and Mornington. Here a more soundly based expansion was geared to the development of Melbourne and the Melbourne market. In 1854 Oakleigh already had a substantial population and this increased rapidly during 1857–61 and more slowly thereafter. Lilydale, Berwick and Mornington were only sparsely populated in 1854 with less than 2000 people in the whole area. The fastest period of growth here was during the next three years to 1857, but the influx of people was minor compared with that to some other divisions, for example Barrabool and Bannockburn. Nevertheless, a steady growth was maintained right through until 1881, when the total populations of both Lilydale and Berwick exceeded those of Barrabool and Bannockburn, and Mornington was not far behind.

It must be stressed that the foregoing figures represent net population movements only; at all times there was movement both into and out of each division, together with variable birth- and death-rates, which were particularly variable where there was a sudden large influx of young people. Contrasting population movements within a division are revealed in some cases in the census figures for birth-places of the people. For example, between 1861 and 1871 there was a gain of Continentals other than French and Germans in both Barrabool and Bannockburn, although both divisions had net population losses. The immigrants in this instance were mainly Swiss.[3] During the same decade in the Bacchus Marsh division, there was a net loss of English and Scottish and a net gain of Irish, while the division as a whole showed a population increase. Contrasting the Lilydale and Berwick divisions for the period 1871–81, it can be shown that the population increase in Lilydale was due to natural increase, and possibly some local migration, as the numbers of foreign-born declined. However, in Berwick, immigration into the area was still evident since there was an increase in foreign-born as well as Victorian-born.

RURAL WORKFORCE

As the population increased in all rural divisions up until about 1861, but decreased in many thereafter—a fact substantiated by reports from 1862 onwards[4] —it is particularly illuminating to examine the population in more detail at this point in time. In 1861 the census recorded a rural population of 57 981 consisting of 32 903 males and 25 078 females. Of the males, approximately one-third were engaged in agriculture, one-third were scholars or were under fifteen years of age and not working, and the remaining third included all other males. Of the third engaged in agriculture, 4599 were independent farmers and 6925 were employees.

In this population it can be assumed that the males aged fifteen and older were the bread-winners for the community. Wives and children certainly assisted the adult males in their work, but within the context of the present discussion their contribution was marginal. Similarly the aged males, say seventy and older, were sufficiently few in number to be unimportant. Therefore, half the bread-winners were directly employed in agriculture, and at least one-third of the remainder were dependent on the agricultural sector for their livelihood. This latter category includes the rural storekeepers, bakers, butchers, implement makers, carters, post splitters, etc., living in the rural areas and catering directly for the needs of the farming people (and of course for one another's needs). Similarly, at least some of the professional people were also dependent upon the farming people for their clientele and hence their income. Thus the prosperity of the rural community was directly dependent upon the prosperity of the agriculture, and this in turn was dependent upon how the 4599 farmers farmed their properties.

The proportion of the bread-winners engaged directly in agriculture altered little between 1861 and 1881. In the Oakleigh division there was an exception to this because of the rapid extension of urban settlement into this area; the 61 per cent of the fifteen and older male age group engaged in agriculture in 1861 had fallen to 39 per cent by 1881. The comparatively low percentages shown in table 9 for the Bannockburn division (50 per cent) in 1861 and for the Sunbury division (46 per

Table 9
Male Agricultural Workers (employers and employees) as a Percentage of All Males Aged Fifteen and Older, 1861 and 1881

Division	1861			1881		
	Agricultural workers	Males 15+	Percentage	Agricultural workers	Males 15+	Percentage
Bellarine	916	1502	61·0	890	1656	53·7
Barrabool	1600	2050	78·0	939	1328	70·7
Bannockburn	967	1936	49·9	858	1355	63·3
Bacchus Marsh	357	613	58·2	411	709	58·0
Werribee	245	318	77·0	406	475	85·5
Sunbury	1341	2941	45·6	856	1660	51·6
Plenty	2804	6568	42·7	2558	6183	41·4
Lilydale	813	1158	70·2	1207	1918	63·0
Oakleigh	1583	2614	60·6	1554	4027	38·6
Berwick	619	832	74·4	1227	1821	67·4
Mornington	279	737	37·9	661	1184	55·8

Sources: Census, 1861, Occupations, Ages; Census, 1881, Ages; Stat., 1880, Production

cent and 52 per cent) in 1861 and 1881 are due to quarrying activities there. Similarly in the Plenty division the low percentages (43 per cent and 41 per cent) are due to the employment of a number of the bread-winners in quarrying together with the inclusion of statistics for the inmates of Pentridge Gaol and the Yarra Bend Asylum. The low percentage for the Mornington division (38 per cent) in 1861 is due to the presence of government officers, and quarrying and construction men, mainly associated with the quarantine station at Point Nepean.

Despite these anomalies, the point remains that the fluctuations noted previously in the total population were paralleled by fluctuations in the agricultural workforce. Approximately, in the divisions south of the Yarra River, after the 1850s, there was a prolonged and steady growth in the rural workforce, while in the other divisions the workforce available to agriculture declined. The relative employment opportunities in these latter divisions apparently were insufficient to retain the workforce that was already present. Not that there was always an unqualified surfeit of labour in these areas. Much of the work, such as shearing, harvesting and vintage, was seasonal in nature, and many of the potential workers, particularly viticultural workers, were lacking in the skills appropriate to the various tasks they wished to undertake.

All types of agricultural workers did not leave (or enter) agriculture at the same rate. R. Bićanić has noted the tendency for the agricultural population to decrease in developed countries and has pointed out that those who leave first tend to be the unpaid family workers and then the hired labourers, while the owner operators are the most stable.[5] Evidence relating to the ages of the most mobile groups (next section) and in some divisions to the stability of the total number of holdings (see chapter 7) suggests that the same pattern was true of the decreasing rural population in the Port Phillip region. However, a point was reached in some divisions, and Barrabool was one of them, when very small holdings, particularly tenant holdings, became unviable and the only solution was for the occupants to leave some of them so that these holdings could be regrouped into larger, more viable, units. It is also true that the population as a whole was by nature more mobile than those with which Bićanić was dealing.

Wherever there was a population loss during the 1860s and 1870s the land utilization underwent at the same time a change from cropping to grazing or to mixed farming with a large grazing component, with the consequent lower requirement of labour per unit of land. Conversely in those areas where the population increased, land use became more intensified and, unlike the 1850s, also more specialized. Relatively labour-intensive forms of production such as dairying, orcharding, market gardening, and onion growing, all developed where rainfall, soils, and market possibilities gave them the best chances of economic success.

It was the lot of the farmers to adapt to these changes. Unfortunately the census figures do not give a detailed description of this group of people as such. Nevertheless the farmers did constitute 20 per cent of the males aged fifteen and older, and the farmers together with their employees constituted, in many divisions, well over half of the males in this age group. Therefore an analysis of this group will give some indication of the characteristics of the farmers and of their employees and, in particular, of their family responsibilities, their age and their standard of education—three personal factors that can be important in determining how a farmer adapts to change and manages his farm.

ADAPTABILITY TO CHANGE

Age and responsibility

Approximately 20 per cent of the males aged fifteen years and older were making the farm management decisions which affected the rural prosperity of the whole region. Between 1861 and 1871 the percentage of males in this age group fell and the responsibility per bread-winner, on the average, increased (see table 10). Taking the figures for the Bellarine division, in 1854 the average bread-winner had to provide for himself plus 1·7 dependants and by 1871 this had increased to 2·6 dependants. From a quantitative point of view these figures have limited meaning because they include unmarried sons, independent young men, and fathers with

Table 10
Males Aged Fifteen and Older as a Percentage of the Total Population

Division	1854	1861	1871	1881
Bellarine	36·7	31·2	28·0	31·2
Barrabool	33·8	32·3	28·4	31·0
Bannockburn	—	34·7	28·1	30·7
Bacchus Marsh	—	35·3	29·7	31·6
Werribee	—	37·0	36·4	32·6
Sunbury	—	40·5	28·6	34·5
Plenty	—	40·1	36·5	36·5
Lilydale	—	37·0	34·7	33·8
Oakleigh	—	33·9	30·5	31·8
Berwick	43·5	36·0	32·5	37·2
Mornington	42·0	41·0	34·5	31·3

Sources: Censuses, 1854, 1861, 1871, 1881, Ages

families of ten or more. Nevertheless they do indicate the very real trends within the community towards increasing demands on the bread-winners.

This increase in dependants was to be expected. Table 11 shows that the people who settled in the rural areas before 1861 were young. Having settled they proceeded to have families. However, people then began leaving the area, but they left in disproportionate numbers. In the two decades 1861–71 and 1871–81 in the

Table 11
Males Aged Forty and Older as a Percentage
of Males Aged Fifteen and Older

Division	1854	1861	1871	1881
Bellarine	24·8	29·8	44·1	41·2
Barrabool	30·2	31·1	40·9	43·3
Bannockburn	—	27·5	39·4	42·5
Bacchus Marsh	—	22·7	39·6	43·4
Werribee	—	28·3	30·1	40·2
Sunbury	—	25·2	37·3	42·9
Plenty	—	30·4	39·9	42·4
Lilydale	—	27·7	37·8	41·7
Oakleigh	—	31·6	40·3	39·8
Berwick	25·0	27·2	38·3	37·6
Mornington	23·6	26·5	38·8	44·0

Sources: Censuses, 1854, 1861, 1871, 1881, Ages

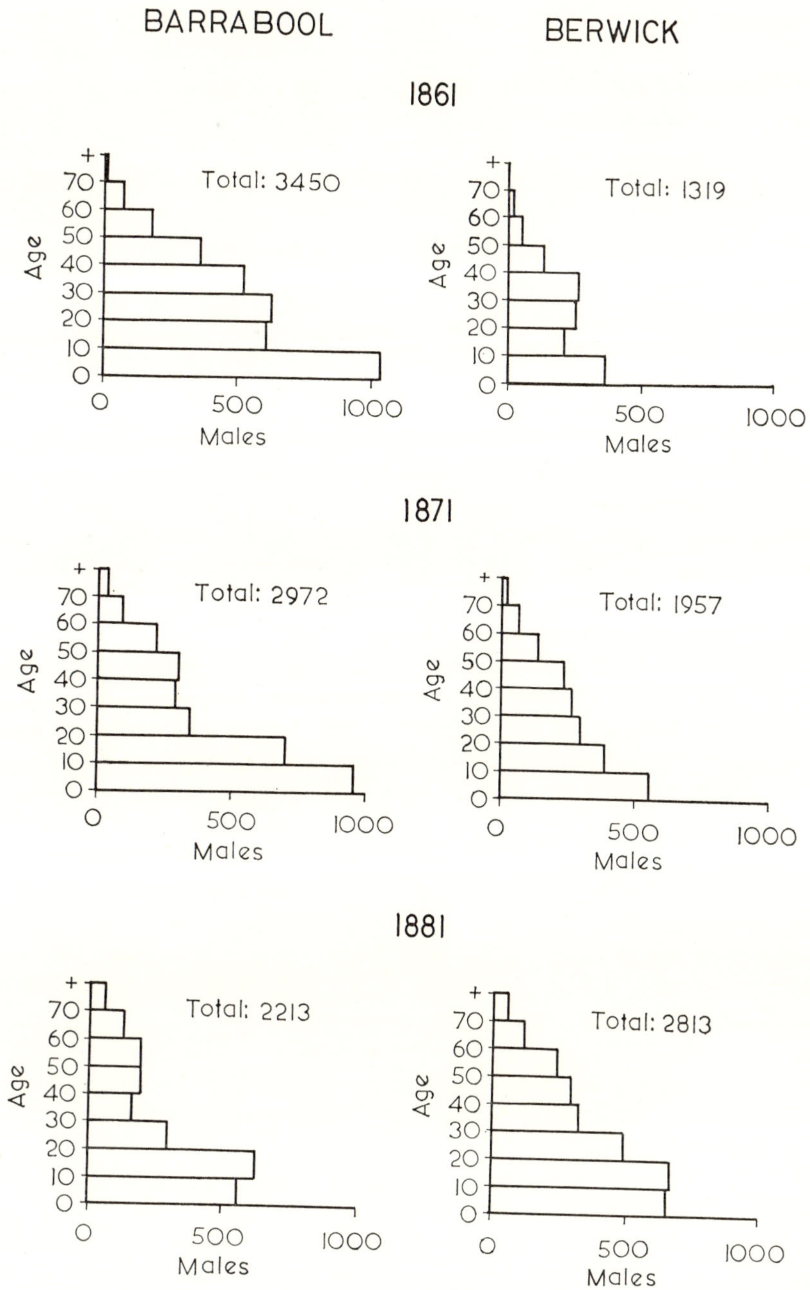

Fig. 1 Male Age Pyramids for Barrabool and Berwick Divisions, 1861, 1871 and 1881

Barrabool division, only 47 per cent and 46 per cent, respectively, of the men aged twenty to twenty-nine at the beginning of the ten-year period were there at the end, and wherever the population was decreasing, the major exodus tended to be in this age group (see fig. 1). Therefore, as a comparison of tables 10 and 11 shows, the situation arose during the sixties and seventies whereby the bread-winners were becoming older and older and at the same time were increasingly under pressure to provide for dependants. By 1881 family responsibilities had started to ease as the children grew up and entered the workforce or left the farms, and during the eighties the immigrant fathers were to give way to the first generation of locally born Victorians.

Recent work in rural sociology and allied fields has demonstrated that there is a close correlation between increasing age and the decreasing ability of a farmer to adapt his farm management to changing situations. It has also been shown that people under stress, for example, to produce, may increase their level of performance under moderate pressure, but become less efficient when the pressure becomes severe.[6]

An opportune time to introduce radical change on a family farm would be when the younger generation took over control from the older generation. But during the early 1860s, when radical changes became necessary on many farms in the Port Phillip region, it was the people who had been on these farms for something like ten years, and not their sons (who mostly were still too young) who had to make the changes. The implications of this are a slower rate of change with greater resistance to change than otherwise might have been expected. For instance, during this period when wheat growing became most unprofitable, there was an apparent reluctance on the part of the farmers to give up wheat growing in favour of other, more profitable, enterprises. This reluctance appears to have stemmed from the traditions and virtues of wheat growing as discussed in chapter 3, and the fact that these farmers had grown wheat sufficiently long to have become accustomed to wheat production. A few years more and their sons, less fettered by Old World notions and spurred on by youthful interest in new methods and ideas, would probably have made the change much more rapidly. Similar examples might also be cited of the viticulturists whose sons eventually uprooted their vineyards. National tradition played a part here, but so too did age and a changing generation. Also once wheat growing had been abandoned in favour of livestock grazing and mixed farming, it was the younger men who were most likely to introduce the integrated livestock and rotational cropping systems; the older men tended to adhere to more straightforward grazing or simpler farming methods. Where family responsibilities allowed, this could approach a form of semi-retirement, an example of which is given in the next chapter.

Education

In a different context George Russell was certainly aware of the realities of management when, before leaving for a visit to Britain, he instructed his deputy 'to do little or nothing with your hands, but keep your *eyes*, *ears*, & *brain*, particularly the *latter*, wide-a-wake.' Or, as the old saying went, 'Let the hands use the spade,/But the head direct the plough.'[7] A high level of education and diversity of experience were a definite advantage in directing the plough and overcoming the problems of change and adaptation.

During the twenty years 1861–81 the technical aspects of farming were continually changing—pleuro-pneumonia, rust, caterpillars, phylloxera, and other pests had to be contended with, while reapers, strippers, threshers, double-furrow ploughs, and steam power were all possible additions to the farm. Various forms of fertilizer were being considered by the advanced farmers who were also putting more and more land under pasture.

Each individual farm occupant had three main ways of learning about these and other advances in farming. He heard about them, read about them or deduced them from his own knowledge and experience. For the present we will ignore the first point, important though it is, and consider only the second and that part of the third which involves the farmer in keeping written records. An example of how a farmer learnt from his records is available in the diaries of James Stewart Johnston, a former vice-president of the Board of Land and Works, who owned a vineyard at Sunbury, climatically a difficult area for grape harvesting. In January 1870, after keeping a daily record of his activities for five years Johnston was able to conclude,

> We aught to begin pruning about 6 June & put on strength enough to get finished about 1st Aug. Commence Tying down canes about 1st Aug & finish by the 25th at the *latest*! It takes fully 3 weeks. Pruning takes about 8 weeks The Vines begin to bud about 10th Sept. that is the buds swell. The tying up of the shoots aught to be begun about 20th Oct. & . . . [8]

But how many farm managers were capable of keeping records and learning from the farming books, journals, newspapers and pamphlets? The best indication we have of this is in an estimate of the literacy of males fifteen years and older, based on the census information as to whether people could both read and write, read only or not read. As might be expected, literacy and level of education tend to be closely related to a farmer's ability to manage his farm and adapt to change.[9] This is not to deny the existence of the illiterate but prosperous farmer, who certainly existed as many an old farmer will recount. Nevertheless the descriptions by I. Batey of many of his farming neighbours in the Sunbury division serve to illustrate the general conclusions of the rural sociologists.[10]

Traditionally agriculture has been the province of the less well educated. The comment 'he hasn't any brains so we'll put him on the land' is still all too common[11] and the immigrant population at Port Phillip very rapidly sorted itself out according to this dictum. By the census of 1851, 89 per cent of males in Melbourne aged 21+ could read and write, compared with only 72 per cent in the country areas of County Grant (that is, the rural divisions around Geelong).[12] The percentages of males aged 15–39 and 40+ who stated in 1854, 1871 and 1881 that they could both read and write are given in table 5 in the appendix (the 15–39 group of 1854 would be approximately the 40+ group of 1881, ignoring population movements). In general the literacy rate continued to be higher in Melbourne than in Geelong, and much higher than in the country divisions. The lowest literacy rates tended to occur in the divisions around Geelong and north of Melbourne in the areas where population decline and other depressive tendencies have been noted. However, although a marked discrepancy in level of education probably continued long after 1881, at least by that date the percentage of males in the rural divisions aged 15–39 who could both read and write had risen by some 10 per cent, since 1854, to exceed 91 per cent, and in some divisions was approaching that in Melbourne of 97 per cent. The educational system and more particularly the Education Act of 1872 (36 Vict., no. 447), which had decreed free, secular and compulsory education for all 6–15-year-olds as from 1 January 1873, had certainly achieved some results. The literacy of the 40+ group had also risen but was still some 10 per cent behind the younger age-group.

The discrepancy in literacy rate between the two age-groups is particularly important because with the rapid emigration of young people from some divisions, the benefits from the increased literacy of this group tended to be lost and even a decline in the overall literacy of the male workforce in some areas may have occurred after 1861. Where there was a net immigration of young people, for example into the Berwick division, the opposite effect of rapidly increasing overall literacy would have been achieved.

The literacy rate as given in the appendix is probably an over-estimate of the literacy of those engaged in agriculture, since the figures include about 16 per cent of people who were employed in government, the professions and trading, and therefore were presumably literate. If this percentage is deducted from the 'beyond Melbourne' males for 1854, the percentage for the remainder of the males in the 15+ age-group is reduced from 86 per cent to about 83 per cent. Unfortunately education and occupation figures of sufficient detail are not available together in any one census for use in the areas defined, but a reduction in estimates of the literacy of the agricultural workforce, as above, appears to be quite valid.

The relative literacy of the farmers was low, and particularly so in the more depressed rural areas. A low standard of education, a lack of innovation, and poor farm management are usually associated with a low literacy rate in these circumstances, and some farmers, at least, were very limited in their adaptability simply because they could neither read nor write. The farmers who most needed to alter their farming methods and adjust to the changing situations were least able to do so.

Before 1850, farming at Port Phillip had evolved in two separate directions—cropping (particularly wheat) and grazing. During the upheavals immediately before and after the gold discoveries in the 1850s, land tenure with regard to the grazier was changed and there was an enormous increase in the number of people taking up small cropping farms. From the earliest years the cropping farmers had represented a relatively unprosperous sector of the community, and amid short-lived optimism, high prices, and Old World values and ambitions, this group quickly swelled. But the unsoundness of this rapid intensification of land settlement was the basis for widespread future poverty. For it was founded on wheat cultivation, the one commodity that was easily imported from elsewhere to the burgeoning city, whereas the slower, sounder development in the eastern divisions was founded on the production of more perishable commodities over which competition from elsewhere was far less likely. But, as the next chapter shows, the impoverished farmers of the 1860s were not just the victims of the economic, political and social milieu that led them (enthusiastically) into a rash farming settlement; they were also the victims of a rapidly changing farming technology which of itself was making their small farms outmoded. When circumstances became really difficult for them during the 1860s, the resulting demographic situation and the personal inadequacies of those left behind in the western and northern parts of the region tended to maintain the situation of relative poverty.

Fortunately, however, some reform of the farm structure was made possible by the opportunities for people to find work in the city and to settle elsewhere in Victoria. This is not to say that in the long run those people who took up new farms under the selection Acts were any more successful—it is doubtful that much of this closer settlement was more soundly based—but it did provide some opportunity for improving the farming system where the land was vacated. This process, it should be emphasized, took decades. Farms were still being amalgamated after 1880—correcting the indiscretions of a very few years in the 1850s.

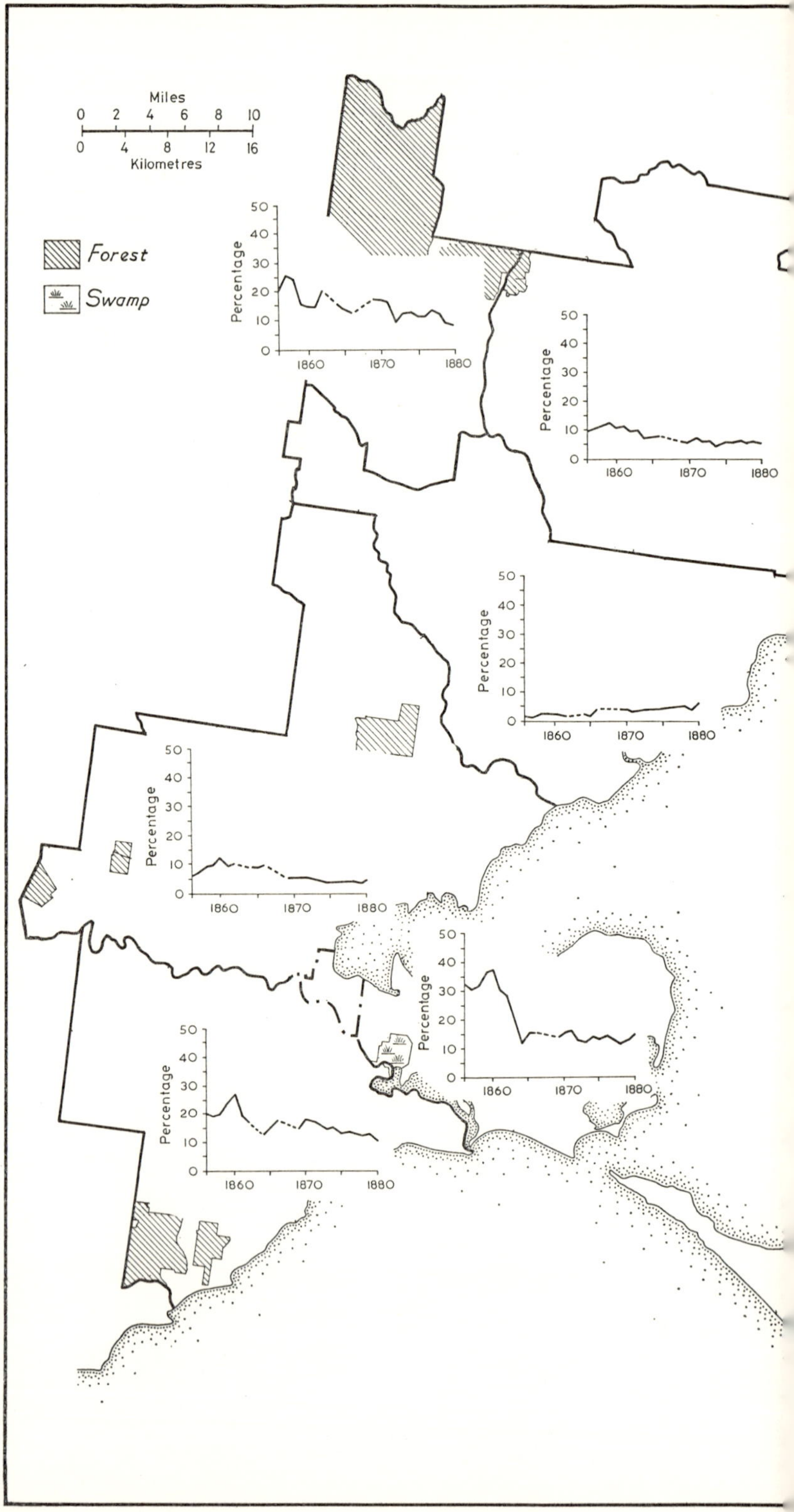

Map 12 Percentage of Freehold, Occupied Land Cultivated, 1856–80
Agric. Stat., 1856–80

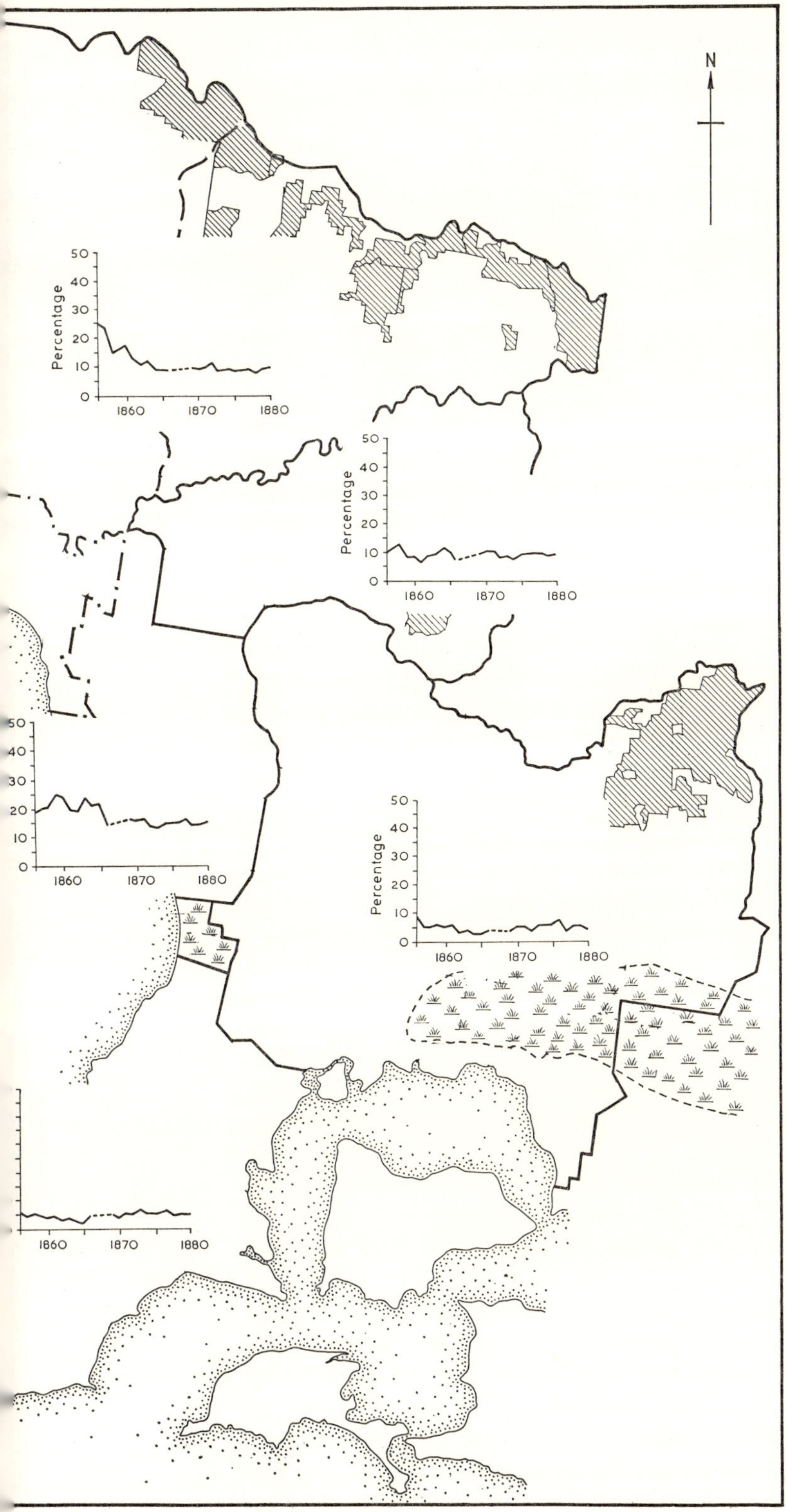
N
50
40
30
20
10
0
Percentage
1860
1870
1880
50
40
30
20
10
0
Percentage
1860
1870
1880
50
40
30
20
10
0
1860
1870
1880
50
40
30
20
10
0
Percentage
1860
1870
1880
1860
1870
1880

6 : Production

Many of the farms taken up by the new settlers during the 1850s were less than 50 acres in area, and the majority in the closely settled divisions were less than 100 acres. On these small farms the land was cultivated in a multitude of small paddocks, thus giving a patchwork appearance to the countryside. Around Geelong in 1856, 43 per cent of farmers cropping the land were cropping only 1–10 acres each, 72 per cent were cropping no more than 30 acres each, and only six occupants or 0·004 per cent were cropping more than 250 acres each.[1] Nevertheless 38 473 acres were cultivated in this area alone. At this time cropping was concentrated in the older cropping divisions of Bellarine, Barrabool, Bannockburn, Sunbury, Plenty and Oakleigh, with 5500–39 000 acres being cropped in each division. In the remaining five divisions less than 3000 acres were under crop in each division. Thus the distribution of cropping reflected the movement of people into the older cropping divisions.

During the next few years, from 1856 to 1860, more and more people took up small farms. In the older cropping divisions already occupied, farmland was subdivided further to make new farms. Here the area of occupied farmland was increased by no more than 32 per cent in any division. In the remaining divisions Crown land sales proceeded apace and the increase in occupied farm land was 94–345 per cent. (Occupied farmland was land alienated from the Crown, held in holdings of one acre or more, and occupied for agricultural purposes at the time the agricultural statistics were collected.) The five divisions Bacchus Marsh, Werribee, Lilydale, Berwick and Mornington were sparsely settled by comparison with the older cropping divisions and represented the areas of more gradual development on bigger farms, and largely without the tenant farming element so apparent in the Bellarine, Barrabool, Bannockburn, Sunbury and Plenty divisions, but not in Oakleigh (see chapter 7).

The increases in the number of farms and in the area of occupied farmland during this period were accompanied by an increase in the area of land cultivated in all divisions except the Plenty division. In the older settled divisions cultivation spread more rapidly than the increase in farmland so that by 1860 a higher percentage of the land was under cultivation than in 1856 (see map 12). The Plenty division is an exception here because, being so large, it embraced two areas of contrasting development. Plenty West was characteristic of the older cropping divisions and in fact included the oldest cropping area, while Plenty East was characteristic of the new, sparsely settled, cropping divisions. In the five divisions of sparser settlement, the extension of cropping into the newly alienated farmland was only just able to keep pace with or else fell behind the extension of the occupied farmland. Here much more clearing was necessary and the general development work, already carried out over the years in the older divisions, still remained to be done. In these divisions in 1860 only 2–15 per cent of the farmland was cultivated compared with 11–38 per cent in the older cropping divisions. And even within these five divisions three different types were apparent—and were distinguished basically by environment. Cultivation in Bacchus Marsh was centred on a relatively large but isolated area of river flats at the point where the Werribee River leaves the surrounding hill country before it cuts its narrow course through the basalt plain. In this division in 1860 15 per cent of the farmland was cultivated. In the Werribee division on the dry basalt plains only 2 per cent of the farmland was cultivated, and the population density was correspondingly low. However, the three eastern divisions—Lilydale, Berwick and Mornington—were more of the same type. Land alienation was much more gradual, and population growth was relatively slow, although steadily upwards. Here, of the land occupied as farmland in 1860, 4–9 per cent was cultivated.

By 1860, then, the larger part of the rural population was concentrated in the older settled cropping areas around Geelong, north of Melbourne, and in the Oakleigh division, where most of the cropping was being done on small farms. Cropping and grazing were still essentially separated, and where the land was not being cropped, if suitable, it was used for grazing mostly in holdings of several thousand acres or more.

As map 12 shows, after 1860 there was a sharp fall in the proportion of cultivation on farmlands and this fall continued until about 1865. Thereafter there were still minor fluctuations but the notable feature of the fifteen years from 1866 to 1880 is the relative stability in the proportion of farmland that was cultivated each year in each division.

Throughout the region in 1856 the farmers who cropped their land were growing cereals. Of the total cultivated area, 45 per cent was sown to wheat, 30 per cent to cereal hay (largely oaten) and 15 per cent to oats for grain. All other crops were limited to the remaining 10 per cent of the cultivated area, a situation reminiscent of the 1840s. The uniformity of this cereal cropping throughout the region is illustrated in figure 2. From 1856 onwards, however, as shown in this figure, the situation changed. By 1860 wheat had fallen a little in popularity although cereal cropping was still paramount. Then between 1860 and 1870 major changes occurred. Wheat growing dropped to a minor activity, oaten hay production became increasingly important, and by 1870 a substantial proportion of the cultivated land was being sown with introduced pasture species. The main feature of cultivation from 1870 to 1880 was the increasing diversity of crops sown, and the spread of sown pasture. If the graphs shown for each division in 1880 are compared with those for 1856, in figure 2, it can be seen that by 1880 each division had developed its own characteristic pattern of cropping, in contrast to the uniform cereal cropping of 1856.

From these observations three major overlapping phases of agricultural change and development become apparent. They were, firstly, a decline in wheat growing throughout the region during the early 1860s as inexperienced farmers on tiny farms and with heavy debt burdens were forced, by falling prices, pests, diseases, overcropping, technical disadvantages and adverse seasons, to abandon wheat growing, and often farming. Hay production was slightly more rewarding than wheat

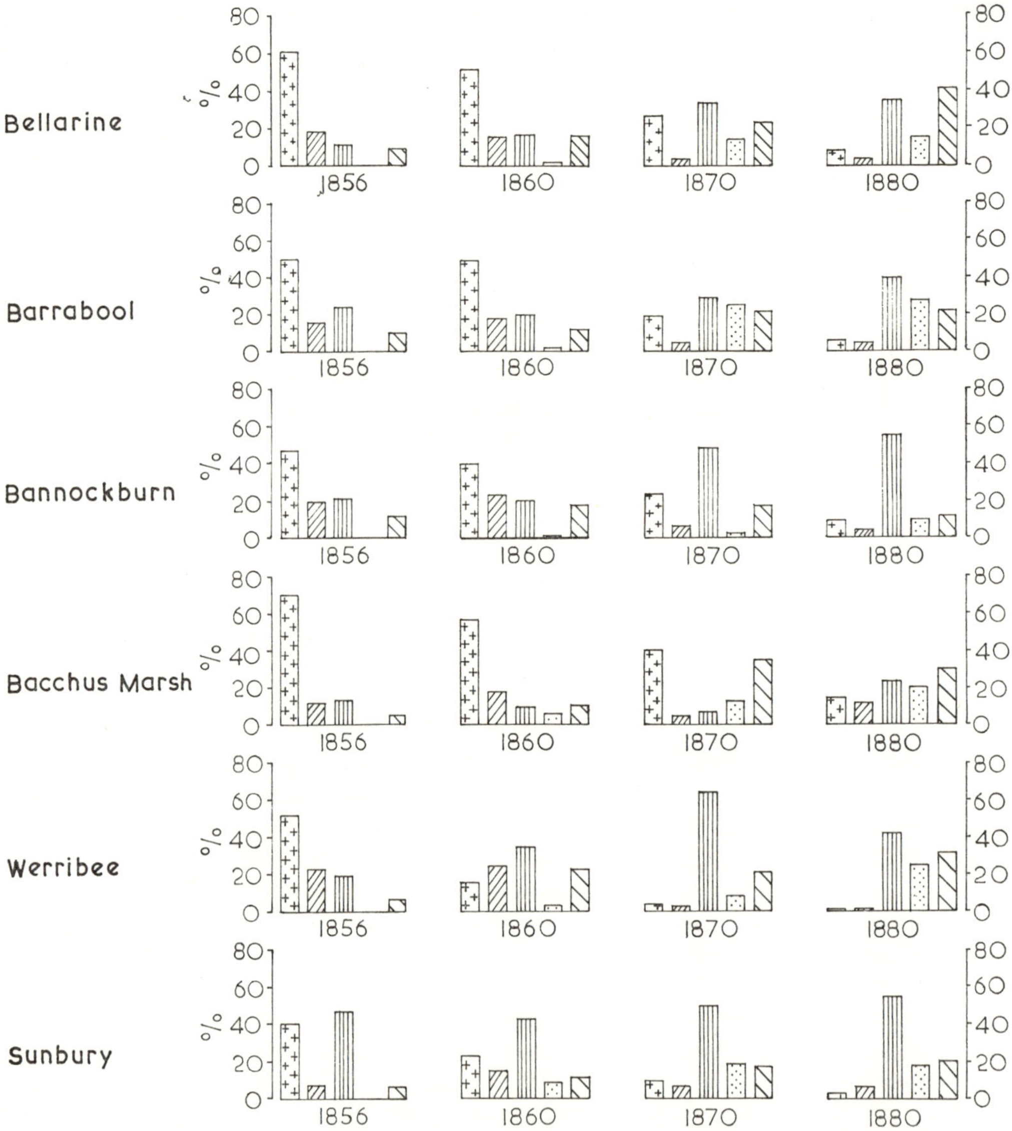

Fig. 2 Proportion of Cultivated Land Sown to Wheat, Oats, Hay, Pasture and Other Crops in 1856, 1860, 1870 and 1880

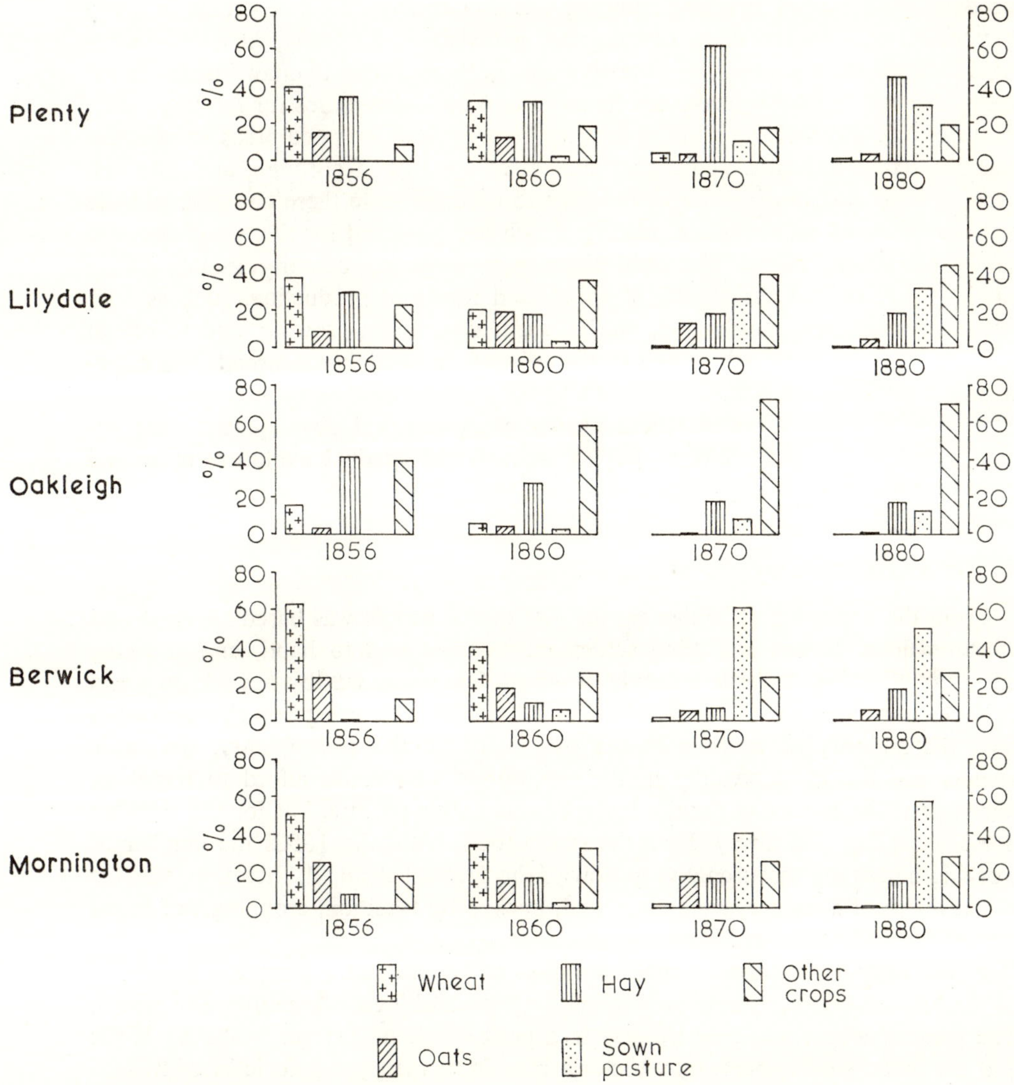
Plenty
Lilydale
Oakleigh
Berwick
Mornington
%
80
60
40
20
0
1856
1860
1870
1880
Wheat
Hay
Other crops
Oats
Sown pasture

production so the fall in wheat cropping was accompanied by an increase in oaten hay production in the main cereal-growing divisions. Secondly, in order to rehabilitate the land ravaged by excessive and indiscriminate, if unavoidable, cereal cropping, and to establish sounder financial and biological bases for farming, sown pastures and livestock were introduced to the previously cropped areas from about the mid-sixties onwards. Judiciously integrated systems of cropping and livestock grazing were developed on larger holdings to accommodate these changes, and the old separation of cropping and grazing, which had persisted for three decades, was finally brought to an end. The third phase of development occurred mainly during the 1870s. This was the growth of specialized forms of production, such as fruit growing, whole milk production, market gardening, onion growing, and so on, in specific localities peculiarly suited to the type of production concerned, and catering for a particular market.

As we have already seen, these phases of agricultural development were accompanied by marked shifts of population and the gradual evolution of settled rural communities.

WHEAT AND OATEN HAY

From the beginning of settlement the diet of the people was based on meat and wheaten flour. It was a grazing settlement so meat was to hand, and cropping efforts were mainly towards a supply of wheat. Transport was by bullock-dray and bullocks were used for ploughing. Few working horses were kept on sheep-runs; in fact, the majority of working horses were kept by the constabulary, the cattle owners and the more wealthy in the community who could afford to travel on horseback. The basic diet for the bullocks was native pasture, but for the working horse oaten hay had always been the staple food. Until the 1850s the number of working horses increased only very slowly; the greatest demand, therefore, was for wheat for local human consumption, and, backed by tradition, cropping was based on this demand.

In the early 1850s came a massive influx of people and a complete disruption of the balance between home production, imports and local consumption of wheat. The price of wheat rose year by year to a peak of about 23s per bushel in 1855; and net bread-stuff imports into Victoria rose from their pre-gold level of 37 000 to 75 000 bushels wheat equivalent per year (1845–50) to 2·2 million bushels wheat equivalent in 1856, with South Australia being the main supplier.[2] At the same time more and more draught and riding horses were to be found in and around Melbourne and Geelong. Roads were being improved and bridges were built over the rivers and creeks, better iron ploughs were becoming available, and horses were able to replace the bullocks for the lighter work on both roads and farms.[3] The number of working horses multiplied rapidly and with it the demand for oaten hay to feed them. Thus in the 1850s a strong local demand for oaten hay developed alongside the increased demand for wheat.

In considering the supply situation of wheat and hay, the difference in the nature of the trade in these two commodities is important. Wheat was an item of international commerce, a world-wide basic component of human diet, whereas hay, particularly oaten hay, was an animal fodder of far less international significance. The relative costs of transport, too, and prices received during the more normal course of commerce were in favour of wheat. For example, even in 1856, when hay prices at Melbourne, compared with wheat prices, were still relatively high, a ton of hay was worth 200s whereas a ton of wheat was worth 367s (with wheat at 10s per bushel and hay at £10 per ton). This difference in the value of unit weight, together with the difference in bulk between the two commodities, meant that costs of transport, overland or by sea, provided greater incentive for trade in wheat.

It is not surprising, then, that supplies of wheat were more easily mobilized and shipped to Port Phillip, as news of the market demand for it spread abroad, than were supplies of hay. Although some hay was shipped to Port Phillip from Launceston, the trade in this commodity in no way compared with the large shipments of wheat and flour that arrived from such places as South Australia, Chile and California. Consequently, for a short period during the early 1850s, when local agriculture was greatly disrupted, the price of a ton of hay in Melbourne exceeded the price of a ton of fine, first-quality flour. For example the market quotations for 4 February 1853 were fine flour £22–25 per ton, and hay £24–27 per ton, or on 31 March 1854 fine flour £35 per ton, and hay £36–39 per ton.[4] The following year, however, local farming settled down, more hay became available and its price was halved.

Wheat

As a result of the wheat and flour importations, Melbourne wheat prices were gradually brought into line with the prevailing world prices. Thus, following the high prices of 14–23s per bushel in 1855, the wheat price in Melbourne fell to as low as 8s 6d per bushel in 1856. Thereafter the price remained generally within the range of 4s to 9s 9d per bushel—the same range as for the Adelaide and United Kingdom markets. The only exception occurred in 1864 after a sudden and almost total crop failure; shippers were unprepared for the sudden extra demand and the price rose to 12s 6d per bushel. By the late 1870s the dry inland wheat areas of Victoria were being developed and the colony was becoming an exporter of wheat. In 1880 the average price range for wheat in Melbourne was only 3s to 4s 8d per bushel, the lowest since 1850.

With so many people taking up small cropping farms during the 1850s, the downturn in wheat prices became a matter for some concern. Until detailed farm accounts are found the profitability of wheat growing on a tenant farm during the late fifties can only be estimated. The estimate for a small farm on the Barrabool Hills in 1859 does not present a picture of prosperity. For this hypothetical small rented farm, say thirty acres in area, we will assume an area of ten acres planted to wheat, and a rent of 22s per acre with the land capable of the average wheat yield which in 1859–60 was 18·4 bushels per acre (a good season in the Barrabool division). The 1860 wheat price will be assumed at 8s 6d per bushel. For labour assume 20s per acre for reapers and 8d per bushel for threshing with rations extra.[5] Costs that have not been included are: rations for workmen (10 lb flour, 12 lb meat, 2 lb sugar and ¼ lb tea per person per week,[6] plus alcoholic inducement), stooking and stacking before threshing, bags for the grain, transport to market, and the costs of cultivating and sowing. At some stage the farmer had purchased or hired his plough, horses, dray, and other equipment. He also had an extra £22 rent to pay for the remaining 20 acres on part of which he had his dwelling and sheds and ran his cow and draught animals if he owned any.

	Per acre
Wheat yield	18·4 bu.
Minus seed	1·4 bu.
	17·0 bu.

Gross return at 8s 6d per bu. = 144s 6d per acre

Costs:	reaping	20s
	threshing	12s
	rent	22s
		54s

Net return = 91s per acre

Net return for 10 acres = £45 10s

This wheat crop would return less than £45, yet it could well represent almost the entire farm income on a farm such as this. The cow, poultry, pigs and vegetables providing for little more than the requirements of the farm household.[7] By comparison, in 1860 shepherds were receiving £35–38 per year with rations, and gardeners £60–65 per year with board and lodging.[8] Certainly the farmer who had entered into a contract when prices were high, as many had, was in an unenviable position, and his concern to maintain wheat prices at boom levels reflected this.

As the price of wheat fell, some farmers began organizing to press for a protective duty on wheat imports. The most outspoken group was the Bellarine Farmers' Association, formed in 1856 and re-formed in 1858 into the Victorian Association for the Protection of Native Industry.[9] This group had the backing of the *Geelong Advertiser*, the local daily newspaper, but in 1858 the farmers had by no means universal sympathy, for free trade had been the popular policy of the 1850s. One of the Melbourne daily papers, the *Age*, and its associated weekly, the *Melbourne Leader*, adopted the attitude that 'If grain growing is not sufficiently profitable in Victoria, why not grow something which will be so?'[10] The wider ranks of the farmers were often unclear in their demands. Following a meeting of farmers (presumably from the Sunbury division) at Essendon in February 1860 to consider what might be done about 'the very low rate of prices for farm produce generally', the local paper reported that 'an association was formed and a committee appointed to carry out certain objects, which, however, being by no means clearly stated, we are unable to define.'[11] By 1860, however, unemployment had become widespread in Melbourne in the wake of the gold boom and the farmers had been joined by a number of manufacturers and artisans in their demands for protection, and the press had become more kindly disposed towards the idea. But no immediate action was taken by parliament to protect wheat, and soon the farmers were distracted from the cause by even more pressing problems.

Falling prices were only the first setback the new farmers had to face. Many still had to learn by bitter experience the important part such mundane things as soil fertility, weather and disease played in determining their livelihood year by year. For many farmers, learning these simple lessons was a shattering experience, for their idyllic pictures of rural life were broken in pieces around them, and they were left disillusioned and depressed. It took time to develop the experienced farmer's philosophical outlook.

In many areas the decline in soil fertility was an insidious thing. On virgin soil or with a lot of fertilizer added, wheat yields of 30–40 bushels per acre could at times be obtained in good seasons.[12] During the early years of settlement and on the largest farms this natural fertility was exploited by ploughing up new ground each year. However, as explained in the first chapter, Victorian soils are deficient in phosphorus. Also, as G. B. Clarke and T. J. Marshall have shown, the first two or three cereal crops taken from new land result in a sharp fall in the nitrogen content of the soil; thereafter the decline is at a far slower rate.[13] Therefore, once the first few high-yielding crops had been taken from the land, the subsequent lowering of yield became more gradual and less obvious, particularly if the yields from one year were compared with those for the immediately preceding year. It was this type of problem that many new farmers faced in the older settled divisions, where one or two crops had very likely already been taken from the land some time earlier. Furthermore, the greater the nutrient deficiency, the less able the crop was to withstand a dry season, and so with every successive crop the farmers took from the land (without replenishing the soil nutrients), the greater their losses were likely to be as soon as the inevitable dry season came.

In the most depleted areas the problem of soil fertility was already recognized. By 1859 the general opinion was that 'Where farming has been carried on for any length of time in the colony, the exhaustion of the soil, by a succession of crops, has ensued, and is felt to be a serious evil, while in many instances those crops have ceased to be remunerative . . .'[14] And throughout the countryside this land, if at all sandy, was marked by a prolific growth of sorrel *Rumex acetosella.* But the ominous spread of sorrel did not deter many of the farmers from continuing to take cereal crop after cereal crop each year from the same land. The predicament of the small farmer was, of course, considerable. Often his available area was so small he had to crop the same land, and he saw cereal crops as practically his only livelihood. Guano was the recommended fertilizer for the depleted lands, and it was used extensively wherever 'prize' farming was attempted, but it was expensive. An application of 2 cwt per acre of guano in 1859 cost 31s excluding the cost of cartage—a costly proposition for our hypothetical farmer of the Barrabool Hills with no capital to draw upon.[15] The alternative of animal manure was very limited when so few animals (probably only several horses or bullocks and maybe a cow) were kept in comparison to the area cultivated, and the profitable change from cropping only, to a combination of livestock raising and cropping, was beyond the physical capacity of many of the small farms and the financial capacity of their occupants under the prevailing circumstances. This mixed farming concept was still limited to a very few prosperous farmers.

In 1856–7, the first season for which reliable statistics are available (see table 12), wheat yields were good—20–25 bushels per acre in the main wheat-growing divisions of Bellarine, Barrabool, Bannockburn, Sunbury and Plenty—and probably reflected the good season and the extension of cropping into relatively uncropped land. These average yields, however, were not again attained in the main wheat-growing divisions. From 1857–8 to 1860–1 the yields tended to be 16–19 bushels per acre, although the range was 9–22 bushels per acre. In 1861–2 a lack

Table 12
Acreage and Yield of Wheat in Selected Divisions
1856–7 to 1880–1

Year (1800s)	Bellarine		Barrabool		Bannockburn		Sunbury		Plenty	
	Area (a.)	Yield (bu./a.)	Area (a.)	Yield (bu./a.)	Area (a.)	Yield (bu./a.)	Area (a.)	Yield (bu./a.)	Area (a.)	Yield (bu./a.)
56–7	7 403	22·3	8 674	22·1	4 237	20·5	6 037	24·8	15 649	23·1
57–8	7 518	17·5	8 564	17·9	4 698	18·3	5 579	18·8	12 469	15·2
58–9	5 853	15·9	6 708	15·8	3 553	9·0	2 894	13·1	7 663	18·5
59–60	6 494	18·5	8 406	18·4	4 324	17·0	3 582	21·8	9 100	19·3
60–1	7 930	16·8	11 606	15·6	5 925	16·4	4 819	18·9	11 886	13·8
61–2	8 169	15·6	12 049	15·3	8 472	17·0	5 618	16·9	11 349	14·0
62–3	5 846	9·9	9 325	14·3	5 494	15·0	3 130	16·3	4 690	10.0
63–4	5 270	0.2	8 179	1·6	5 457	2·6	2 754	4·9	4 308	1·7
64–5	1 600	10·8	3 530	13·2	3 026	11·6	1 508	10·2	1 368	7·2
65–6	2 907	19·9	6 323	19·4	4 516	19·3	1 621	14·1	1 980	18·4
66–7	3 879	6·7	6 512	10·4	4 657	14·7	2 060	17·6	3 763	18·4
67–8	—	—	—	—	—	—	—	—	—	—
68–9	—	—	—	—	—	—	—	—	—	—
69–70	2 324	18·0	3 992	14·1	3 042	14·8	1 961	15·4	2 968	18·8
70–1	2 486	7·4	3 937	7·3	2 956	9·0	1 424	8·8	1 083	6·4
71–2	2 401	9·5	4 509	12·1	3 893	11·3	1 951	7·5	2 028	7·0
72–3	1 511	12·2	3 931	10·8	3 333	10·6	911	10·8	966	13·6
73–4	1 475	12·2	3 420	9·8	2 632	11·2	662	11·0	718	12·2
74–5	1 178	18·9	2 243	14·3	1 966	15·0	614	9·8	637	16·9
75–6	607	15·5	1 317	12·8	1 403	14·8	100	11·6	159	13·4
76–7	672	17·9	1 044	14·0	840	13·1	212	13·0	221	17·8
77–8	1 200	15·7	846	16·9	853	9·3	347	12·7	218	15·2
78–9	1 014	15·0	1 514	11·9	1 558	9·2	244	10·5	46	6·9
79–80	486	21·0	1 027	18·6	812	17·6	124	11·5	265	26·6
80–1	753	14·0	870	12·2	952	12·1	255	16·4	322	11·5

Source: Agric. Stat., 1856–80

of rain in late spring and early summer reduced wheat yields to 14–17 bushels per acre, and some hay crops were attacked by blight.

By the 1862–3 season the wheat growers' position had become extremely serious with prices down and crops yielding only about two-thirds of what the growers had probably expected when commencing to farm. Many farmers were to learn for the first time what a serious effect the weather could have on their crops:

> a cold and wet winter set in, and many fields which I saw at that time were so brown (the seed to a certain extent having perished) that the farmers thought they would have to re-sow or plant some other crop. A sudden change took place, and from one extreme to another—extreme dry weather followed, so much so that the land got such a crust on it that vegetation was seriously retarded, and had it not been for some favourable showers of rain many would not have been able to put in their crops this year.[16]

The average wheat yield in the main cropping divisions was only 10–16 bushels per acre.

The 1863–4 season commenced with brighter prospects. The summer was wet and, apart from April, good rains fell throughout the year with some heavy falls in December. Until December the crops did particularly well, but the storms of that month took their toll and greater disasters followed. At about Christmas time rust spread through the wheat crops and then, just at harvest time, the caterpillars appeared. In the main cropping divisions the wheat yield ranged from less than 1 to 5 bushels per acre, and in many cases this was insufficient to return the seed sown.

To make matters worse, the following summer was again wet; rust appeared and was only partly checked by drier weather. The collector of statistics reported, 'The produce of the land under cultivation this season is also so affected by caterpillars, blight, and rust, that in many parts of the district, the crops might justly be reported as almost a total failure.'[17] The wheat yield for the 1864–5 crop in the main cropping divisions was again only 7–13 bushels per acre.

Rust has been an intermittent scourge of the Australian farmer since the earliest days of wheat cropping. In southern Australia the long dry summers tend to prevent the growth of host plants and the carry-over of rust from one season to the next, but it is believed that in exceptional years with a high summer rainfall the growth of volunteer wheat crops on the stubble provides a host for the early development of the disease which is then able to affect the newly sown crops in autumn. Millington and others have suggested that 'when self-sown crops are infected at seeding time, the hazard of rust in that year is very high. Whether or not an epidemic develops will depend on the weather conditions in the spring.'[18] On this criterion the year 1863 was ideal for a rust epidemic and apparently for caterpillars too, another scourge of the Australian farmers long prevalent in the colonies. Both were widespread throughout Victoria in 1863.

Following the rust outbreak in 1864–5 the collector of statistics concluded from his inquiries that 'the red varieties of wheat are less liable to be affected than white varieties, and that early sowing is preferable to late sowing.'[19] These observations were further supported by an inquiry conducted by a Board of Agriculture committee which concluded that 'the red spring wheat, Spaldings, the red [and white?] Tuscan, the Uxbridge, the Pedigree, the rough chaff wheat, are amongst those generally free of rust; while the golden drop, the white prolific . . .,'[20] 'the club-eared, and Windslows wheat, suffered most from the disease.'[21]

The farmers who persevered with wheat growing quickly changed to the earlier-maturing varieties and by 1866 the collector of statistics was able to report, 'The "prolific" variety of wheat which was so universally sown in 1864, and proved so subject to rust, has given way to the "purple straw" and "white tuscan", which yield a handsome grain, although not so heavy a crop as "prolific", when successfully cultivated.'[22] Thus disease had forced a change in a further factor contributing to yield, the variety of grain sown.

The persistent farmers were finally rewarded, for in 1865–6 the average wheat yield in the main wheat-growing divisions was 14–20 bushels per acre. Yet few farmers had survived to reap such a reward. The 45 657 acres of wheat harvested in these divisions in 1861–2 had dwindled to 17 347 acres by the harvest of 1865–6, and from a monetary point of view there was little cause for rejoicing as the minimum price for wheat had dropped to 4s 6d per bushel, the lowest it had been for sixteen years (see fig. 3).

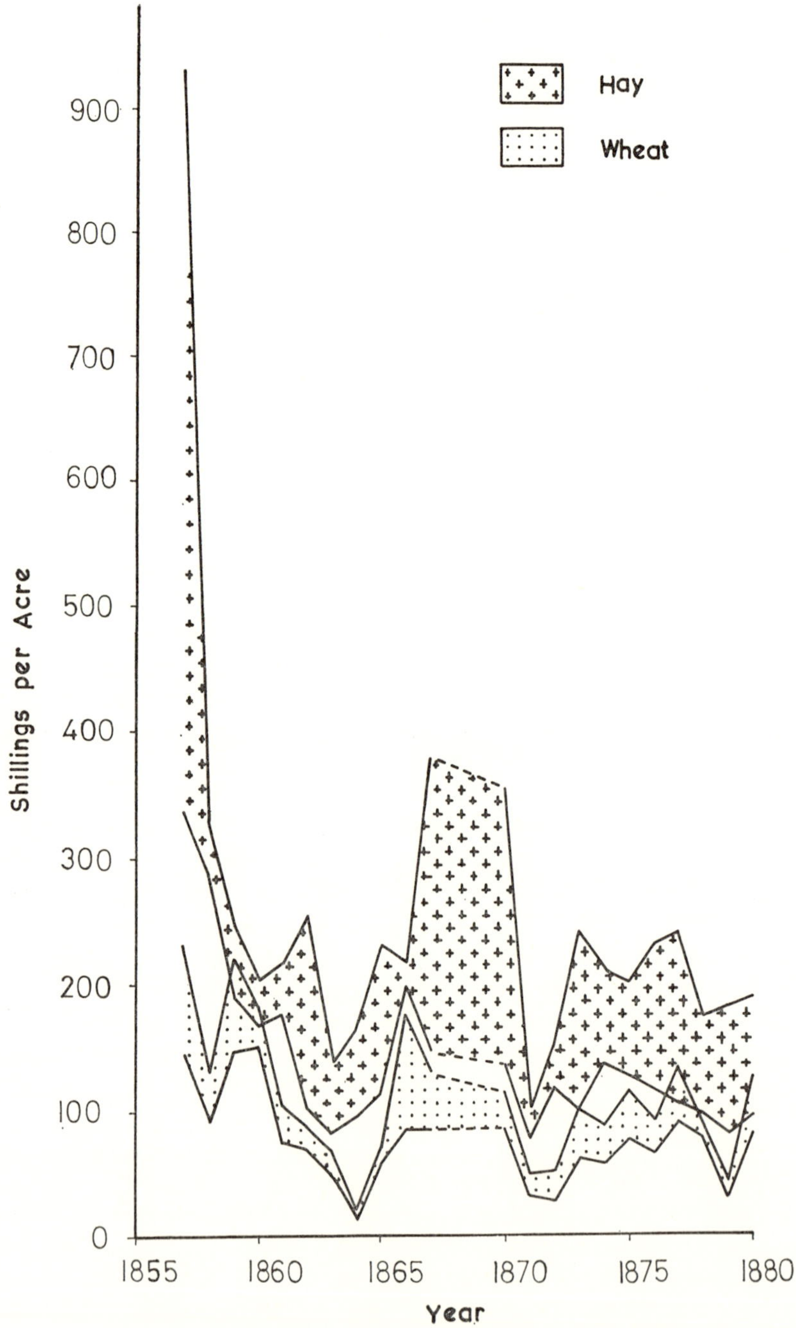

Fig. 3 Gross Returns per Acre (average yield × price range) from Oaten Hay and Wheat in the Plenty Division, 1857–80

During these crucial years of the late fifties and early sixties the Port Phillip region was by no means a technological backwater. Like most commodity prices, the wage levels for farm labour had fallen as the rush to the gold-fields had eased. A reaper who in 1855 was receiving 25s per week plus rations, was receiving only 10–12s by 1863. Nevertheless, spurred on by the high cost of labour and attracted by the high prices for produce in the mid-fifties, the wealthier farmers had been quick to import the latest British inventions in harvesting machinery. Mr Bankin of the Barrabool Hills had imported a steam threshing and winnowing machine for the 1856–7 harvest. It was one of 'R. Hornsby and Son's Patent Combined Threshing, Shaking, Riddling, and Dressing Machines [and] cost as nearly possible, £600 landed here, that is, including the steam-engine for working it.'[23] It had a threshing drum fitted with tubular beaters and a sophisticated system of shaker and riddles and was 'capable of threshing and bagging with twelve men employed, one thousand bushels per day.'[24] The simpler horse-works thresher had been used in the colony since the forties, although the flail had remained the most common method of threshing on the smaller farms.

However, around this time portable threshing machines rapidly gained in popularity, particularly among the leading farmers. In 1862 'That eminent agriculturist, Mr William Wade [remarked that] "If I had not a threshing machine to send round the country for hire, I could not have paid my way by any profit derivable from farming this year." '[25] And following the next harvest the collector of agricultural statistics in the north of the region reported,

> Thrashing machines have also increased in number, and the improvements in their construction are remarkable. It is certainly not very pleasant to stand alongside on a windy day whilst smutty wheat is being thrashed, but it is certainly very entertaining so to do, on a fine day, when you see a machine alongside a stack, and the grain going into the bag fit for the miller, and the straw being stacked to a height of 30 feet, and the smut cleaned out from the grain, and all this done by one power and at one time.[26]

Combining a thresher and winnower in one portable machine was indeed an advance, and threshing by contract was quickly adopted.

It should be noted that with the introduction of machinery there was not a sudden dramatic fall in the number of harvest hands needed. Rather, at times even more hands were needed, but over shorter periods. Thus Mr Bankin's thresher required twelve men to work it as it did within a day what one or two men might have spent weeks doing on a small farm with a flail and hand winnower. This had the effect of enabling larger areas of crop to be handled within the optimum period for harvesting, but it also tended to increase, and condense in time, the seasonal demands for labour. To meet these demands farmers helped each other—and so strengthened local unity—and casual seasonal workers moved through the countryside.

Mowing and reaping machines were introduced more slowly than the threshers. As a trial of locally made reaping machines showed in 1860, they had their advantages and were 'capable of cutting and sheafing at the rate of an acre in forty-one minutes',[27] but they were as yet unreliable. Of the three machines at this trial, one worked satisfactorily, one worked but had 'an accident', and the third was unable to proceed, also because of 'an accident'. These machines cut and sheafed the crop but the sheaves still had to be tied by hand.

Reaping machines gained in popularity and by the harvest of 1865–6 in the Sunbury division and in the developing wheat area immediately to the north, the grain crops were generally reaped by machine. But elsewhere, and subsequently here too, as the acreage under cereal crops fell, enthusiasm for the more elaborate machines dwindled. 'The great falling off in the extent of land under crop, and the little attention given to the cultivation of cereals, account for there being no agricultural machinery used in the district, except the ordinary thrashing-machines worked by horses.'[28]

Wheat-cropping practices in Victoria as a whole were soon adapted to the changing circumstances of the late fifties and sixties, but wheat growing in the Port Phillip region did not benefit. By 1863 in the unsettled district of the Murray, an area in northern Victoria where wheat growing was increasing, there was reaping by machine 'all over the district'. The machines chiefly used were 'the Adelaide stripper and the side delivery [reaper] . . . The stripper is, no doubt, of great advantage where the straw is not considered of much value and hands are scarce. . .'[29] The stripper, however, could only be used successfully in a dry climate such as that of northern Victoria, or South Australia where the stripper had been developed in 1843; in the wetter southern areas the heads of grain often would not strip properly. With the stripper there were only two operations involved in grain harvesting—stripping the ripe grain off by means of a comb and revolving beater, the chaff and grain being collected in the large box behind the comb, and winnowing.

The usual method of harvesting wheat was far more laborious. Firstly the crop was reaped by hand or machine before full maturity and tied by hand into sheaves. The sheaves were then stooked and left to dry for several weeks (in the southern areas). Carting in and stacking followed, and finally threshing was carried out by the travelling machines under contract, the farmers themselves finding the dozen or so men necessary for the work and supplying them with food. One advantage that remained in favour of reaping rather than stripping was that the straw was saved and, with the good growth of straw in the coastal Port Phillip region this was a marketable commodity. Nevertheless, as the railways were extended into the interior (reaching Bendigo and Ballarat in 1862, St Arnaud in 1878 and Horsham in 1879) the saving in costs by using the stripper instead of reaping made it more profitable to grow wheat in the inland areas or in South Australia and ship or rail it to Melbourne than to grow it within twenty miles of Melbourne and reap and thresh it. Thus a technical factor became partly responsible for the cessation of wheat growing in the Port Phillip region.

The essential difference that developed between wheat growing in the Port Phillip region and in the drier areas of Victoria from the 1860s onwards was similar to that which developed between wheat growing in the United Kingdom and in the western areas of the United States. In the United Kingdom intensive cultivation prevailed with emphasis by the leading farmers on careful ploughing and cultivation, drainage, crop rotation, fertilization and livestock—in general 'high' farming. In the United States extensive, exploitative cultivation was practised, largely made possible by the development of machines peculiarly suited to harvesting grain in these dry climates. In the dry areas of Victoria it was the stripper, complemented by the reaper; in western United States the header. In both areas the machines made possible rapid harvesting of large areas, often of low-yielding crops, and cultivation was kept to a minimum as the new lands were brought under the plough. Intensive farming could not compete; despite an average wheat yield of about 30 bushels per acre in the United Kingdom the wheat acreage there was declining during the seventies while it was expanding rapidly in the United States and the drier parts of Victoria where the yield was less than half that of the United Kingdom.[30] Meanwhile in the United Kingdom the cereal crops were being replaced by grassland; the same thing happened at Port Phillip, except that, despite the endeavours of members of the Port Phillip Farmers' Society and similarly inclined people, 'high' farming was never adopted to the extent that it was in England.

Hay

During the mid-nineteenth century in England the term 'hay' usually meant pasture hay, whereas to Victorian farmers it meant oaten hay. In this instance the colonial farmers had departed from British tradition at a very early stage. During the early years of settlement at Port Phillip bush hay had been made from the native pasture and sold on the Melbourne market for about one-third of the price of Van Diemen's Land cereal hay.[31] But in 1839 bush hay was being replaced on the local market by locally grown as well as Van Diemen's Land cereal hay.[32] Thereafter the reappearance of grass hay on the local market was dependent on the spread of sown pasture, and even then there appears to have been a time-lag before grass hay was widely accepted. The lag was probably associated with technological developments, the demand for cereal hay and chaff for horse feed, and the changing patterns of livestock feeding; but these changes belong to the decades after 1880. Suffice it to say that up to the eighties, apart from some lucerne hay, very little hay was made for sale from pasture species, although increasing amounts of rye-grass hay appear to have been made during the seventies for the farmers' own use.

The mechanics of harvesting oaten hay varied little throughout the colony. In growing the crop the climate of the southern, Port Phillip region was an advantage; it gave a good growth of straw and in general the hay growers in the region were in a sound position during the late sixties and seventies. Despite the grumbles of the Gisborne farmers 'of the expense and trouble attending [the] removal [of hay] to Melbourne, a distance of 30 miles, necessitating keep of men and horses for two days and nights on the road, with four tolls to pay twice . . .',[33] best Colonial (trussed) was the only hay quoted among the average prices of the leading commodities in Melbourne during the years 1862–5. By contrast, during the same period, wheat (Victorian, Adelaide, Chilian and Californian), barley (English and Cape) and oats (Colonial, Californian, English, Scotch, and Irish) were all quoted at one time or other.[34]

Hay farming in the region, in contrast to wheat growing, fared much better from technological developments. Mowing machines were introduced more slowly than reapers, and in the mid-sixties the hay growers still found it in their interest 'to use the scythe, as it cuts closer than the mowing machine'.[35] But these machines were gradually improved and they gained in popularity during the seventies. In the Plenty division in 1872 there were 94 mowing machines; by 1880 there were 215. The corresponding figures for reaping machines (including combined reapers and mowers) were 62 and 51 respectively.[36] Hay at this time was still sold in trusses. A truss of old hay was 56 lb and of new hay (until 1 September) 60 lb; a load was 36 trusses. When oaten hay was shipped or sent inland, it was often pressed into bales of 3–4 cwt and in this form sold at a premium over the trussed hay.[37]

Handling oaten hay in sheaves did not become common until the eighties after the introduction of the reaper and binder with a twine-knotter.

During the 1870s the local inventors were busy trying to find a means of mechanically tying sheaves. By 1874 they were able to gather the cut crop into a sheaf and pass the twine around it mechanically, but the twine ends still had to be tied by hand. Soon afterwards, during the 1878–9 season, the American-manufactured McCormick harvester and self-binder, and the W. A. Wood patent harvester and binder were imported for use on Victorian farms.[38] These self-binding wire-operated machines were far superior to anything of local manufacture then available. One result of their introduction was a concerted agitation on the part of the farmers to have reapers and binders exempted from the 20 per cent ad valorem import duty on agricultural implements, and in this the farmers were successful. Meanwhile in America, in 1878, John F. Appleby had perfected his twine-knotter, and the reaper was transformed from a machine for the grain grower to a machine for the hay grower. Thereafter twine-operated machines quickly replaced the wire machines, thus eliminating the problem of wire appearing in the chaff. By the mid-eighties several American and English twine-operated, mechanically tying reapers and binders were available on the Melbourne market.

In the Port Phillip region, then, the climate was well suited to oaten hay production; the bulkiness of the product gave the local growers an advantage in transport costs over any competitors farther afield, and since the relevant technical advances were readily applicable within the region the growers suffered no disadvantage in this respect. With a large metropolitan market close at hand, oaten hay was retained by the farmers as a cash crop and was incorporated into the mixed farming system which became necessary for them to adopt in order to restore exhausted land, maintain fertility and meet changing market requirements.

PASTURES AND LIVESTOCK

As the grain crops returned less and less and the repeatedly cropped paddocks grew sorrel and thistles, the farmers became increasingly concerned, for the old dichotomous system of agriculture, developed in the thirties and forties, which separated grazing from cropping, was still paramount at the beginning of the sixties. But obviously on the older farmlands at least, the initial pioneering, exploitative phase was ending:

> there is a diversity of opinion as to the best mode of husbandry to be pursued under circumstances in which agriculture is at present placed.
>
> The rotation system of husbandry is engaging the attention of some of the leading agriculturists, and a large number of farmers appear anxious to combine grazing with tillage pursuits, believing it to prove more profitable than the present anomalous system.[39]

These comments about the old farms in the Bellarine and Barrabool divisions were made in 1857, but as conditions on the farms deteriorated further they were repeated more and more frequently throughout the region, until in 1864 at Mornington and elsewhere, as the collector of statistics noted, changes were becoming apparent: 'I marked a great change for the better in some of the small farms where sheep-keeping had been combined with agriculture . . .'[40]

The transition from the old cropping regime took various forms. A prime reason for this was that 'adequate capital is as essential to successful farming here as in the mother country, and it is most desirable the farm should be of sufficient extent to combine grazing with agriculture. . .'[41] One practice, albeit a temporary one, was virtually to abandon the land.

> Extensive fields are everywhere throughout the district thrown out of cultivation . . . but unfortunately, from ignorance, want of capital, or from the uncertain tenure under which many tenants hold their land, the extent laid down with artificial grasses is comparatively limited—the greater part is left in a great measure unproductive, particularly in such a dry season as this, so unfavourable to the native grasses.[42]

A more productive approach, which many adopted, was the introduction of sheep and cattle to the cropping lands, and in many instances this was associated with amalgamation of the smaller farms (see chapter 7). This was a major change and was accomplished by the introduction of farming systems of varying degrees of complexity. The simplest was to use the land exclusively for extensive sheep grazing, primarily for wool. But more important was the introduction of sheep and cattle in conjunction with cropping, primarily for meat production. On some farms sheep were simply introduced to the farms and were grazed on the native pastures and stubbles. On other farms pastures were sown specifically to graze sheep and cattle, while the most complex system was known as rotational husbandry.

Josiah Mitchell,[43] a man of wide agricultural and horticultural experience (he served a while under Sir William Hooker at Kew Gardens in England and was the lessee of the government-sponsored Experimental Farm near Melbourne from 1863), was one of the few men who had a sound practical appreciation of farming and who publicly stated their views in opposition to the more popularly held ideas about small farms. Mitchell practised rotational husbandry at the Experimental Farm and advocated it strongly: 'the base of all our operations in cultivation in this climate *must be grass*', he stressed. The farmers

> want the grass to feed the herd of dairy cows or the flock of sheep—according to the fitness of local conditions—to manure the cultivated land. It is now long since I expressed the opinion—and I have since seen no reason to alter it—that 640 acres of real good land, fifteen or twenty miles from a market, would be but a small farm under the present circumstances of the country.

About one-fifth of such a farm could be cultivated and by means of the livestock 'a portion of the fertility could, without any cost of labour, be transferred from the grass to the cultivated land . . .' Phosphates lost to the farm in produce sold off it were to be returned in bone-dust or phosphatic guano. The rotation actually adopted by Mitchell on the Experimental Farm was, 'first, oats; second, green crops, chiefly mangels, heavily manured; third, oats; fourth, grass; fifth, grass. The oats are cut for hay, and the grass pastured—my object and interest, owing to position [within 2½ miles of Melbourne] being crops bulky of carriage, and milk.'[44]

In this way, under systems of varying intensity, livestock and particularly sheep were introduced to the smaller farms, and on some farms pasture was sown specifically to feed these animals.

Fencing, watering points and buildings

Whatever form mixed farming took, the first requirement was fences to separate livestock from crops and livestock from livestock—not just boundary fences but subdivision fences and yards as well. A second requirement was watering points for the livestock, and in some instances extra buildings were also needed.

The type of fencing adopted reflected the nature of the countryside and the materials most readily to hand. Despite the introduction of wire fencing during the fifties, post-and-rail fencing had remained popular with many farmers and had become more competitive in price as the costs of labour fell after the gold rushes. In areas close to a supply of good timber, post-and-rail fencing or a combination of post and rail and wire was common. With increasing distance from a timber supply, less timber was used in fence construction and wire fences, or stone walls in the stony country, became more common. Again where less stone was available, stone wall and wire fences were combined, with the stone wall portion consisting of anything from a single row of stones to a substantial wall three or more feet high with only one or two wires on top.

During the late sixties timber for fencing in the vicinity of Sunbury was supplied from the Mt Macedon area. Sunbury was also at the edge of stony country and therefore split timber, stone and wire, were all common fencing materials. Typical of the costs of fencing at Sunbury during the years 1864–8 were:[45]

4 rails fence	£1 12s per chain
2 rails and 3 wires	£1 6s per chain
stone wall	£1 14s per chain

The standard in post-and-rail fencing was eight posts per chain. By 1880 the cost of erecting a stone wall was still reckoned at about 30s per chain, 'the stone being, of course, found on the premises'.[46]

In the United Kingdom various species of hedge plants had for many years been used for fences and at Port Phillip during the late sixties and seventies many farmers believed that the post-and-rail, wire, or combination fences should gradually be replaced with hedges to obtain the optimum in permanent fencing.[47] The 'value and utility of hedges as shelter for stock from the cold, or for pastures and crops from hot winds, has been well taught to colonial farmers by experience'.[48] In practice this meant planting hawthorn or white thorn *Crataegus oxyacantha*, furze or gorse *Ulex europaeus*, Cape or African boxthorn *Lycium ferocissimum*, Osage orange *Maclura aurantiaca* or other hedge plants along the fence lines in conjunction with the more usual type of fencing, which the hedges then overgrew and slowly replaced.[49] But the hedges were a mixed blessing, for already at Port Phillip using farm labour to trim hedges was becoming a luxury. Gradually towards the end of the century the hedges spread untended beyond the fence lines, and eventually a number of the hedge plants were proclaimed as weeds. Eradication, however, was not enforced and many examples of unkempt hedges overgrowing post-and-rail, wire, or combination fences can still be seen in the former closely settled areas.

On the farms lacking the advantage of a water frontage, small wells and waterholes were dug to provide water for the livestock. At first small holes were dug by hand with the aid of a plough. By 1875 Wilding and Company's 'Patent Champion

Excavator' was on the market and by 1880 at least seventy-eight earth scoops of varying types were in use in the Port Phillip region.[50]

Various new buildings were also needed on the farms as production was diversified. By 1880 on one highly improved farm on the Plenty River, where about thirty cows were milked for butter production, pigs were kept, a few sheep were run and about forty acres were cultivated (besides the sown pasture on drained swampland), there was quite an array of buildings. This included a stone dairy, harness rooms, a blacksmith's and a carpenter's shop, a storeroom, a potato house, a cart-shed, a stable and a barn housing a threshing machine, corn-crushing mill and chaff-cutter. In addition there were the men's quarters and the homestead.[51]

The continuing fencing activity, the sinking of waterholes and wells, the erection of various farm buildings and the purchase of the various implements and machines, together represented a very considerable capital investment in the improvement of the land and the development of the farms. During the collection of agricultural statistics for the year ending 31 March 1873 an attempt was made to evaluate this investment for the first time, and the farmers were asked to place an approximate value on their implements, machinery and improvements. This and subsequent inquiries showed the average value of the total investment in implements, machinery and improvements to range from about 12s per acre in the Werribee division to about £4 8s per acre in the Oakleigh division for the years 1872–4, with the value for most divisions being about £1–2 per acre. During the next few years the average total value of implements, machinery and improvements increased in all the divisions except Barrabool, where the opposite happened, reflecting the reversion of closely settled and cropped land to extensive sheep grazing. In this instance the change was so marked and uncompromising that former improvements were abandoned and left to degenerate with time. By 1878–80 the value of the total investment was £1–2 per acre for all divisions except Oakleigh, and for Oakleigh it had increased to £4 10s per acre (see table 13).

If these figures are broken down into two categories—implements and machinery, and improvements—it can be seen that the value of buildings, fencing, sheep-dips, wells, dams, etc., was about 16s to £1 18s per acre during the seventies in all divisions except Oakleigh, where intensive dairying, orcharding and market gardening had prompted an investment of about £4 per acre in these items. When it is appreciated that this type of farm development and improvement was five to ten times as expensive as implements and machinery, and sometimes much higher, the costs of establishing and developing farms are brought more into perspective. The costs of implements and machinery seem small by comparison, yet these would be the costs many new farmers would be more likely to provide for than the greater but less apparent and definite costs of the other improvements—a dangerous trap for the inexperienced. Of course on the basis of an acre of cultivated land, the value of the implements and machinery was high, ranging from £1 8s to £3 10s per acre of cultivated land in the various divisions during the seventies. But the sixties had proven the fallacy of isolating cropping from livestock husbandry in the Port Phillip region, particularly in the absence of heavy fertilization.

Sown pasture

Investment in fencing, waterholes and farm buildings, however, represented only the beginning of the capital outlay necessary to bring a farm into profitable pro-

Table 13
Average Valuation of Improvements, Implements and Machinery, 1872–4 and 1878–80

Division	Years (1800s)	Implements and machinery		Improvements*		Total A + B per acre occupied	Ratio A:B
		A Total (£)	Total per acre cultivated (£)	B Total (£)	Total per acre occupied (£)	(£)	
Bellarine	72–4	16 686	1·9	77 783	0·8	1·4	1:4·7
	78–80	23 320	2·7	103 962	1·5	1·9	1:4·5
Barrabool	72–4	36 749	2·1	204 308	1·9	2·2	1:5·6
	78–80	25 183	1·7	190 580	1·6	1·8	1:7·6
Bannockburn	72–4	19 542	1·7	162 765	0·8	0·9	1:8·3
	78–80	19 691	2·0	199 397	0·9	1·0	1:10·1
Bacchus Marsh	72–4	9 462	1·6	68 035	1·3	1·5	1:7·2
	78–80	8 544	1·7	93 462	1·8	1·9	1:10·9
Werribee	72–4	11 712	1·7	90 003	0·5	0·6	1:7·7
	78–80	12 151	1·4	239 821	1·4	1·7	1:19·7
Sunbury	72–4	22 869	1·9	255 020	1·2	1·3	1:11·2
	78–80	25 144	2·3	268 781	1·4	1·5	1:10·7
Plenty	72–4	55 490	2·2	384 988	1·4	1·6	1:6·9
	78–80	55 554	2·2	487 034	1·7	1·9	1:8·8
Lilydale	72–4	20 007	3·1	145 208	1·8	2·1	1:7·3
	78–80	24 710	2·5	190 638	1·8	2·0	1:7·7
Oakleigh	72–4	27 916	3·5	226 502	4·0	4·4	1:8·1
	78–80	31 354	3·2	260 489	4·0	4·5	1:8·3
Berwick	72–4	14 284	1·6	167 225	1·0	1·1	1:11·7
	78–80	18 927	1·7	250 594	1·2	1·2	1:13·2
Mornington	72–4	9 650	1·7	120 634	1·3	1·4	1:12·5
	78–80	12 208	1·9	152 038	1·2	1·3	1:12·5

* Value of buildings, fencing, sheep-dips, wells, dams, etc., but not cost of clearing or cropping
Source: Agric. Stat., 1872–4, 1878–80

duction under a mixed farming system during the 1860s and 1870s. Further outlay was subsequently required for sowing pastures and purchasing good-quality livestock to take advantage of the other improvements. In some areas further clearing of the land was also involved.

The cost of sowing pastures varied considerably depending upon the seed mixture used, the sowing rate and the preparation of the soil. Initially the 'fashionable' methods and ideas used in England were adopted at Port Phillip, and attempts were made during the sixties to put them into practice. People in England had observed the wide variety of species in the old permanent pastures on well-watered fertile land and, in an attempt to reproduce these mixed swards, many rural observers had recommended using similarly complex seed mixtures for sowing new permanent pastures.[52] Since the English rainfall was good, a heavy sowing could be sustained, particularly on reasonably fertile land. Therefore the main characteristics of the 'fashionable' English pasture were a sowing rate of about 50 lb of seed per acre, a wide range of species (12–14 grasses and about 5 legumes), and the species primarily suited to a good rainfall (more than 25 inches, well distributed and in a cool climate). The soil, too, would be thoroughly and deeply ploughed and brought to a fine tilth.[53]

This, then, was the type of pasture that the agricultural leaders of the Port Phillip region hoped to establish in the early sixties, both on their own farms and at the Experimental Farm. In 1860 the following seed mixture was sown in field no. 2 at the Experimental Farm, after some difficulty in procuring a wide range of seeds:[54]

		lbs.
Perennial rye grass, per acre		13
Italian ditto,	"	13
Cocksfoot ditto,	"	4
Timothy ditto	"	2
Red clover	"	3
White ditto	"	3
Cow grass	"	2
Alsike	"	1
Lucerne	"	2
Trefoil	"	1
Parsley	"	½
Total per acre		44½ lbs.

The costs of this pasture—the then fashionable deep ploughing, it will be noted, added considerably to the costs—and of the pasture sown in field no. 4 were as follows:[55]

	£	s.	d.
No 2, containing 13a. 2r. 13¼p.*			
Seed per acre	2	18	11
Half cost of subsoiling in 1859	2	0	0
Half cost of manure in 1859	1	7	10
Sowing and harrowing, 1860	0	10	0
Total cost per acre	£6	16	9
No. 4 field, containing 12a. Or. 21¼p.			
Seed per acre	2	8	2
Labor, etc., per acre	2	6	3
Total cost per acre	£4	14	5

These costs appear to be representative of pastures sown during the 1860s on well prepared land. Half an acre of lucerne sown in 1865 at Sunbury cost about £3 or the equivalent of about £6 per acre.[56] Obviously much capital was needed for improvements of this nature.

One of the first things that became apparent about the 'fashionable' pastures sown in the Port Phillip environment was that they were not permanent. This disappointed their advocates, for to them the very best English pastures were perman-

*a. = acres; r. = roods; p. = perches
1 perch = 30¼ sq. yards; 1 rood = 40 perches

ent—in England 'there was particular virtue in aged pasture'.[57] Of the species in the field no. 2 pasture after six years,

cocksfoot, perennial rye grass, white clover, and lucerne, alone remain. The pasture this season, from the rapid spreading of the 'trefoil burr,' as it is commonly called, and the gradual disappearance of the better sorts of grasses, gives unmistakable evidence of the necessity of again ploughing up the land and putting it through an improving course of tillage.

I may state that, although the grasses of this field are now failing fast, it has been the best pasture on the farm, and two years ago resembled, more than anything I have seen in the colony, a rich English pasture.[58]

The trefoil burr was almost certainly burr or rough medic *Medicago polymorpha*. In 1853 this introduced species was becoming dominant in the native pastures along the flats and banks of the Moorabool River as some of the native grasses disappeared under grazing pressure, and there is evidence to suggest that it was already prevalent in the country beyond Bacchus Marsh as early as 1847. The burrs of this medic became entangled in the sheeps' wool and the graziers tried to shear earlier, before the seed set, to overcome the problem. This plant, it should be noted, is best adapted to a 14–20-inch annual rainfall.[59]

The gradual dying out of the preferred English species was experienced elsewhere and in time the life of pastures comprised of these species came to be reckoned at about five to eight years, although it varied in different localities. This in turn lent a further impetus to the rotational or ley farming. As one prize-winning farmer (beyond the region to the north-west) maintained in 1874, 'it would be impossible to determine upon any undeviating course of cropping. For instance, if clovers are found to prevail over rye-grass, when the sown down land comes to be broken up again, instead of a green crop, he would take a crop of wheat from the clover lea.'[60]

As a result of both a shortage of seed, and practical experience, the complex mixtures of pasture seed were soon modified; probably only very few acres were ever sown to more than about ten species at one time. Soon after Josiah Mitchell took over the Experimental Farm in 1863, he sowed some areas of it to simpler mixtures. In 1864, for example, he sowed one paddock with 'prairie grass, 20 lbs., rye grass, 10 lbs., red clover, 4 lbs., and white clover, 4 lbs., to the acre.'[61] Three years later J. S. Johnston at Sunbury sowed his land with 'Rye 12 lbs Lucerne 4 lbs. white clover 1 lb Cocksfoot 3 lbs Yorkshire Fog 2 lbs prairie grass 20 lbs. per acre. Total weight of seed per acre 42 lbs.'[62] By the mid-seventies a bushel of rye-grass seed, 2 lb of white clover and 2 lb of either cow-grass or cocksfoot was more typical, with prairie grass in wetter areas.[63]

Prairie grass (*Ceratochloa unioloides*)—the one species not commonly grown in the United Kingdom—was gradually introduced into the pastures in the early sixties. A native of South America, it was introduced to the colony by Josiah Mitchell in 1853 and possibly by others at an even earlier date.[64] During the mid-sixties Mitchell sowed it at the Experimental Farm both as a pure stand and in mixtures and commented favourably about it in his reports. At the same time a farmer on the Mornington Peninsula was growing it successfully.[65]

In discussing the species sown in pastures, it would be wrong to ignore completely the native kangaroo-grass *Themeda australis*, for this species had long been recognized as a highly nutritious and palatable grass although easily over-grazed.

It was suggested for inclusion in trials with pasture species, but its seed—difficult to harvest and of low percentage germination—was unavailable on the commercial market and so was not tried; if sown at all, it was only to a very limited extent.[66]

Although the pasture mixtures were modified, a heavy and expensive sowing of seed was continued. This probably was a sound practice in the areas where sown pasture was most extensively laid down. If a pasture sown on the Experimental Farm by Mitchell in 1865, consisting of '20 lbs. perennial rye, 5 lbs. prairie grass, 4 lbs. cow grass, and 2 lbs. white clover, to the acre, without a crop',[67] is compared with a pasture mixture recommended for the Gippsland district of Victoria nearly a century later—namely, 12 lb perennial rye grass, 6–8 lb H-I rye grass (a hybrid between perennial and Italian), 4 lb cocksfoot, 2 lb white clover and 2 lb cow-grass[68]—a considerable similarity in composition and sowing rates is evident. Leaving aside the strain improvement, the one major difference is that the latter pasture mixture was recommended for a district of 30–40-inch annual rainfall or more, while the former was sown in a 26–27-inch annual rainfall area. Thus in order to adapt the English type of pasture to Port Phillip conditions the farmers had to learn that a heavy sowing of seed, and species such as cocksfoot and white clover, were only suited to the higher rainfall areas. This the farmers gradually learnt from experience and in time the introduced pasture species were sown most extensively in the eastern areas of the region where the rainfall was best suited to them. For the time being the farmers in the driest areas had to continue to rely on the native pasture species and the introduced aliens, such as burr medic, which were spreading of their own accord where the environment was suited to them.

At least one section of the rural press failed to appreciate this aspect of the local situation. As late as 1885 the agricultural staff of the *Australasian* could give no better advice than to quote extensively from English writings on pastures, recommending on the one hand the complex pasture mixtures of that country and condemning on the other hand the lack of real permanence in the local pastures and the widespread use of rye grass—the plant that in practice had shown by far the best adaptation to the new environment, a fact recognized by the farmers in their use of it.[69] Another plant more tolerant than most to the lower fertility and drier conditions—Yorkshire fog-grass—was also roundly condemned, and herein lay the difference between pastures in theory and pastures in practice, a difference, incidentally, that was also apparent in Britain where, despite the fashionability of complex mixtures among the 'experts', the simple rye-grass and white clover pasture was still the most prevalent.

Fortunately not all agricultural writers were mesmerized by the British scene. Abraham Lincolne, the respected seed merchant from Kirk's Bazaar, and a regular columnist in the *Journal of the National Agricultural Society of Victoria*, was one of the writers alive to the realities of local pasture production and was able to offer sound practical advice on pasture management. He appreciated the limitations of the various pasture species, but perhaps even more importantly frequently recommended that sown pastures be top-dressed with phosphatic fertilizer.[70] In the light of the present-day use of superphosphate in Victoria, the report on manures from Kirk's Bazaar for 30 June 1877 is worth repeating as an indication of the state of the trade at that time and the availability of phosphatic manures to the farmers. The manufacturers, it will be seen, were producing well in excess of the local demand.

Manures—Very few orders are coming to hand for artificials; a good export trade is being carried on. The present rate of prices is as follows:—Bone dust and animal guano, £7 per ton; 7s. 6d. per cwt. Phosphatic guanos, £6. 10s. per ton; 7s. per cwt. Super-phosphate, £9. Refuse salt, £3 per ton.[71]

In 1877, 4111 tons of bone-dust valued at £27 750 was exported from Victoria, and over 3000 tons of guano was imported.[72] By 1879 the agent for 'The Victorian Bone Mill Co.'s and Messrs. Cum[m]ing, Smith & Co.'s Superphosphate Manures' was advertising as follows:[73]

Bone Dust	£6 10s. per Ton
Animal Guano	£6 10s. „ „
Lacepede Island Guano	£6 10s. „ „
Super-Phosphate	£7 10s. „ „
do do containing 7½ per cent. Sulp. Ammonia	£8 10s. „ „

The price of superphosphate was falling, and informed opinion strongly favoured it in preference to the traditional bone-dust, but up until the end of the century bone-dust remained the most commonly used artificial manure.

In order to restore and maintain fertility, then, the land was sown with introduced pasture grasses and legumes. Initially an attempt was made to sow the types of pastures advocated by the leading English writers for the farmers in England, and throughout the sixties and seventies there were people in the colony recommending this transplanting of English methods. Local practice, however, soon proved that this proposition was unsound and the farmers came to appreciate the great importance of local variations in environment and to sow their pastures accordingly. This led to the farm enterprises most dependent on well balanced pasture growth, such as whole milk production and fat lamb production, and the complex rotational systems, being concentrated in the eastern half of the region where the climate was best adapted to the introduced pasture species. But since no other satisfactory pasture legumes were then available, species such as rye grass and white clover were also sown in small areas in the drier hay-growing divisions in order to help maintain fertility. But in the driest parts, for instance the Werribee division, these pastures were short-lived, and the grazing of livestock on natural pasture and on forage crops, and the application of fertilizer also played an important part in maintaining fertility in conjunction with hay growing. Furthermore much of the expansion of hay growing in these areas was on previously uncropped land and the farmers therefore did not face the problem of rehabilitating already depleted soils. All the same, the proportion of the land cultivated in the drier divisions remained low, and the extensive grazing of the native pastures predominated.

Sheep

During the fifties and sixties interest had increased in the various breeds of sheep available in the United Kingdom. Cotswolds, Southdowns, Lincolns and Leicesters were all imported from Britain during this period, and the Border Leicesters slowly replaced the old type of English Leicesters previously prevalent in the colony.

In a trial at the Experimental Farm during 1861, 50 Cotswold/Merino cross, 30 Southdown/Merino cross and 60 Merino ewes were mated with one Cotswold and one Leicester ram. These sheep were bought on 31 December 1860 and sold in December 1861. They grazed continuously on thirty-seven acres of sown pasture, and 125 lambs were sold. The Cotswold ram cost £20 and the Leicester ram £15. The result of the trial was:

	Cotswold/ Merino	Southdown/ Merino	Merino
Purchase price (ea.) Dec. 1860	15s 6d	14s	15s 6d
Selling price (ea.) Dec. 1861	19s 1d	16s 6½d	9s 6d
Average weight of fleece	5 lb 8¾ oz	5 lb 2 oz	3 lb 2¾ oz
Average value of fleece	4s 3½d	5s 11d	4s 6d

During the trial the Merinos were far more restless than the crossbreds and when sold were only in store condition whereas the crossbreds were fat.[74]

The farmers with sown pastures and mixed husbandry systems soon sought the British breed sheep in preference to the Merinos, and in particular they sought the longwools. 'Not only are these not so dainty as to what they eat as the merinoes, they yield a larger quantity of wool, which fully compensates for the difference in the price obtainable, and fetch higher prices when fattened up for sale.'[75] By the late seventies Leicesters, followed by Lincolns, were the most popular of the longwool pure-breds, while the majority of the sheep on the mixed farms were Leicester/Merino or Lincoln/Merino crossbreds.

Therefore, the introduction of sheep to the arable farmlands brought only a small increase in the Merino flock. Instead more British breed sheep were imported and there was a major increase in the number of these sheep and their crossbreds, particularly in the eastern divisions.

The basis for the expansion of mutton, lamb and beef production was, of course, the growth of the Melbourne meat market. During the fifties sheep and cattle were driven down to the Victorian gold-fields and city markets from as far north as Queensland. These animals were channelled down through the Riverina district of New South Wales, and then on to Melbourne, frequently via the Glenvale road through Wallan Wallan and Yan Yean. After about 1860, however, this traffic began to decline as the fat-stock prices fell and Victorian production increased.[76] The local livestock producers meanwhile were in a good position. The quality of the animals being sent to the butcher varied considerably, and obviously a Leicester/Merino animal specially bred for the meat market, fattened on specially sown pasture and driven twenty miles was in a far better position to command the top prices than a Merino bred as much for its wool as its meat, fattened on whatever native pasture was available, and driven (or later railed) hundreds of miles to market. The same advantage applied to the local fat lambs and fat cattle.

Therefore by the seventies, with better pastures, fodder crops and improved breeds of livestock, it had become possible to keep quite small flocks and herds of sheep and cattle on the mixed farms for lamb, mutton and beef production in the higher rainfall areas. Small specialized flocks could be incorporated into the mixed farming systems, helping to maintain overall farm fertility and also increasing farm income. No longer was sheep farming exclusively a broad-acre enterprise.

Dairying

In the early years at Port Phillip many townspeople had kept their own cows and grazed them on vacant land near their dwellings or on the town common in the care of the town herd. By 1859 controlling the town cows had become a well regulated business, and tenders were frequently called for the various positions of town herd. For Richmond, the Melbourne suburb, the following conditions applied: 'The land is to be grazed by milch cows only, and the stock so depasturing are to be tailed, and prevented from trespassing on the footpaths and drains, and kept off the streets except when being driven to the houses of their owners. The charge for each milch cow is not to exceed 1s. per week.'[77] During the night the cows were kept in stalls and yards near their owners' dwellings. In 1841, it will be remembered, William Greig had hoped to have a cow-shed built at the urban cottage he intended renting. From the fifties onwards, however, with the rapid growth in Melbourne's population, many houses were soon built without facility for keeping a cow, and similarly, with the growth of the city and sale of Crown land, the vacant lands and commons were no longer sufficiently large for grazing all the cows, even if space had been provided to house them. By the sixties, therefore, comparatively few cows were owned by the city dwellers, particularly in the inner areas, although on the larger blocks this was still possible. J. S. Johnston of Sunbury had his town residence in the suburb of St Kilda and in 1870, when living there more or less permanently in preference to Sunbury, still kept two or three dairy cows at Sunbury and supplied his St Kilda home with milk by bringing in a cow from Sunbury after she had calved and there stabling and milking her until it was time to send her back to Sunbury and replace her with another cow.

From the early years of settlement, supplies of dairy produce from the town cows had been supplemented by produce from a few specialized dairy farms at the edges of the towns, and further supplies also came from some stock-holders, similarly situated, who had made use of a provision in the 29 March 1848 regulations giving holders of purchased lands a commonage right to graze vacant adjacent Crown lands. During the early fifties, for instance, within ten miles of Geelong a number of people purchased or leased small allotments in the vicinity of unalienated Crown lands 'with a view chiefly to graze cattle' there.[78] But with the fairly rapid sale of Crown lands these 'squatting' cow-keepers were forced to move on, and in fact it became very difficult for any small farmers to keep more than one or two cows close to the city for this reason.[79] Therefore just as the demand for dairy produce was rapidly increasing, the old sources of supply were, if anything, decreasing.

In the short term, as with wheat, the difference was made up with imports. In 1860, for example, there was a net import of 285 tons of butter valued at £37 593 into the port of Geelong, and of 3225 tons of butter valued at £364 040 into the port of Melbourne.[80] By the end of the sixties Victoria as a whole was still importing large quantities of butter and also cheese, but during the seventies the situation was slowly reversed and by 1881 the colony had a net export of 869 tons of butter. The imposition of an import duty on butter (initially of 1d per lb from 1866 to 1871, and then 2d per lb throughout the seventies) may have had some bearing on this but, as might be expected, there appears to have been a consumer preference for the fresher local product over the imported, more heavily salted butter.[81]

Until the critical period of the early sixties the majority of farmers had paid little attention to dairying apart from providing for their own needs. Their interest had been centred on wheat. Besides, to keep more than one or two dairy cows on a cropping farm would have meant extra yards, fences and other facilities, and the cows themselves would have cost about £12–14 per head during the latter fifties.[82] As outlined above, the milk, butter and cheese requirements were supplied instead by the town cows, the small dairying 'squatters', a few larger commercial producers, and by imports. This situation did not go entirely unrecognized. In 1857 the annual report of the Port Phillip Farmers' Society bemoaned the fact that 'until very recently the breeding of neat cattle could not be properly regarded as within the province of the agriculturist.'[83] And in the same year, after the Geelong and Western District Agricultural and Horticultural Society's autumn show, it was reported that 'The produce of the Dairy was but scantily represented. No Salt Butter or Cheese having been sent. We hope soon to see this department of the farm well represented. Why should we import so much butter and cheese! We trust the dairy will not be so much overlooked now that there are doubts about wheat paying the farmer.'[84]

As the doubts about wheat paying the farmer were well justified, the dairy very soon was not 'so much overlooked'. Spurred on by the assured demand for dairy produce and even more so by the need to find an alternative to cereal cropping as a means of earning a living, the farmers turned to dairying. And with this many also associated pigs, poultry, bee-keeping, wood-cutting, and paling-splitting in an endeavour to make a living, particularly during the sixties. Commercial dairying developed in several forms. In some areas the dairy herd became the major source of income; in other areas it became just one of a number of minor enterprises on the farms. Likewise, depending upon access to the market and the type of environment, fresh milk was sold, or cheese and butter were made on the farm.

The most highly specialized form of dairying that developed was the large-scale production of fresh milk for the Melbourne market. Since it was so specialized, it probably arose more in response to the demand for milk for the increased urban population than as an alternative enterprise for poverty-stricken small farmers. Two requirements influenced the development of this type of dairying. Firstly, the cows had to be milked sufficiently close to the city to enable a twice daily delivery of fresh milk to the main centres of distribution (this was most necessary during summer), and secondly, adequate supplies of good-quality fodder had to be available all the year round to maintain milk production at a high level—that is, irrespective of the seasonal variations. This was particularly important for the large producers who became established and were dependent on orderly marketing facilities and a regular clientele; to maintain these a consistent supply of milk was essential.

In response to these two requirements, dairy farms were established close to the city, a number within the boundaries of the Melbourne division as defined, on high value semi-urban land, and particularly to the east of Melbourne in the vicinity of the tongue of 30 inches or more annual rainfall reaching across the Lilydale and Oakleigh divisions. By 1866 some dairy farmers in this area had as many as sixty or seventy milkers and were renting extra paddocks near their farms.[85] They fed their cattle upon a combination of native and sown pastures. If phosphatic fertilizers were applied to these intensively grazed pastures as recommended, the sown pasture species would have spread and soon displaced the native species. In winter the pasture feed was supplemented with hay or chaff and mangels, and in summer with green fodder crops of oats and maize.

However, not all the animals had to be kept close to the city all the time, and numbers of the farmers also owned or rented land farther out, or had agistment arrangements, so that their dry stock could be sent away, leaving only the milkers to be provided for close to the city. By 1874, for instance, cattle were being sent from Heidelberg twenty miles farther up the Yarra valley to Yering for autumn grazing on the river flats; the agistment rate was 12s 6d per head for three months.[86]

Near Werribee a different type of dairying enterprise developed. Here, particularly on land rented from the Chirnsides and Staughtons, a number of farmers relied on butter production for their main source of income although they also produced hay and most kept pigs. The herds were quite large, one farmer had 64 head of cattle and 37 pigs, another about 58 head of cattle and 37 pigs. There were few sheep on these farms. The climate near Werribee, in contrast to that of the city milk-supply area, limited these farmers to supplementing the native pasture feed for their milking cows either with roots, particularly mangels grown on small flats along the Werribee River, or with cereal chaff and hay grown elsewhere on the farm. Altogether in 1872, when an outbreak of foot-and-mouth disease occurred, these farms did not present a very prosperous appearance; fences were broken down and improvements were minimal. (The foot-and-mouth disease was eliminated by the destruction of animals and the quarantining of farms.)[87]

On many other farms throughout the region dairy cows were gradually introduced to diversify the former single cropping enterprises, but they tended to play a less significant part in the whole farm economy than on the farms mentioned above. The collector of statistics reported in 1867, for example, that bordering the southern banks of the Yarra River in the Lilydale and Oakleigh divisions,

> The best farms in the district are certainly those on the creeks. . . On these oaten hay seems to be the staple . . . but the product has been so large elsewhere, and the low prices obtained, make it not a lucrative business . . . Invariably these farmers keep a few cows, and the produce from the dairy is a good stand-by.[88]

Similarly to the south-east of Melbourne,

> Where once large wheat-stacks and other cereals met the eye, nothing now is to be seen but stacks of firewood, and the farmers are more or less engaged in it . . . To produce a small stack of hay for their horses, and a few potatoes, is their greatest effort. All have a few cows, and rely much on their dairy and firewood to help them out.[89]

In the sixties a number of these farms were eventually deserted, but in the areas with a more favourable natural environment, more stable and prosperous mixed farms, such as those in the western portion of the Plenty division, were gradually developed.

Here, by 1880, a little cultivation (up to about 70 acres but usually much less) was engaged in with oats, peas and potatoes forming part of a rotational system which usually ended in sown pasture. The flats along the Plenty River, for instance, tended to be 'put under cultivation for three or four years, and then sown down with artificial grasses as pasture for milch cows—dairying being looked upon as a far more important industry than fattening stock for market.'[90] The dairy herds numbered about 20–40 cows each. One herd of well-bred Durham cattle produced about 5 lb of butter per head per week, on an average for the year, while individuals in this herd produced as much as 9 lb per week. Throughout the seventies butter, the main dairy product of the area, was sold to Melbourne dealers who visited the farms at regular intervals, usually weekly. The price varied according to the time of the year and the state of the Melbourne market, the range being from 6d to 1s per lb by 1879.[91]

But dairying was only one enterprise among several, and by no means all farmers ran dairy cattle. W. H. Budd, senior, who owned Strangeways, one of the largest properties near Wallan Wallan, had purchased the property in 1846 and in the 1851 fires had lost all his livestock and crops; his house had been saved but many years had passed before he was able to make good his other losses. By 1879 he owned nearly a thousand acres, part of which he rented to another farmer, and the remainder of which he worked himself. The land was well grassed and subdivided; it was used mainly for grazing and breeding Shorthorn cattle, and very little had been cultivated for a number of years. Being an older man, the relatively straightforward grazing of cattle together with the added income from leased land probably suited the owner's desire for a more leisurely life. By contrast, on the adjoining property, Lovely Banks, the younger more active W. H. Budd, junior, had cultivated twenty acres in 1879, sowing half of it with oats and the remainder with peas and potatoes. He had some good Clydesdale horses on the property and a dairy herd of well-bred Durhams. Close to this farm was that of T. Hogan who rented four hundred acres from W. H. Budd, senior, of Strangeways. This land was a mixture of timbered hill country and cleared flat land. The latter was first ploughed in 1836 but by 1879 had not been cultivated for some time. The pastures contained a mixture of native and artificial grasses. Besides this rented property, Hogan also possessed about a thousand acres in Gippsland. He was well known as a breeder of longwooled sheep of which he ran over a thousand head, and he also had Clydesdale horses, including a stud stallion, and prize-winning pigs, predominantly of the Berkshire strain.[92] These three farms serve to illustrate the varied complexity of farming by 1880 in the Plenty division with its climate and soils suited to the introduced pasture species, and the added advantage of small patches of fertile river flats.

Dairying, although an enterprise turned to for economic relief after crop failure, was itself beset by the ravages of disease. Pleuro-pneumonia had been known in Europe for over a century, and following the importation of diseased cattle into England in about 1840, it spread throughout that country causing heavy losses. In 1858 an infected cow, imported from England, was landed at Melbourne and taken to a farm near the Plenty River. From there the disease spread rapidly throughout the colony. The collector of statistics for Mornington reported in April 1864 that 'The general spread of pleuro-pneumonia has left many paddocks this year unstocked, as parties seem unwilling to speculate for fear of that disease.'[93] But by then the worst had passed and the collector from the Sunbury division in the same year was able to write,

> I am happy to inform you that pleuro-pneumonia was not so virulent when we were going through the district as it had previously been; many have suffered greatly by this disease, but since I finished the collection, I met a gentleman from Derrimut, who informed me that he had lost twenty-seven of his best milkers (that is the most serious loss that I have heard of), since I was there.[94]

More cases were reported in 1865, but by 1866 there were very few reports of deaths from the disease, and although this was by no means the last that would be heard of it, by April 1867 the livestock were described as being 'remarkably healthy and free from disease'.[95] Thereafter solitary cases continued to appear and occasionally there were more serious outbreaks, but by 1874 many thought the disease to be of a milder type than when it first appeared, probably because after the animals had been once affected they showed immunity, whereas in 1858 all cattle would have been highly susceptible, and because many owners by then were inoculating their cattle.[96]

The timing of this outbreak could not have been worse for the farmers. Staggering under the blows of lower prices, drought, rust and caterpillars, they turned for relief to dairying, only to be hit by pleuro-pneumonia. The precise importance and influence of this outbreak is difficult to assess, but pleuro-pneumonia undoubtedly contributed to overall rural distress and was the final blow that forced some farmers to leave the land. After all, twenty-seven milking cows were worth from £81–216 in 1864, and if they were the 'best milkers', their replacement cost was probably close to the top of this range.[97]

'Got new cow "Poly" home price £8', wrote J. S. Johnston in his diary on 30 September 1866, and probably to the majority of cow owners at this time the cow was just 'Poly' or 'Alice' rather than an Alderney or any other distinct breed. Provided she gave 'lots of milk', as did the above 'Poly', the owner was happy. Nevertheless, as with sheep and other animals, some people imported dairying stock from the United Kingdom, and established herds of Alderneys, Ayrshires, Brittanys and Shorthorns. In the mid-fifties 'Rusticus' had recommended Durhams (Shorthorns) as the best dairy breed, and the bulk of the cattle being milked were undoubtedly of this descent.[98] But during the sixties and seventies the stud Shorthorn animals in the region had been imported and grown for their beef and, although certain English strains of Shorthorns were well known for their milk production, it was mainly left to the other breeds to improve the milking herds at Port Phillip.

In the Sunbury division at Tullamarine two Ayrshire studs were founded which by the end of the century were still acknowledged as the leaders of the breed. Three young Scottish immigrants, John and Duncan McNab and John Grant, all bought land adjacent to one another at Tullamarine in about 1849, and their association was further strengthened by marriage. John McNab's property was known as Oakbank, his brother's was Victoria Bank, and John Grant's was Seafield. All three men bred Ayrshires, but it was the Oakbank and Seafield studs that achieved Australia-wide renown.[99] Many years later the circumstances of the foundation of these studs were recorded:

> The late Mr. Grant was looked upon as the 'father' of the Ayrshire in Victoria; and often I have heard the veteran breeder tell the story of the purchase of his first Ayrshire cow, Annie, from Captain Hutton, on the sailing vessel *Martin Luther*, in 1848. His purchase afterwards presented him with a bull calf by a Scottish sire. . .[1]

To this humble beginning more illustrious importations were added as the Oakbank and Seafield herds grew.

Another property renowned during the sixties was Arundel (afterwards purchased by Robert McDougall of beef Shorthorn breeding fame) which was a showplace running a variety of well-bred stock ranging from Alderney cattle and Lincoln sheep to asses, mules and Chinchilla rabbits. At the sale of this property in 1868 one Alderney cow sold for £34 and the first sixteen brought a total of £240 or an average of £15 each.[2]

Therefore, although the majority of dairy stock were still of very mixed parentage based on early Durham stock with an infusion of many a ship's cow, a few breeders were importing high-quality stock from the United Kingdom and by the seventies the benefits from these importations and their descendants were slowly diffusing through the dairy herds of the region. This, together with the improvements in stock feeding, probably resulted in a gradual improvement in both the quantity and quality of milk produced, which no doubt played a major part in the transition of the colony from an importer to an exporter of butter during the seventies.

Livestock studs and beef cattle

Some of the stud properties specializing in the small mixed farm animals such as pigs and dairy cattle were closely integrated with the surrounding farming community. They reflected the efforts of the well established, medium-range farmers in progressively improving their livestock and production, and the development of the studs on these properties was closely linked with the local district shows. But other properties, particularly those grazing beef cattle, tended to be more isolated from the local community; their connections were more colonial-wide and inter-colonial in nature. Not necessarily situated on large areas of land, they tended to be owned by men of capital who often had interests in properties elsewhere as well. The private stock auctions of these men would draw buyers from Queensland and New South Wales as well as Victoria.

This type of stud stock development reflected a similar development that had already occurred in Britain, the United States and elsewhere, and which was reaching its zenith of high prices and inbreeding during the 1870s. Britain was leading the world in livestock breeding at this time, and the most fashionable of all breeds was the Shorthorn. This breed had proved itself in the market-place and with the advantage of published pedigree records dating from 1822 had become the favourite of the wealthy landed gentry. By the 1870s many breeders were diligently proving the descent of their cattle from either the Booth or the Bates strains of Shorthorns. The Australian graziers, with their obvious interest in livestock, had made a point of visiting the famous herds of England on their trips home.[3] There some bought pedigreed animals which they shipped to Australia to up-grade the stock on the large stations, to start a fashionable stud in one of the better-watered regions closer to the coast in emulation of the parent stud, or more likely to do both. For there were fortunes to be made and lost in breeding stud animals, quite apart from the pleasure and the glory.

The various studs built their reputations through exhibiting at the local shows, but more importantly through importing animals of known and fashionable pedigree from Britain. In June 1873 this supply of imported stud stock was cut off when an embargo was placed on importing livestock into Victoria from overseas to prevent the introduction of disease. Immediately the value of imported pedigreed animals already in Victoria and their offspring was greatly increased. The Mt Derrimut Shorthorn stud, based on imported stock of the Bates strain, was one of the leading herds in the colony. Originally established at Mt Derrimut in the Sunbury division,[4] by 1875 its owner, Richard Morton, had moved its headquarters to Kyneton, just north of the region. In February of that year Morton held a sale of stud stock at Kyneton. A special train ran from Melbourne carrying the local and inter-colonial buyers, and, if another stud sale is any indication, a champagne luncheon was provided. And well it might have been, for the highest price for the day was 1650 guineas for a bull, and other prices around 500 guineas were common.[5] Later that year Morton, 'detained in England by the state of his health',[6] decided to sell the whole of his herd, and in October 1875 the Mt Derrimut herd of thirty-seven head was sold by private contract to Robertson Brothers of Colac, in the Western District, for the sum of £27 000. 'The sale included the imported Bates bull Oxford Cherry Duke (32,016) at £2,500, whose calves when from eight to twelve months old at the last auction sale averaged £458.17s., being the highest average ever obtained here or in England for calves of the same age.'[7]

During the next three years the high prices were maintained. At the Robertson Brothers' January 1876 sale, the twenty-six-month-old heifer Roan Duchess, by Duke of Brunswick (an imported Mt Derrimut sire), sold for 2200 guineas, and the seven top bulls sold for a total of £4961 5s. The 293 head auctioned at this sale were soon widely dispersed throughout the Australian colonies.[8] At the Robertson Brothers' January 1878 sale the top price was 2450 guineas for the 24th Duke of Derrimut, and the next nine bulls sold for a total of 5100 guineas.[9] Then in November 1878 the ban on importing cattle from Great Britain was lifted and prices immediately dropped. At the Robertson Brothers' sale in January 1879, nine bulls altogether only realized 1000 guineas. A drop in prices had been expected, but 'few were prepared for such a depreciation in value'.[10]

The suddenness of the slump in stud cattle prices was almost certainly due to the lifting of the import ban.[11] However, a similar general rise in prices had been experienced in the United Kingdom and the United States during the seventies, and there, too, a slump eventually followed the artificial heights, and these movements probably had some influence on the Victorian market. Other factors, therefore, also probably played a part in the local price fall, including the uncertain political situation, particularly with regard to border duties and the fat stock trade.

The importance of the stud industry to the farming community was considerable, and gradually the benefits from the highly priced, even extravagant, importations permeated through the lesser herds and flocks. Although the most highly priced animals were far beyond the reach of the average farmer, less highly priced sires of associated blood line were hired for service by the more prosperous farmers, even if they could not afford to buy them. Furthermore, there is every indication that a tiered system, somewhat analagous to the parent, daughter and general studs recently outlined for Australian Merino sheep, was rapidly developing during the 1870s.[12] A major difference at that stage was that for nearly all the livestock breeds in the Port Phillip region the parent studs were still located in the United Kingdom and most animals were not registered. Of course it did not necessarily follow that the animals that brought the highest prices in the stud auctions would bring the highest returns in terms of commercial farm production. But such questions cannot be pursued here.

Pigs

Pigs had always played an important part in the food supply of farm households once the farms had become reasonably well established, and often a pig would be killed by one farmer and shared with a neighbour. The Berkshire was considered to be the best breed, but the descendants of many other breeds were also present in the colony by 1880. The pigs were fed on a variety of fodders—mangels, pumpkins, bran, maize, skim milk, and anything else that was convenient and cheap at the time, and therefore pig-keeping could be incorporated as a useful sideline into many mixed farming systems. An early practice had been to keep pigs in association with abattoirs and butcheries to eat the offal, but this practice had largely ceased by the sixties, partly because the local residents objected, and also because of stricter health regulations for these establishments.

OTHER CROPS

The local variations in animal and cereal production, which arose as mixed farming spread and became stabilized in the later sixties and in the seventies, were reflected, too, on a smaller scale in more specialized crop production. In particular, orcharding and market gardening spread out to the east and south of Melbourne, with a concentration of market gardening in the Oakleigh division, and on the other side of the bay the Bellarine Peninsula emerged as the main onion-growing region of the colony.

The poor sandy soil in the southern part of the Oakleigh division created a major obstacle to farm rehabilitation in this area after the bad years of the early sixties. The area was so impoverished that it was unsuited to the mixed farming systems introduced elsewhere, and much of the land was left unused while the occupants went wood carting. The eventual salvation of this area was associated with the growth of the city. Firstly the homes of the urban dwellers slowly encroached on the land nearest to Melbourne. Secondly market gardening gradually developed on the land now devoid of timber. This was made possible by the accessibility of the area to the city vegetable market and manure supply, and by a soil and climate suited to vegetable production. Although the sandy soil was deficient in plant nutrients, it was singularly suited in texture to vegetable growing, and the climate tended towards a year-round growing season with only light frosts in winter.

Under market gardening the size of holding was particularly small. The labour requirements could be supplied by the farmer and his family and only hand implements or simple horse-drawn implements were needed apart from the very necessary dray and horse. Hence holding size was dependent on the physical ability of the farmer and his family to work the land using hand methods and to cart sufficient fertilizer for the heavy applications required. A situation reminiscent of the small farms developed during the forties, but in this instance the intensity of production per unit area of land was sufficient for hand cultivation to remain profitable. With the very small holding suited to the agricultural technique for production, a few hundred pounds in cash was adequate to start a market garden of ten to twelve acres in 1854 and, no doubt, in subsequent years.[13] Therefore the low initial capital requirement for land (particularly when the area was first being developed for market gardening) made it possible for the market gardeners to establish themselves without being heavily dependent on borrowed capital or on large landholders to purchase the land and lease it to them. Thus tenure became a minor consideration; the major considerations were hard work over very long hours, a detailed knowledge of market requirements, and an expertise in growing a wide variety of vegetable crops.

The intensive utilization of the land in the Oakleigh division slowly increased throughout the seventies as the city of Melbourne grew. Dependent on the city market, dairying, and particularly orcharding, slowly spread eastward over the undulating clay country, pushing back the bushland, while the market gardens spread away from the city on the sands. In turn the villa residences slowly encroached on the orchards and market gardens. By 1880 the process had reached the point where the mean size of all the rural holdings in the Oakleigh division was only about 64 acres.[14]

A NEW EQUILIBRIUM

During the late 1860s and the 1870s farming at Port Phillip underwent a gradual development in which new equilibriums of man with his surroundings were achieved. An illustration of the degree to which the farmers had established a closer identification and interaction with their surroundings can be seen in the farming that developed in the Bellarine division during the seventies, the one division where the population decline was arrested and reversed. The environmental characteristics of the Bellarine Peninsula were a 22–26-inch annual rainfall, mild weather and little or no frost; gently undulating hills with, among other species, a good natural growth of the golden wattle trees *Acacia pycnantha*; reasonably extensive areas of cracking clay soils which were associated with friable dark soils; and along the shore of the bay extensive deposits of seaweed and shell grit. Following the excessively wet and dry years of the sixties so disastrous for wheat, there were eight consecutive good to wet years, commencing in 1869–70, well suited to the growth of introduced pasture species and other plants requiring a good rainfall. Economically the Bellarine farmers had convenient and rapid access to the ever-expanding Melbourne market. By the seventies roads had been formed and passage over them was faster, but the immediate cash cost of travelling had increased as a result of the local shires collecting tolls to help finance the roads. However the Bellarine farmers were able to save travelling time and avoid a toll by taking their produce to Portarlington on the northern tip of the peninsula instead of to Geelong, and there selling it to an agent who shipped it to Melbourne and other markets. It is perhaps indicative of the success of this traffic that when the Geelong–Queenscliff railway line was proposed in 1875, the arguments in favour of it were based on its advantages for speeding mails from the Heads to the interior, for defence and also for the summer traffic of people from Geelong to the beaches. No mention, however, was made of any possible benefits in transporting farm produce.[15]

In 1856 in the Bellarine division 61 per cent of the cultivated land had been sown to wheat and a further 30 per cent to oats for hay or grain, or a total of 91 per cent to these two cereals under an exploitative system, a cropping regime not very different from anywhere else in the region.[16] By 1875 all this had changed: 'The wheat harvest in this district may now be said to be in full swing . . . Some have commenced gathering in their peas . . . The onions are looking and doing so well that some growers are actually growling about it . . . Some few have commenced digging their late potatoes . . .'[17] Besides these crops, oaten hay was still produced, pastures had been sown down, sheep and cattle were kept to produce wool, meat and dairy products, and bark was stripped from the golden wattle trees and sold for tanning purposes.[18]

In this transformation the onion crop had played a major part, particularly on the northern side of the peninsula. There was a good market for onions in Melbourne and cheap transport for the crop to this market. The soils and climate, too, were well suited to onion growing since the crop thrives best in a well-drained, friable, non-acidic soil in a mild climate. And the farmers maintained the soil fertility and thereby their means of production by collecting the seaweed and shell grit from the shores of the bay and applying it to their paddocks in conjunction with various systems of ley farming.[19] The onion crop was not entirely free from pests and diseases, the wire worm being at times a problem. However, the farmers made allowances for such infestations and, in fact, even feared depressed prices from an over-supply of onions when the crops were too good. Thus the farmers had learnt to live with problems of this nature and to counteract them as best they could by rotating their crops and sowing clean seed.

Not only was the natural environment suited to the crop, and a good accessible market available for it, but the situation of the farmers was also well suited to the techniques of production. The onion crop, it was agreed, 'requires attention, and involves a good deal of labour in the shape of weeding and hoeing, but with moderate weather and a good market the labour is well repaid'.[20] After the failure of the wheat crops, the amalgamation of the farms, and the reversion of portion of the cultivated land to pasture, there were too many people in the region for the work available, as shown by the net loss of population during the sixties. The necessary labour supply was, therefore, already present in the division and, furthermore, by the seventies many farmers who had settled in the division during the fifties now had children to provide valuable assistance with the light but tedious work of weeding and hoeing.

With the harmonious combination of soils, climate, plants, animals, men and market the Bellarine division became the onion supplier for all of Victoria, producing 83 per cent of the onions grown in the colony of Victoria in 1878–9 and 91 per cent in 1879–80, from 66 and 86 per cent respectively of the land sown to this crop.[21] In 1879 a total of 1025 tons of onions valued at £7433 were exported from Victoria—mainly to New South Wales, South Australia and New Zealand.[22] Such stabilized development in the late sixties and the seventies in the Port Phillip region typically replaced the disequilibrium of the preceding fifteen years.

Farming in the Port Phillip region in the fifties reflected man only partly in tune with his environment; if anything he had been rather antagonistic to it. The uniform but dichotomous production of wheat and wool represented, in the case of wheat, an emotional and sociological response by the farmers to their former traditions more than a response to economic realities, and even less of a response to the natural environment. Wool growing, on the other hand, had been more in tune with both the economic and natural environments.

Many of the men producing wool had, unlike their wheat-growing compatriots, had previous colonial experience and were partly adapted to the environment before they even ventured across Bass Strait. Their sparse sheep grazing, too, was a relatively gentle incursion into the old ecosystem compared with the crops of the cultivators.

The outstanding feature of the changes after the fifties is the gradual harmonization of man and his environment and more specifically of the farmers with their economic and natural environments. This had been a severe process in which the least able to adapt had been forced off the land altogether or else condemned to a life of poverty. The remaining farmers, however, had made great progress, and the extent to which they had integrated with their surroundings by 1880 is revealed in the considerable variation and specialization in type of production across the region.

7 : Land Tenure and Farm Size

With the rapid sale of Crown land in the Port Phillip region during the 1850s, the number of rural holdings exceeding one acre had increased to 4126 by 31 March 1857, and within another three years the total was 5625. But then the increase was halted and a further three years passed before a total of 6002 was reached. Thereafter, until 31 March 1881, the number of holdings remained between 5954 and 6800 (see map 13 and table 7 in appendix). But this apparent stability from about 1860 onwards masks a series of advances and retreats in different areas throughout the region. The net result of these changes between 1860 and 1881 in each division is as follows. In the Bellarine, Plenty and Oakleigh divisions the net change was less than 13 per cent; in the Barrabool, Bannockburn and Sunbury divisions, the total numbers of holdings fell by 29, 20 and 30 per cent respectively; while in the Bacchus Marsh, Werribee, Lilydale, Berwick and Mornington divisions the numbers increased by 44, 40, 145, 114, and 269 per cent respectively, thus offsetting the decrease in the Barrabool, Bannockburn and Sunbury divisions. Undoubtedly if it were possible to compare totals on a parish basis, similar discrepancies would be evident within the one division.

Unlike the total number of holdings, the total acreage of freehold land comprised in these holdings rose erratically during the sixties and then steadily up to 1881. Comparing the totals for 1860 and 1881 again, in all divisions there was an increase, and therefore, although the holdings in the Bellarine, Plenty and Oakleigh divisions and in the Barrabool, Bannockburn and Sunbury divisions remained constant in number or declined, they increased in average area. Similarly, in the remaining divisions the average area of the holdings increased in all except the Lilydale division (i.e. the Bacchus Marsh, Werribee, Berwick and Mornington divisions), since there the occupied freehold area increased more rapidly than the number of holdings. Only in the Lilydale division did the increase in the number of holdings exceed that of the area occupied.

While allowing for the vagaries of collectors of agricultural statistics, it is still pertinent to ask how meaningful these totals of holdings and areas occupied are, when the range in holding size was so great. I have purposefully avoided quoting precise figures for the average size of the holdings in each division. Fortunately for historians, if not for the farmers, a Land Tax Act was passed in 1877 under which all freehold estates upwards of 640 acres in one area, or in separate areas not more than five miles apart, and valued for the purposes of the Act at upwards of £2500, were taxed. Under the valuation system all estates exceeding 2500 acres were taxed and therefore were listed in the Land Tax Register; smaller estates on the better land were also included. From the information in this register for 1880,

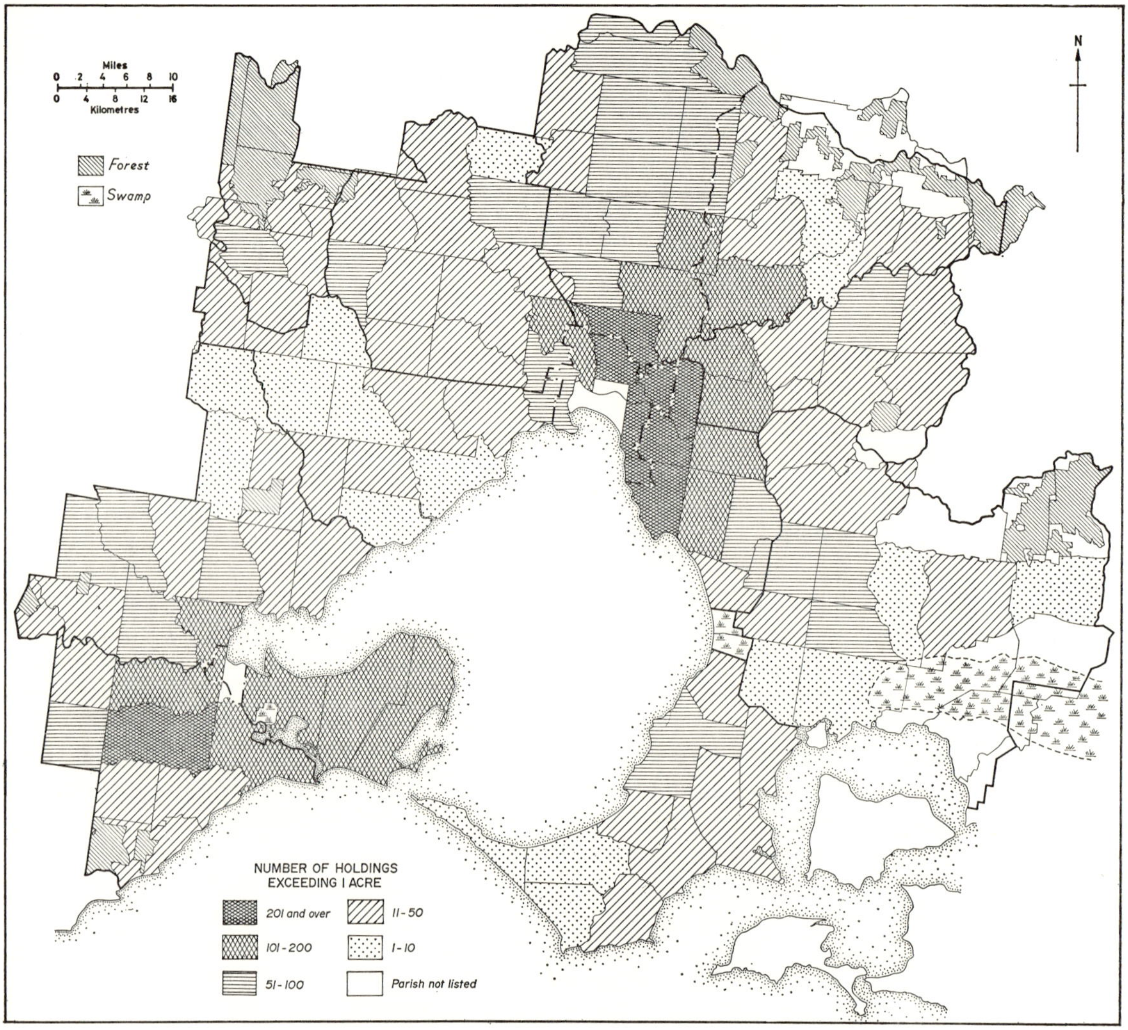

Map 13 Number of Rural Holdings in Each Parish, 1867
Agric. Stat., 1866

seventy estates larger than 2500 acres should have been included in the agricultural statistics for 1879–80, and these estates covered an area of 646 051 acres (see table 14).[1] Subtracting this from the region total, leaves 974 439 acres or 60 per cent of the rural land owned in estates of less than 2500 acres. When the totals given in table 14 are related to the information regarding total numbers of holdings and areas occupied, some perspective at least is given to the latter.

It is probably reasonably accurate to say that by 1880 for the Oakleigh division the average size of all holdings was about 64 acres, and few, if any, of these holdings exceeded 640 acres. But similar statements about the other divisions can be made with less certainty because the estates in the Land Tax Register are not strictly comparable to the holdings in the agricultural statistics. Under the Land Tax Act the freehold owner of the land was taxed, but for the agricultural statistics the actual occupant of the land was enumerated, whether freehold owner or tenant.

Table 14
Holdings Recorded in the 1880 Land Tax Register

Division	Holdings* 640–2500 acres		Holdings 2500–10 000 acres		Holdings 10 000 acres		Total		Adjusted total area† (a.)	Total occupied farm land‡ 1880 (a.)
	No.	Total area (a.)	No.	Total area (a.)	No.	Total area (a.)	No.	Area (a.)		
Bellarine	1	1 440	2	6 357	—	—	3	7 797	7 797	67 771
Barrabool	4	4 262	6	23 224	1	11 093	11	38 579	38 579	114 561
Bannockburn	8	11 734	5	20 962	6	112 141	19	144 837	144 837	227 684
Bacchus Marsh	3	3 627	1	2 877	—	—	4	6 504	6 504	50 659
Werribee	5	7 175	2	12 523	4	124 791	11	144 489	150 120	186 350
Sunbury	12	14 918	6	28 958	3	160 123	21	203 999	146 082	184 827
Plenty	24	35 179	11	50 479	—	—	35	85 658	110 912	270 304
Lilydale	4	6 435	3	14 393	—	—	7	20 828	20 828	108 882
Oakleigh	—	—	—	—	—	—	—	—	—	64 929
Berwick	5	6 966	13	50 101	—	—	18	57 067	57 067	214 897
Mornington	1	2 103	7	28 029	—	—	8	30 132	30 132	129 626
Total	67	93 839	56	237 903	14	408 148	137	739 890	712 858	1 620 490

* Holdings in this category were taxed only if they were on the better land
† Division acreages adjusted for Clarke's holding which extended over three divisions and beyond the region, but with the homestead in the Sunbury division
‡ From appendix, table 8
Source: *Victoria Government Gazette*, 1880, pp. 2937–63

If the land was totally unoccupied, it was omitted. Since Clarke, Chirnside and Staughton, at least, all leased part of their land at one time or another to small farmers, and since there was nothing to prevent people amalgamating land leased from several owners into one holding, it is not valid to subtract the Land Tax Register estates from the agricultural statistics holdings to arrive at the average size of the holdings of less than 2500 acres.

LARGER ESTATES

Of the seventy estates exceeding 2500 acres, only fourteen exceeded 10 000 acres. The areas of these fourteen estates, together with the names and addresses of their owners are given in table 15 (for their approximate location see map 14). George Russell was another landholder in this category in 1880, but his 28 356-acre Golf Hill estate lay outside the region, immediately to the west of the Bannockburn division. The men listed owned between them 408 148 acres.

Three of the founders of these estates have already been referred to—W. J. T. Clarke, Thomas Chirnside and Simon Staughton. Clarke died in 1874 and was succeeded by his sons, William John Clarke inheriting his father's Port Phillip estate, and the other sons succeeding to his New South Wales, New Zealand, and Tasmanian interests. William had acted as manager for his father in Victoria since about 1862. At Sunbury he built a large mansion, Rupertswood, and commuted

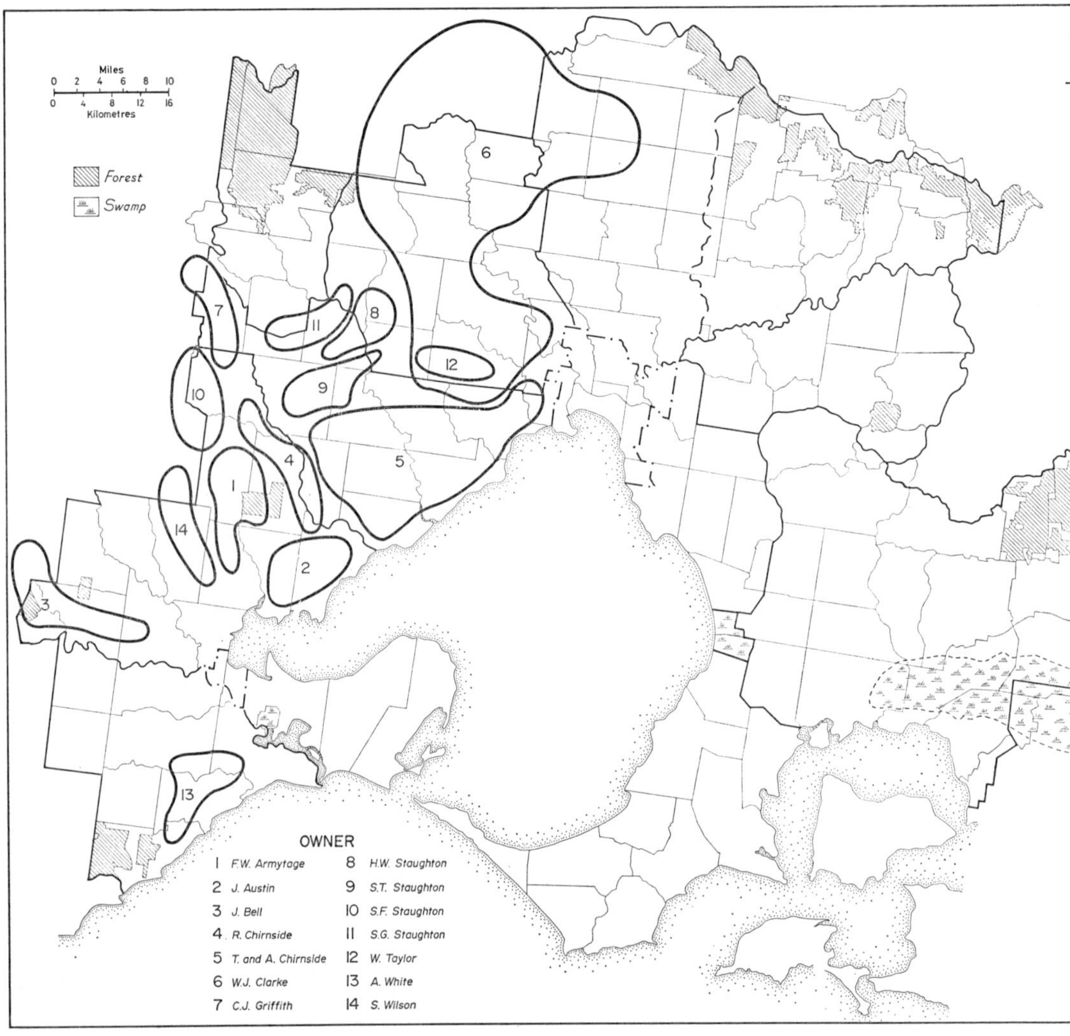

Map 14 Approximate Location of Freehold Estates Exceeding 10 000 Acres, 1880
Victoria Government Gazette, 1880, pp. 2937–63

between there and his city residence, Cliveden. One of the leading citizens of Melbourne, he was elected to the Legislative Council in 1878, although he was never particularly active in politics. Instead he was more widely known for his extensive business interests inherited from his father, for his encouragement of farming—he was patron of a number of agricultural societies—for his philanthropic activities and for his wide participation in public affairs generally, including his presidency of the organizing commission for the Great International Exhibition held in Melbourne in 1880. In 1882 he was created a baronet.[2]

Thomas Chirnside, who with his brother Andrew had become renowned for his race horses, also thought it appropriate to erect a home befitting a country gentleman. The result was Werribee Park, a two-storey stone mansion of seventy rooms. Robert Chirnside of Mount Rothwell, Little River, was their nephew.

Table 15
Holdings Exceeding 10 000 Acres, 1880

Number	Area (a.)	Owner	Address
1	22 768	Armytage, Frederick William	Duck Ponds
2	23 528	Austin, James	Avalon Lara
3	21 646	Bell, James trustees of the late, namely, Stephen Vine Buckland, Charles Meredith Poynter and George M. Bell	c/o S. V. Buckland, solicitor Geelong
4	12 959	Chirnside, Robert	Little River
5	81 068	Chirnside, Thomas and Andrew	Werribee Park Wyndham
6	136 310	Clarke, The Hon. William John (also owned 4096 acres of Jamieson's special survey in the Mornington division, and 3180 acres in the Berwick division)	27 Queen Street Melbourne
7	11 508	Griffith, Charles James, trustees of the late, namely, Arthur Wolfe Chomley (9897 acres owned by Molesworth Richard Greene)	Temple Court Melbourne (Grey Stones Bacchus Marsh)
8	13 462	Staughton, Harry Werribee	Melton
9	21 322	Staughton, Samuel Thomas	Eynesbury Melton
10	16 844	Staughton, Simon Frederick	Brisbane Ranges Anakie
11	10 893	Staughton, Stephen George	Brooklyn Melton
12	10 351	Taylor, William (also owned 3753 acres in the Berwick division)	Over-Newton Keilor 117 Collins St West Melbourne
13	11 093	White, Andrew	Connewarre
14	14 396	Wilson, The Hon. Sir Samuel	Oakleigh Hall St Kilda
	408 148		

Source: 'Land Tax Register', *Victoria Government Gazette*, 1880, pp. 2937–63

Simon Staughton died in 1863 and his estate was divided among his four sons. This still left each son with an estate ranking among the fourteen largest in the region. The Staughtons took an active interest in local affairs, and the popular Samuel T. Staughton, a staunch conservative, served as a member for West Bourke in the Legislative Assembly.[3]

Members of the Armytage, Austin and Bell families were already farming in Van Diemen's Land at the time Port Phillip was first settled, and younger members of these families joined the rush to Port Phillip, shipping sheep across Bass Strait and occupying a number of runs to the west of Geelong. As with the Chirnsides, these people had become well established in the Western District by 1880. They had extended their interests from the Western District into the Port Phillip region during the late forties and the fifties by purchasing Crown licences or leases, and subsequently the freehold titles to land, mainly from the Crown but also from private individuals.[4]

C. J. Griffith first occupied the Glenmore run in 1840 in partnership with a Mr J. Moore, but within the next two years had formed what was to become a long and close partnership with his nephew Molesworth Greene, a well-educated man of letters. Together Griffith and Greene leased the Mooradoranook run, and Greene later acquired Moore's interest in Glenmore. They eventually purchased this land from the Crown and established themselves on adjoining estates.[5]

William Taylor arrived at Port Phillip from Scotland in 1840. He too acquired interests in various runs before he purchased his Overnewton estate in 1849, where he made his permanent home. He also bought land in New South Wales. Active in public affairs, he twice served on the Legislative Council.[6]

Samuel Wilson, a later arrival, came to Port Phillip from Ireland in 1852. In Ireland he had owned a small farm and had gained experience in linen manufacturing and the law. He tried gold mining in Victoria, with some success, and then went to manage his brother's sheep-run. The Wilson brothers subsequently built up extensive holdings in Victoria and New South Wales and eventually Samuel Wilson purchased the well-known Ercildoune property in the Western District and made it his home; the estate within the Port Phillip region was just one of many. A noted philanthropist and public man, he was knighted in 1875.[7]

Andrew White's estate was somewhat different from those of the other large landholders. Although extensive in area, the land was comparatively much less valuable. The soils were mainly hard-setting loams in association with sandy ridges on mottled yellow clay subsoils, and the land was extensively covered with forest and heathy scrub. White bought this land, which was scattered in a number of allotments, from private individuals. A latecomer for a first generation large landholder, he served on the local shire council from 1878 to 1886.[8]

With the exception of Andrew White's estate in the poorer country in the Barrabool division, these large estates represented the eastern extremity of the large estates in the Western District of Victoria. In family ties and in middle-class British origin, the owners were of the Western District fraternity. In background they were yeomen farmers, butchers, merchants and engineers. Initially they made their fortunes in Victoria by grazing sheep on licensed and leasehold land. Then they invested their money in purchasing their estates and in the sixties and seventies built their country mansions and city residences, took an active part in politics both at the local and colonial level, promoted education and other community interests, and in general they, or their sons, enjoyed the fruits of their pioneering efforts. The majority visited England at least once; some returned there to settle permanently. For example, James Austin bought the abbey and house at Glastonbury in his home county of Somerset (his son Frank ran Avalon near Werribee), while Sir Samuel Wilson purchased the estate of Hughendon in England. These people were of the region and yet their horizons were much wider; they took a paternalistic interest in local small farming but they identified themselves more with colonial interests as a whole and with the social life of the gracious city and country homes.[9]

Why were these holdings concentrated in the Bannockburn, Werribee and Sunbury divisions, while none lay to the east of the bay? The very nature of the basalt plains seems to have determined this differentiation of occupation from the beginning. As seen in chapter 2, already by the time of the census of 1841 this area represented the sheep country, cultivation was on the cracking clay soils and cattle were in the wetter areas of the east and south-east. Those who first brought livestock to the colony were sufficiently good judges of the new country to divide at a very early stage the land best suited to sheep from that best suited to cattle. The cultivators, too, chose well under the prevailing circumstances. Those who did try Merino sheep in the south-east found, to their loss, that they suffered from fluke and did not thrive. It is reasonable to suggest that when the land was eventually sold, that best suited to intensive farming brought too high a price to be attractive for extensive sheep grazing even from the long-term point of view, and hence the absence of large estates on the Barrabool Hills, the Merri Creek–Plenty River area, and also the areas brought under cultivation in the Bellarine and Oakleigh divisions, although the reason in the latter case was more due to the climate and nature of the terrain.

The eastern part of the region was cattle country. It had a heavier rainfall, poor coastal plains rising into hill country, thickly timbered in parts, and a longer, coarser vegetation. In short, it was country alien to a sheepman, and it was the sheepmen who had established themselves and gained experience of the environment in the crucial, early years of the colony. As W. J. T. Clarke pointed out, for the first fifteen years cattle were not very profitable for the market was too limited, but wool could be shipped to England.[10] Hence when the land was sold it was the more successful of the sheepmen who were in a position to utilize their accumulated capital and/or their credit backing in purchasing large areas of land. These men had obtained their capital by grazing operations on predominantly basalt plains country; it was only natural that they should remain on the type of land they knew. Conversely, too, these large estates occupied the area of lowest rainfall in the region, the area least adapted to sown pastures and mixed farming and best utilized for extensive grazing.

SMALL HOLDINGS AND LEASEHOLD LAND

The fourteen largest estates were the ones that consisted of tens of thousands of acres and remained intact up to 1880. Table 14 gives an indication, too, of the number and location of the next group of estates, those ranging in size from about 1000–10 000 acres. The remaining group to be considered are the smaller holdings, the majority of which during the fifties had been in the 30–350-acre range. These holdings were essentially of two types—freehold, and leasehold from private individuals—and thus sometimes derived from some of the larger estates aforementioned.

A considerable area of freehold land was rented to private individuals throughout the sixties and apparently right through the seventies to 1880. On 31 March 1861 the 325 342 acres of land rented in this way represented 30 per cent of the occupied farmland of the region, and on 31 March 1881 the 450 585 acres

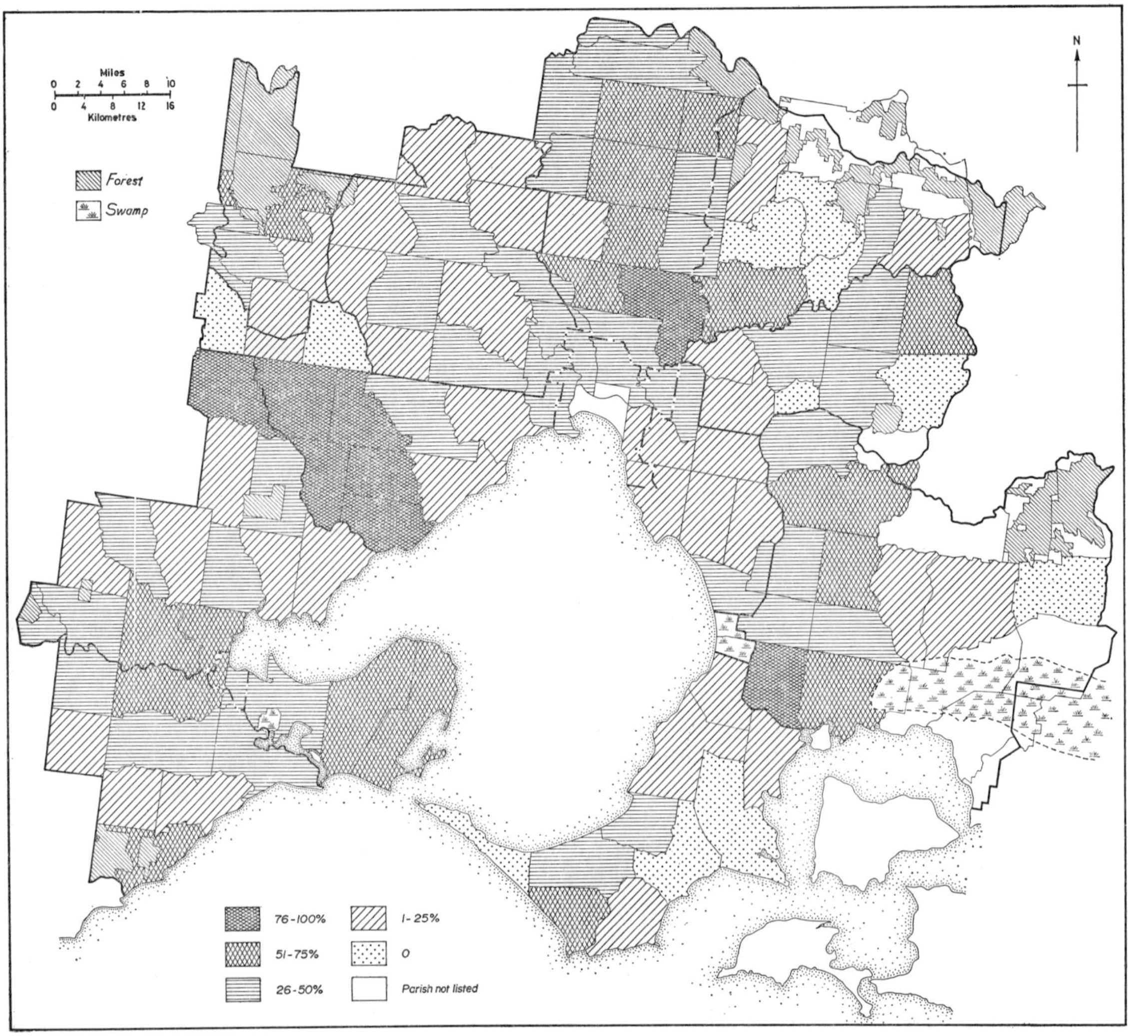

Map 15 Percentage of Freehold Land Rented, 1867
Agric. Stat., 1866

of rented land represented 27 per cent of the occupied farmland (see table 9 in appendix). In the sixties land was either leased out in large areas for grazing or to small tenant farmers. Maps 13 and 15 together show the different areas of broad-acre leasing and small tenant farming. A relatively large number of holdings in a parish with a high proportion of leasehold land almost invariably indicates a number of small leasehold farms in this context. By 1867 the old areas of tenant farming established in the forties and early fifties—to the north of Melbourne, in the Barrabool Hills and on the Bellarine Peninsula—were still predominant in this feature and several more areas had developed as tenant farming centres. They were in a small area in the fertile valley at Bacchus Marsh, on the river flats and adjacent areas along the Yarra and its tributaries, near Berwick, and in a small area north of Werribee on the Werribee River. These areas characteristically occupied the more fertile soils of the region.

Many of the pre-gold leasing arrangements had provided for rent in the form of wheat or permanent improvements. These arrangements had been in part to enable the lessee to develop the land from its natural state into a viable farm. However, by the end of the fifties the system of payment in grain had gone out of favour because of delays in delivering the grain and fluctuations in the grain market. By 1859 most land was let for cash sums, although the system had not yet become stabilized. Some people in the Barrabool Hills and the Bellarine division were still paying up to 50s per acre, a legacy from the high prices of 1854 and 1855, but the average rate was about 25s per acre, and the terms were five to ten years, although few leases were for as long as ten years. There was some agitation for a tenant law to protect the tenant's capital investment in buildings and other improvements, and the owner's land and property from exhaustion and deterioration.[11] But the debate was cut short by the great exodus of the early sixties.

Side by side with the small leasehold farms were the small freehold farms, many of which had been taken up during the fifties. By the end of that decade quite a few of their owners were in serious difficulties because of high interest payments due on land mortgages. Apart from the debt burden, many of these farmers and many of the leaseholders, were also faced with farms that were too small for the changing techniques of farming, a lack of capital to purchase new equipment or make improvements, a serious lack of knowledge of farming, and a standard of living below that which they had known before entering farming.[12] It is therefore not surprising that they were unable to survive the adverse seasons, the rust and the caterpillars of the sixties.

In 1861 some farmers along the Yarra River and adjacent areas sold portions of their farms and went to the new gold-fields in New Zealand or on the Lachlan, the Jordan or the Jamieson. The result was a temporary increase in occupants and small farms as new farmers moved in and bought this land.[13] But in other areas, where people also left, the number of holdings decreased as neighbouring farmers or large landowners such as Clarke bought or rented the vacated lands.[14] Two years later, as the crops failed, some landlords asked for only half their rent, W. J. T. Clarke and Son (son now acting manager) among them. Others owning land along the Yarra River and its tributaries forgave all their rent after extensive floods ruined the crops. Right through the region small farms were abandoned, the land was left uncultivated and the gradual amalgamation of farms and rehabilitation of the land commenced.[15]

The exodus of small farmers from the Port Phillip region was mainly during the years 1861–4, with the greatest movement probably occurring during 1863. By 1865 much of the former cultivation land had been converted to pasture and a number of the small farms had been amalgamated into larger units. But this process did continue at a slower rate at least until 1880. For even if three farms of 50 acres were amalgamated into one holding, this still only resulted in a farm of 150 acres, by no means a large farm for the mixed farming system developing by the late sixties.

Precise figures on farm size are not available and in any case the averages would vary considerably with the type of farming the land was most suited to. However, from the changes in farming systems outlined in the last chapter, the continuing reference to farm amalgamation in the press and other commentaries, and various descriptions of individual farms, together with the evidence of the Land Tax Register, some assumptions can be made about farm size in 1880 as compared with the pattern in about 1860 (see chapter 3). As we have seen, fourteen very large holdings covering tens of thousands of acres were still in existence in 1880. There were some holdings in the range 1000–10 000 acres in 1860 and the number had probably risen considerably by 1880. We do know that there were fifty-six holdings between 2500 and 10 000 acres in the region, but the greatest increase was probably in the 500–1500-acre range, this taking place at the expense of the holdings in the 30–350-acre range. Therefore, where before there had been a conspicuous lack of holdings of about 640 acres, the new integrated farming methods increasingly required farms of about this size or larger, particularly where sheep and/or cattle were combined with cropping.

Land rents, too, were rationalized and from 1870 to 1880 the average rent for pastoral land was 2–10s per acre, for cropping land 5–20s per acre and for market gardening land 20–30s per acre, although by 1880 market gardening land was bringing 40–60s per acre in some areas close to Melbourne. The duration of the leases, however, continued substantially unchanged, varying from about one to ten years but with the emphasis on three- to seven-year terms.[16] There is every indication, too, that side by side with this rationalization of leasing arrangements the leasing of land was taking on a much more diversified character. Although the acreage of land leased does not appear to have changed greatly during the sixties and seventies, the absentee landowner trying to extract the maximum in rent with little thought of the productive capacity of his land did become progressively less significant after 1860. Instead considerably more of the leasing arrangements seem to have involved farmers leasing to one another. The absentee owner meanwhile tended to employ a resident manager and use his land for extensive grazing, or else he leased his land at reasonable rental in larger areas. In this way many farmers who only owned a small area of freehold land were able to extend their activities over a larger, more economic area, their freehold providing the site for many of their major capital improvements in the form of sheds and houses. Other farmers, of course, continued to lease all their land, but they had almost certainly declined both in total numbers and in the proportion they represented of all the farm occupants.

CROWN LANDS AND COMMONS

Commonage rights for the local people involved an age-old tradition in Europe, and this in turn had been respected in the colony of New South Wales and at Port Phillip, particularly in relation to commonage for the townspeoples' cows. Under the first Land Act passed by the Victorian legislature in 1860, the principle of commonage was retained and extended. Crown lands in the vicinity of towns could be proclaimed as towns' commons, and ten or more occupants of not less than five hundred acres of freehold land could petition for Crown land, within five miles of their purchased land, to be proclaimed a farmers' common. The farmers' commons were for the use of all neighbouring occupants of freehold land who cultivated at least one-quarter of their holdings. But use of the common was regulated and all prospective users had to obtain an annual farmers' depasturing licence which entitled the holder to graze horses and cattle on the farmers' common at the rate of one head of cattle for every acre, or one horse for every two acres of purchased land which he had cultivated. For this privilege he had to pay 4s per horse and 2s per head of cattle per year.[17] Sheep, it should be noted, were especially excluded from the commons.[18] The 1860 Act was repealed in 1862, but under the new Land Act of 1862 municipal, gold-fields', towns', and farmers' commons were all provided for under similar principles to the old Act. With all the commons, however, there was always one provision, and that was that the government retained the right to increase or diminish the size of any common and to sell the land at any time. This right the government freely exercised.

During 1861 many commons were proclaimed; the towns' commons varied from about one hundred to five hundred acres, but many of the farmers' commons were much larger, the area depending on the availability of Crown lands. In the Plenty division, the Upper Plenty farmers' common consisted of 21 000 acres of rough timber country; in the south of the Oakleigh division the Mordialloc farmers' common contained 4960 acres while in the north of the same division the Boroondara farmers' common contained only 98 acres.

In some areas these commons were used extensively by the farmers and undoubtedly they provided useful grazing land for the smaller landholders. However, as might be expected where little or no control was exercised over the frequency and intensity of grazing, the smaller commons in the more closely settled areas did not prove to be 'the boon they were expected by the small dairy farmers, in consequence of their being always overstocked during the growing months; the wretched cattle belonging to those who have no other land to fall back upon must, of necessity, die of starvation in a season like this.'[19]

Most commons were short-lived, the land being sold in the sixties and seventies (not without some local opposition) wherever there was a reasonable demand for it. Only in a few less desirable situations, such as heavily timbered country, did the farmers' commons last as grazing land, and towns' commons likewise dwindled except where preserved for recreational purposes. The Belmont town common is one common which has survived to this day, but it is on low-lying land along the Barwon River near Geelong and is subject to periodical flooding.

The proclamation of Crown lands as commons became only a temporary method of utilizing Crown lands in the areas near the major cities until the ever-spreading land sales and alienation overtook these areas. From this point of view the proclaimed commons bore little resemblance to the commons of Europe where they originated. The resemblance was, however, more apparent in the associated desire of the legislators to foster the interests of the small independent farmers who cultivated the land, even if this aim was defeated from the outset by uncertainty about the continued existence of any common.

MORE SMALL HOLDINGS—THE 1862 NOVEL INDUSTRIES CLAUSE

Another favourite project of the legislators of the day was the introduction of novel industries, by which was meant primarily the cultivation of such plants as vines, olives, hops, mulberries, and any other useful plants not generally grown in Victoria, though any other industries would also be considered.[20] Interest for this type of undertaking resulted in the novel industries clause being included in the 1862

Land Act (section 47). Under this clause, leases could be issued for areas of Crown land, not exceeding thirty acres, situated anywhere outside the proclaimed agricultural areas. The rent was to be fixed separately for each individual lease and the right to purchase the leasehold land at £1 per acre after five years was granted to the lessee. In practice within the Port Phillip region this meant the alienation of commons and village reserves.

There was a rapid response to this clause and by the end of the year sixty-two people had applied for leases within the Port Phillip region. When applying for a lease, each applicant had to list the crops he intended planting or otherwise state how he intended using the land. Vines were the favoured crop and twenty-one of the sixty-two people requested their leases for the sole purpose of establishing a vineyard, two other people wished to establish tobacco farms and one person a chemical factory. The remaining thirty-eight applicants all intended trying several crops on their holdings. Vines and tobacco were frequently mentioned and other crops specifically named were olives, oranges, lemons, hops, apples (and apples for cider), almonds, peaches, plums, mulberries (and silkworms), sugar-beet, sugar-cane, ginger, arrowroot, mustard, gram, rape-seed, peas (for splitting), sorghum, teasel, flax, hemp and sea-island cotton. Proposals to establish orchards were only acceptable if the lessee agreed to dry the produce or to convert it into cider, perry or brandy.[21] Such were the intentions.

A few of the applicants, some members of the same family, applied for land in sections adjacent to each other, and in these cases the land was usually intended for viticulture. In the first list of applicants, too, were several of the early viticulturists of the Barrabool Hills and Moorabool River areas who had commenced their vineyards on land leased from private owners in the forties and early fifties. But as subsequent events showed, other people were less experienced and less purposeful in their undertakings.

Many people commenced their operations early in 1863, an unfortunate year in which to commence on a thirty-acre block. By the beginning of 1866 the report was not good. In the Sunbury division, the collector of statistics noted,

> There are a great many blocks of the choicest land taken up under the Novel Industry clause of the Land Act, for the cultivation of tobacco, flax, vines, etc., upon which I find wheat, oats, potatoes, etc., the predominating, and often the sole crop this year; inexperience in the culture, and want of success last year, determining the holders not to attempt such novel crops again . . .[22]

In general these small holdings suffered a similar fate to the other small holdings of this period. Vines, apart from the more common fruit trees already grown in orchards, were the most successful of the crops tried, but even they were a very doubtful financial proposition to 1880 because of uncertain yields from year to year and major difficulties in marketing wine. By the mid-seventies some of the long-established Barrabool Hills growers were, for want of a remunerative market, turning large sections of their vineyards over to sheep.[23]

But the legislators were not to be deterred and in 1871 a royal commission was appointed 'to consider and report, how far it may be practicable to introduce into this country branches of industry which are known to be common and profitable among the farming population of Continental Europe. . .' This commission noted that olives were being grown at Brighton, Heidelberg, Moonee Ponds, Pentridge, and other places in the neighborhood of Melbourne; but, owing to there being no sufficient means available for pressing, the olives have, in most cases, either been allowed to fall from the trees unused, or else have been applied to so poor a purpose as fattening fowls.

Nevertheless the commission recommended

olive culture, and drying and preservation of fruits, the growing and dressing of flax and other fibre plants, the cultivation of the poppy for oil and opium, the beet-root for sugar, plants producing silk, medicinal and dye plants, hops, tea, and cork and Valonia oak, the castor oil bush, and others . . .

Its members were convinced that their labours would

result in paving the way to the establishment in Victoria of various special industries, connected with the cultivation of the soil, which have for centuries been a copious source of national wealth to countries with a like climate to ours, and an unfailing means of comfort and prosperity to the rural population in those countries.

The commissioners appear to have held this view from the beginning. Furthermore they believed 'that the promotion of all such industries would be profitable, in a productive point of view, not only to the State, but also highly beneficial in training the young of both sexes in the habits of frugality and care, which so essentially mark the rural population of those countries where such industries exist.'[24] The commission itself distributed seeds and cuttings and was anxious to publish tracts on how to cultivate these plants. Practical economic problems of production and marketing, and possible social and national differences between the people of southern Europe and the British immigrants, however, were not considered.

The persistence of the legislators in their encouragement of the novel industries contrasted strongly with their disregard for rural distress and the failures of the more common crops. It was one symptom of the great gulf which existed between those familiar with the practical aspects of farming, and the theorists, politicians and agitators who were unacquainted with agricultural realities but were determining government policy relating to rural affairs and influencing people entering farming for the first time.

Probably the salvation of the small-farming areas in the sixties and seventies lay in the opportunities for the small farmers to leave their farms and move way. The extreme difficulties the farmers faced in the early sixties forced many of them to do this. Many of these men had been enticed to Victoria by gold, and since farming increasingly proved to be a hopeless undertaking for them, a return to the goldfields in Victoria or New Zealand was a practicable proposition, at least in the short term. The other main avenue of escape, to a larger land selection elsewhere in the colony under the new Acts, was also attractive, particularly to a leaseholder. Both of these propositions allowed the farmers to maintain their independence, and—of importance to the least skilled—new skills were not required, as was often the case when seeking a city position, although no doubt many did go to the city too. It probably can be argued that those who did move to new land selections often just transferred the small-farming problem from one region to another and from one generation to the next, their continuing lack of capital being a major factor in this. However, such propositions must remain little more than conjecture until detailed studies have been made of the regions of closer settlement.

Because of the movement of people out of some divisions and into others, and the continuing sale of Crown lands, particularly during the seventies in the eastern part of the region, a reasonably fluid land system was maintained. A rigid social system of land inheritance had not developed before 1880, for the people were an immigrant generation and their attachment to the Port Phillip land was still in its infancy. Many people in their old age found themselves more attached to this land than to that of their birth, but others preferred to return to the United Kingdom for their retirement, and for some this meant selling their colonial interests.

All this, then, contributed to a reasonably active land market catering for some six thousand individual holdings within the region, an active market which provided an opportunity for the amalgamation of farms and the adjustment of farm sizes to those best adapted to the prevailing techniques and economics of farming. Likewise the alternative opportunities open to leaseholders, and the difficulties of farming profitably, forced an adjustment in the pattern of land tenure such that leasing arrangements became far less exploitative both of the farm and the tenant, and probably more localized in nature. The large capitalist renting land to numerous small farmers gradually ceased to dominate the scene.

Within this main stream of events the commons created a few eddies in the diminishing current of Crown lands alienation, while the novel industries selections remained very minor backwaters soon to be engulfed again in the main stream of the land system.

8 : Institutional Influences

GOVERNMENT

In the United Kingdom government intervention in agriculture had developed as part of the evolution of government as an institution within British society. A long series of corn laws dated back to the fourteenth century, and by the seventeenth and eighteenth centuries these laws had become quite complex. When the British government extended its influence to New South Wales, the early difficulties in obtaining a food supply, the desire to create a stable rural community, and the problems of land alienation heightened the British and New South Wales governments' interest in rural affairs.

When the Port Phillip region was settled in 1835 the initial concern of the government was with regulating land occupation and alienation. This continued to be a major concern, but as Port Phillip society developed, further government regulation in the British tradition was deemed necessary. Laws already enacted for the more developed society around Sydney (but enforceable at Port Phillip) became increasingly important and were further extended and consolidated after 1851 by succeeding Victorian governments. Such matters as boundary fencing, establishment of markets and public abattoirs, prevention of livestock stealing, control of diseases in livestock, and the eradication of thistles were brought under government control. In this way the government helped to create an ordered community within which the farmer could operate effectively with the minimum of disruption from anti-social neighbours. As in the United Kingdom, pressure for government intervention in rural affairs grew because of the very great importance of agriculture to the economic and social life of the community.

As governments in many countries became increasingly involved in rural affairs, more information about rural activities was needed and by the mid-nineteenth century the international climate of opinion was firmly in favour of the national collection of agricultural statistics, although in Ireland it was the potato famine and in England a cattle plague that finally prompted the collection of agricultural statistics on a regular basis from 1847 and 1866 respectively.[1] In Australia a tradition of collecting statistics had arisen out of the ordered nature of the original penal settlement and the need to send regular reports back to the British government. Thus one of the responsibilities of the first government representative at Port Phillip had been to report upon the number of people present in the new settlement, the livestock they owned and the land they cultivated. From then on regular reports were made to Sydney on these matters, even if for some years they were of very doubtful accuracy. By the time the Victorian government was installed in 1851, a tradition had been established of taking censuses and collecting agricultural statistics. This collection of data was continued and improved. In this way a vast amount of information was made available to the government and any other interested parties. The use that was made of this information is uncertain, although probably it was used selectively to back up preconceived notions more than to evaluate proposed courses of action. Certainly the obsession with small farms and novel industries continued despite an abundance of detailed up-to-date information on rural affairs.

A continuing extension of government activity led to the growth of local government bodies and the construction of roads and railways from which all could benefit. During the fifties and sixties local roads boards were formed wherever enough citizens were resident to petition for the establishment of such boards, and gradually the whole municipal system of cities, towns, boroughs and shires developed. These locally elected bodies were empowered by Acts of Parliament to collect rates from local landowners and tolls on the roads, and were responsible for the construction of roads and other local public utilities.

Railway construction was first attempted in Australia by private companies, but the distances to be covered in relation to the population density were so great that most of these companies were financial failures and the governments had to take over railway construction at a very early stage.[2] In the field of transport, therefore, public bodies played a very vital role; only in water transport was the population served by private enterprise. The construction of a railway line from Melbourne to Hawthorn in 1861 aided the expansion of the fresh milk industry in that direction, and eventually a similar advantage resulted from the belated opening of the railway line linking Melbourne with the Gippsland railway at Oakleigh in 1879. The other railway lines opened in the region by 1880 went from Melbourne to Geelong (1857), to Sunbury (1859) and farther north, to Williamstown (1859), and through Wallan Wallan (1872) to Wodonga (1873) and eventually to Albury to meet the New South Wales line from Sydney (1883). Several short suburban lines radiating from Melbourne to Port Melbourne, St Kilda and Brighton Beach were also constructed, and other lines were built from Geelong north-west to Ballarat (1862) and south-west to Colac (1877). The line along the Bellarine Peninsula to Queenscliff was opened in 1879.[3]

With better transport facilities, travelling time was shortened and therefore perishable products, such as milk, eggs, soft fruits and fresh vegetables, could be taken greater distances to markets. Also the cost of transporting goods fell and it became economical to produce various goods at increasing distances from the markets. Transport also became more reliable throughout the year and this led to a more even supply of goods to the markets, with fewer delays during the wet winter and spring months. In general these improvements made possible greater diversification of production on the farms at ever-greater distances from the markets. However, as better transport facilities, especially railway lines, were extended beyond the region, the farmers within the region had to contend with increasing competition from those beyond. As discussed earlier in the case of wheat and hay, this prompted the local farmers to concentrate increasingly on producing goods that were both well adapted to the local environment and perishable or expensive to transport.

Promoting and maintaining a well-ordered community and providing public facilities such as transport were costly. Funds for this came mainly from Crown lands sales and leases and from customs and excise revenue. By the second half of the seventies customs and excise was providing about twice the revenue coming from Crown lands. Until 1855 the only items bearing import duty in Victoria were alcoholic beverages, tobacco goods (excluding tobacco for sheep-washing), sugar and sugar products, tea, coffee and chicory; gold bore an export duty. This situation was altered little until 1866 when import duties were placed on a much wider range of goods, and thereafter until 1880 both the range and severity of these duties were increased. By 1880 a complex tariff schedule was in operation with many items being subject to 20 or 25 per cent ad valorem duties, while others were taxed at specific rates.[4]

During this period the Victorian tariff was regarded as protectionist while New South Wales was considered to have a free trade policy. This juxtaposition in itself has always created some interest. However, historians have recently come to debate how much the Victorian tariff was the result of a deliberate protectionist policy and how much it was imposed simply to raise revenue. Certainly there was ample propaganda for protectionist policies during the sixties and seventies, and the politicians accepted the principle of encouraging native industries both by the award of bounties and by protective duties, but at the same time heavier import duties tended to follow budget deficits, and there is evidence to suggest that the revenue motive was far stronger than the protection motive in prompting tariff increases. This same need for revenue was also responsible for the Land Tax Act of 1877, which levied a tax on the unimproved value of land held in large holdings.[5]

From the revenue point of view the farmers in the Port Phillip region benefited from the ordered community and public facilities provided by the government. In terms of protection, however, the tariff appears to have been of little benefit to the local farmers and quite possibly was detrimental to them. The duty of 2s per 100 lb on barley after 1871 (3s for pearl and scotch barley) did not promote an increase in the barley acreage within the region. The duty on butter may have played a minor part in the expansion of butter production, but the duty on wheat, first introduced in 1866, was of no significance (see chapter 6). The duty on wine had only a small influence on the wine industry, the problems of which were more related to difficulties and costs of production and a very limited local acceptance of its products than to import competition. The local people did not like the local dry wines and were prepared to pay quite dearly for imported sweeter wines. British tariffs were probably of greater significance to the wine producers than the local tariffs.[6]

Of more importance to the majority of farmers were the increased costs of the items they needed to buy. In particular such things as agricultural implements and machinery, and steam-engines, were taxed. In 1878 the duty on wire was lifted, but a duty was imposed on bags and sacks which had formerly entered free of duty. The duty of 20 per cent ad valorem on agricultural implements and machinery during the seventies played a part in fostering the development of local agricultural implement and machinery manufacturing. The popularity of ploughs designed and manufactured in Melbourne by Hugh Lennon, the local manufacture of strippers (for the northern areas), and the early development of the dray are all examples of the development and acceptance of items specifically designed for local conditions. However, British and American manufacturers did have the advantage of more highly developed metallurgical and engineering industries, and for the more complex machines, such as steam-engines, the overseas manufacturers retained their monopoly in the local market. Similarly in the all-important field of harvesting machinery the local Victorian manufacturers were not well advanced at this time compared with developments overseas, and the tax of 20 per cent on imported machines was a heavy tax indeed for the farmers when it was becoming so essential to mechanize operations. Within the region this was of less importance because cereal cropping, apart from hay, had dwindled, but it was a major cause of the formation of the farmers' unions at the end of the seventies, following the development of the reaper and binder in America.

As indicated above, the government did accept the idea of protection for local industries and did offer bounties for both agricultural and manufactured products. During the fifties and sixties acclimatization societies were established in the Australian colonies, reflecting a world-wide interest in such activities, and were given financial assistance by the colonial governments. As early as 1851 the government of Western Australia had offered a bonus of £60 to the first importer of two male and eight female alpacas. Between 1859 and 1863 the New South Wales government spent £21 303 7s 10d in an attempt to establish llamas, alpacas and vicugnas in New South Wales, while the Victorian government granted £2000 in 1861 to the Acclimatization Society to introduce the same species into Victoria—all without lasting success.[7]

With such men as Edward Wilson, proprietor of the *Argus*, William Lyall, a wealthy landowner, and scientists Professor McCoy and Baron von Mueller at the head of the Victorian society, its influence on the government was considerable. Thus in 1862 £5500 was granted for zoological and acclimatization activities, and further grants were made in subsequent years. Meanwhile the *Yeoman and Australian Acclimatiser* newspaper (after 1 October 1864 the *Australasian*) kept the public well informed on acclimatization activities.

The government's interest in acclimatization was important, not for the new industries and animals that were introduced, but for the general climate of opinion it fostered and reflected, particularly during the 1860s. Typical of the official view of Victorian agriculture were the notes on agriculture distributed by the commissioners for Victoria at the International Exhibition in London in 1862. Firstly, in only four lines, attention was drawn to the samples of wheat, oats and barley in the exhibition and the prizes awarded to these samples. No mention was made of the extent or mode of growth of these crops in the colony. Then followed:

> *Vineyards*—About 2,000 acres of vineyards are already planted and in a thriving condition. New ground is being daily prepared for vine cultivation, so that no doubt exists of this important branch of husbandry extending over a large portion of Victoria . . .
> *Cotton.*—Many parts of the colony are well adapted for the growth of cotton, and steps have been already taken by some of the colonists to introduce this important branch of cultivation . . .
> *Silk.*—Attention is being directed to the rearing of the silk-worm, which is found to thrive exceedingly well both on the black and white mulberry.
> *Arrow-Root.*—Samples of arrow-root are exhibited from various parts of the colony. The plant thrives well, and can be easily and profitably cultivated.
> *Tobacco.*—The cultivation of the tobacco plant is now being carried on in many parts of the colony . . .
>
> The olive, orange, lemon, pine apple, and other tropical fruits are now being cultivated with great success.[8]

An immigrant from London on arrival in Victoria could be forgiven if he thought himself to be in the wrong country.

During the 1870s direct government encouragement for the introduction of new crops and livestock gradually waned; the embargo on importing livestock no doubt had an influence on this, and also such matters were becoming increasingly the prerogative of the Department of Agriculture which was established in 1872. This, however, was a gradual process, and for some time bonuses were offered for various undertakings. For instance, for the year 1874–5 a sum of £5000 was voted for bonuses for the manufacture of beetroot sugar and £1000 for the production of flax and silk.[9]

It is not appropriate to explore here the reasons for the government's pre-occupation with esoteric plants and animals. But it is difficult to believe that the local Victorian politicians were very aware of or concerned with the logistics of empire trade, and trading with countries such as China, as their English counterparts were. A cursory investigation certainly gives no indication of this. Instead, on present evidence, the popularity of zoological and botanical interests among the English gentry, and the social benefits to be gained from emulating and communicating with these people appear to have been of far greater importance. Members of societies such as the Acclimatisation Society of Great Britain (founded in 1860) and the French Imperial Acclimatisation Society (founded in 1854) were interested in animals, birds and plants from all parts of the world. For Victorians with pretensions to power and influence there were two benefits to be gained from adopting the same leisure-time activities as these people. One was the opportunity to make the new colony more like 'home' by acclimatizing the familiar song-birds, fish, plants, etc., and the other was the social opportunity for associating with people of similar interests who were highly placed in overseas society.[10]

With other forms of assistance to agriculture the government was very wary of becoming closely involved in the welfare of any rural industry. Following the 1840s depression, an Act had been passed by the grazier-dominated New South Wales legislature giving a preferable lien on wool from season to season and allowing for mortgages on sheep, cattle and horses. This was an important step because it enabled the graziers to get credit more readily.[11] A similar Act was passed by the very different Victorian government of 1865 providing for liens on yearly crops, and thus giving the cultivator the same advantages in raising credit as the grazier. The government had just passed new land legislation under which it was proposed to lease 'agricultural' lands, and since the lessees would be unable to mortgage their land, it was felt that the Liens on Crops Act would provide them with the means to obtain credit.[12] In other words, the legislation was in response to a theoretical future need and not to a very real present need, though no doubt it helped to satisfy the latter.

When it came to direct assistance for farmers already on the land the government would not become involved. The financial affairs of private citizens were not its concern. Thus repeated requests for assistance for the farmers near Geelong to buy seed wheat were passed on to the Board of Agriculture with the suggestion that the board could spend an amount on assistance equal to its next year's grant if it forwent that grant during the next year (which it refused to do),[13] or else the request was dismissed outrightly, with the Chief Secretary, James McCulloch, stating that 'it was a matter distinctly beyond the function of Government' and that 'it was highly objectionable to lay down a principle that the state should assist to relieve the distress of any particular class of the community.'[14]

Thus the government was willing to foster new developments and act from a broad theoretical basis, provided it was also expedient so to do, but the rights of the individual to remain free from interference were zealously protected, and this meant the right to succeed and the right to fail. The paradox of this, however, was that in championing small allotments for farmers and in passing such measures as the novel industries clause, the government was partly responsible for creating pockets of rural poverty. Once created, however, the government was able to absolve itself from all responsibility for these areas of poverty.

SOCIETIES AND SEMI-GOVERNMENT ORGANIZATIONS

The formation of local agricultural societies, and the advocacy of government action to help farmers increase their production were features of eighteenth-century rural affairs in both Great Britain and the United States. And when British people settled at Port Philip they continued the tradition of organizing to promote knowledge and disseminate information about agriculture.

As early as 1840 the Pastoral and Agricultural Society of Australia Felix was formed, but it was premature and was disbanded in 1842 after an unsuccessful show.[15] A more permanent society, the Port Phillip Farmers' Society, was established in 1848. The farming districts all around Melbourne were well represented in this society, but it was nevertheless a society for the wealthier farmers and landowners, and membership was at the high rate of £2 per year.

Primarily this was a non-political show society which held a general exhibition each year. After 1856 the organization of this exhibition was based on that of the exhibitions conducted by the three principal agricultural societies of the United Kingdom. The entries were systematically classified and a descriptive catalogue listed the names of the exhibitors, the pedigrees of the livestock, and the prices of the implements.[16] In the machinery section the exhibits were tried out in the field before the awards were made, while in the livestock sections the wealthier farmers were quick to adopt the system of 'show-yard fashions' evolved in the United Kingdom, a system which in that country had 'induced a pressure of demand for the breeding stock of the favoured herds'[17] with the concomitant financial benefits to their owners.

Regular ploughing matches were also held, usually in May, in the various districts together with a general match at Brunswick. Although these matches were well supported by contestants and became the major publicity avenue for the plough-makers, the society nevertheless tended to bemoan the lack of spectators and the fact that the matches had not become large functions of social importance.[18] Other encouragements to finesse of cultivation and quality of product were provided in the prizes for the best-cultivated farms. In awarding these prizes the judges looked for the neatness and style with which the land had been cultivated, as much as for the quality of the crops grown, thereby carefully fostering the traditions of European cultivation.[19]

Further overseas influence also became apparent when, in the fashion of the Highland and Agricultural Society of Scotland and of the Royal Agricultural Society of England, an analytical and consulting chemist was appointed to the society in 1856–7. Under the agreement the fee for a quantitative analysis of any sample of soil, manure, etc. was to be £10 and for a qualitative analysis from £1 1s to £1 10s. Although agricultural chemistry was still in its infancy, the work of J. von Liebig, J. B. Lawes, J. F. W. Johnston and others had been noted in Victoria. Further, it was 'contemplated to have a series of lectures on agricultural chemistry delivered under the auspices of the Society.'[20]

During the latter half of the fifties, in sympathy with the prevailing enthusiasm for farming, the Port Phillip Farmers' Society became a very active body with considerable parliamentary influence; the president and vice-president were both members of parliament in 1857–8. In 1859, after consultation with the society, the government passed legislation establishing a Board of Agriculture. Already in 1857 the government had granted £3192 10s for the establishment of an experimental farm, largely at the instigation of the Port Phillip Farmers' Society, and the secretary of the society, Thomas Skilling, a diplomate from Queen's University in Ireland, had been appointed the first director of the farm.[21]

By the end of the fifties several branch societies had been formed, and also a number of independent agricultural societies located throughout the colony. Like the original society, they were all primarily non-political show societies. The government provided financial assistance to these societies (in proportion to their income) to stage their shows, and in 1859 twenty-one societies received grants. This proliferation of local societies, however, resulted in a declining interest in the Melbourne-based Port Phillip Farmers' Society. Its last exhibition was held in 1867 and finally in 1870 it was disbanded. The local societies meanwhile continued to hold shows and ploughing matches.

The Board of Agriculture was composed of representatives from all the agricultural societies in the colony, together with a minority of government nominees. Often members of parliament acted as representatives of their local agricultural societies on the board. From the board (of some forty-three members in 1859) an executive council of thirteen members was elected, and in practice this council became all-powerful. In establishing the board, the government had proposed wide powers for it, including the distribution of the annual vote in aid of agriculture, control of the Experimental Farm and of an agricultural museum, and the collection and compilation of agricultural statistics. However, at its first few meetings the council decided that the collection of agricultural statistics should remain in the hands of the registrar-general, and, apart from a provision for the local agricultural societies to examine and approve the statistics collected in their districts, no further action was taken in that direction, the registrar-general continuing as before. Similarly, the agricultural museum did not materialize, and the efforts of the board were directed towards the distribution of the vote in aid of agriculture among the agricultural societies, and towards the control of the Experimental Farm, together with short-term forays into the promotion of prize essays, the awarding of premiums for novel industries, investigations into disease outbreaks and their control, the analysis of soils, and similar matters of topical interest.[22]

The Board of Agriculture received an annual grant of £6000 and distributed the major portion of this to the various agricultural societies in proportion to their respective incomes from non-government sources. Following the abolition of the board in 1870, the government continued to support the agricultural societies in this way.[23]

The Experimental Farm was situated at Royal Park, two-and-a-half miles north-west of Melbourne, and contained 142 acres. The aim in establishing this farm had been to investigate new varieties of plants and breeds of animals, the best method of cropping, the application of manures, the merits of implements and machinery, and generally, by means of experiments, to arrive at data 'whereon to establish a system of husbandry suited to the soil and climate of the colony.'[24] Initially the director of the farm had been responsible to the Chief Secretary and therefore in practice had been reasonably independent. But soon after operations had commenced on the farm, it was brought under the control of the newly created Board of Agriculture, whereupon the agricultural societies represented on the board were invited to recommend experiments that should be carried out on the farm and were encouraged to 'describe minutely how the experiments should be conducted'.[25] Upon the request of the farm committee, established by the council of the Board of Agriculture, the services of the director of the farm were transferred to the committee, and the director was called upon to furnish the committee with detailed monthly reports. At the same time the committee assumed close control of all business and technical details.[26] From then on matters went from bad to worse. In Skilling's own words,

> The first series of experiments was drawn up by a farm committee, composed *at that time* principally of practical farmers . . . After some time had elapsed the members of the first farm committee gradually retired from the management, and were replaced by others entertaining totally different views concerning it;—the experiments on cropping, draining, and sub-soiling, were condemned in unmeasured terms, and peremptorily suspended, while instructions were at the same time issued, that the growth of mulberries, olives, tea, and coffee plants, was to form the principal feature in future operations; the remainder of the farm, with the exception of twenty acres, to be thrown out of cultivation and laid down with grasses.[27]

The director's salary, too, was reduced, and the director finally submitted a resignation, whereupon the farm committee decided to dismiss him, and a select committee was appointed to inquire into the farm.

After Skilling was dismissed the council decided that the farm should be self-supporting and, from 1 January 1862, let it to a tenant to work it in an approved manner.[28] But the first tenant spent too much money and his lease was terminated. Finally in 1863 Josiah Mitchell took up a long lease of the farm on more independent terms and worked it successfully as a model farm until the expiration of the lease in 1870. After a one-year renewal of the lease the government resumed the land. Mitchell's success at the farm during this period was mainly due to his own sound knowledge of agriculture and largely despite the Board of Agriculture.[29]

Before Mitchell's tenure, the conduct of the farm under committee management had been farcical. The director, originally appointed as a responsible person in control of operations, was ignored by the farm committee and treated as its servant whose duty it was to carry out orders without question. However, the committee, which was appointed annually, at times completely reversed the decisions of the previous committee—that is, when a quorum was present, and often it was not. Further, some people sanguinely expected to have experiments which private farmers could not afford, conducted on the farm, and yet at the same time to have the farm self-supporting within the ordinary commercial farm environment. Such a dichotomy of aims and expectations could not be harmoniously reconciled.

From its inception the Board of Agriculture was an unwieldy body with well over half its members attending less than half the meetings of either the board or its council. By 1866 it was being generally discredited for ineffectiveness and being an expensive way of distributing funds to the agricultural societies.[30] The following year a Bill to alter the board was introduced into parliament but the Legislative Assembly deleted all clauses except the one abolishing the old board; however, the Bill was thrown out by the Council. Meanwhile the £6000 grant continued to be passed with Supply, mainly because expenditure was usually incurred by the societies in anticipation of the grant. Finally in 1869 it was agreed that no further grant would be made to the board, and in the following year parliament abolished the now inoperative board.[31]

The idea of a minister of agriculture had been put forward in the Supply debate in 1866 and had arisen from time to time thereafter, but no immediate action was taken to replace the Board of Agriculture. The Experimental Farm lease had expired by 1871 and the farm was resumed by the government, and the grants to the societies could be made directly. Furthermore, the Port Phillip Farmers' Society, long the moving force behind the Board of Agriculture had also ceased to exist. Nevertheless the government was granting financial assistance to the botanical gardens and to the acclimatization, horticultural and agricultural societies, and it still wished to encourage such things as flax production. Therefore, it was felt that some body to co-ordinate the activities pertaining to agriculture was desirable. Ultimately the Commissioner of Crown Lands and Survey in the Francis ministry, Mr J. J. Casey, proposed a department of agriculture and on 19 June 1872 became the first minister of agriculture.

Initially Casey's ideas were loosely defined, and during the Supply debate in August 1872 he asked only for £300 for a secretary's salary and £100 for expenses for an honorary advisory council which he hoped to appoint to advise him on rural matters. The main purpose of the secretary was to provide facilities so that such a body could be appointed.[32] One of the main functions of the department, he thought, could be to disseminate information. 'An intelligent department could collect knowledge from the experience of other nations, and distribute it so that it would reach all the farmers in the country.' But for the time being Casey envisaged only a very minor department. He 'did not expect that the department would reach its maximum utility this year or next year; it must grow gradually'.[33] A number of his colleagues, however, did not share his views, and amid passing references to the United States Department of Agriculture suggested that the new vote should be nearer £4000 or £40 000 than £400. The £400 vote was approved as requested by Casey, but later in the year a further sum of £5316 13s 4d was also approved, the money to be spent on setting out the government domain, on caretakers for the state forests, on encouraging the growth of flax, and for the salary of the Secretary for Agriculture, which had been raised to £500, the same amount as that of the curator of the government domain gardens. Casey meanwhile proceeded to select the first permanent head of the Department of Agriculture by means of an essay competition. Three gentlemen judged the essays (Casey being too busy), and Alexander Robert Wallis was duly appointed.[34]

Such an official was very necessary and Wallis was an excellent choice. The old Board of Agriculture had already failed under haphazard committee control, and the same fate may well have overtaken the infant Department of Agriculture during the 1870s if its development had been dependent upon the minister in charge. Casey already had a very full workload as Commissioner of Crown Lands and Survey and in practice had very little time to devote to his position as Minister of Agriculture (without salary). Furthermore, enthusiasm for the new department waxed and waned among parliamentarians as evinced in the successive debates on Supply, and frequent changes in ministries added to the uncertainty. Three different ministers held the portfolio (in conjunction with Lands and Survey) in five different ministries between 1872 and 1880.

Wallis was an energetic man who came to his new post with some formal training in agriculture. In England he had passed examinations in agriculture, agricultural chemistry, geology, surveying, and veterinary science, and he also had a reasonable knowledge of overseas agricultural institutions.[35] During the 1870s his major work was in establishing contacts with other institutions and generally making others aware of the existence of the Department of Agriculture. Locally he travelled the countryside and made contact with the farmers and their societies; further afield he wrote to the leading agricultural societies and institutions requesting information and copies of publications and offering copies of his own annual reports in exchange. Gifts of seeds were also solicited and obtained, for instance from the Japanese agricultural officials and from the United States Department of Agriculture and the various American State Boards of Agriculture. In his annual reports Wallis stressed the need for agricultural colleges, basing his arguments on European and American examples, and was anxious to encourage the formation of farmers' clubs where farmers could discuss their methods and other matters affecting them. None of these ideas were particularly new, but their strong advocacy, with frequent reference to overseas experience, kept them before the public and before parliament in particular. Gradually these efforts bore fruit and in December 1876 £1500 was voted for establishing an experimental farm at Mt Major in northern Victoria.[36] Ultimately this farm became a combined research centre and agricultural college.

Despite the efforts of the Secretary for Agriculture, and his suggestions for establishing the department on lines similar to the United States Department of Agriculture by formal legislation, the department developed only very slowly under the changing ministries, and its responsibilities remained ill-defined. From 1872–3 to 1876–7 the total expenditure on the agricultural division was only £3460 2s 7d and on the forests division £16 268 14s 8d. Half of the working time of the Secretary for Agriculture, the clerk and the messenger was devoted to work in the forests division, and two-thirds of the time of the chemist and analyst. The other matters administered by the department were the votes in aid of the various societies and votes for the encouragement of flax production and the invention of a reaper and binder. Administration of the diseases in livestock regulations was no concern of this department during these years.[37]

The eventual appointment of a chemist to the department reflected the prevailing interest in agricultural chemistry. From the 1850s farmers in the colony had been having samples of soils and fertilizers analysed; the Port Phillip Farmers' Society and the Board of Agriculture had both been active in this field. Towards the end of the 1870s the Hon. W. J. Clarke (son of W. J. T. Clarke) had brought, at his own expense, an experienced agricultural chemist, R. W. McIvor, to the colony from England to lecture on agricultural chemistry.[38] McIvor toured the colony lecturing and contributing articles to the newspapers and journals and almost certainly played a major part in creating an awareness of the comparative merits of the various phosphatic manures just at the time when superphosphate was being manufactured in Melbourne, and an increasing number of fertilizers were being offered to the farmers. These fertilizers varied considerably in phosphate content and solubility, and McIvor was able to present to the farmers the concept of differing rates of phosphate release and how to capitalize on this in selecting a fertilizer, and timing its application, according to the soil type present and the crop or pasture to be fertilized.[39] Meanwhile people continued to send samples to the new department, as they had done to the earlier institutions, to have them analysed. However, expectations were beginning to outstrip scientific knowledge as some of the less well-informed argued in favour of widespread soil analyses on the assumption that the crops best suited to a soil could be determined from the results of a chemical analysis.[40] Nevertheless, a beginning had been made, science was slowly being allied to farming and the groundwork was being laid for future advances, even if somewhat tardily and lacking in direction from a world-wide point of view.

In 1871, the year following the demise of the Port Phillip Farmers' Society, a new central society, the National Agricultural Society, was organized, and it took over the assets of the old society. It aimed to be widely representative rather than local in nature and its councillors were mainly well-known stud breeders from all over the colony. Its annual show was soon established as the major show in the colony and it did much to promote the interests of the stud livestock industry, although in 1877 the Australian Sheepbreeders' Association was formed and Merino breeders in particular favoured the association's show earlier in the year. Meanwhile the local societies continued to hold their own shows and ploughing matches, their fortunes rising and falling in accordance with the enthusiasm of local farmers.

The local societies were non-political (for years they had received government subsidies and their constitutions disallowed political activity) and very few did anything other than organize their annual shows and ploughing matches. Several farmers' clubs, devoted more to discussing technical problems, were established during the seventies in the colony, but none were within the Port Phillip region. Therefore there was no real forum available for the farmers to discuss general matters affecting them. The groupings of the late fifties and early sixties had been short-lived during that period of rapid change.

By 1879 the government of Victoria faced a serious financial deficit, and a political crisis had arisen in which the protection movement was deeply involved. Higher tariffs were threatened on many goods including wheat bags and agricultural implements, and the farmers were coming to regard many items in the tariff as very burdensome. A drought, too, was increasing their difficulties. During the 1878–9 season the American-manufactured McCormick reaper and self-binder had been introduced to the farmers and displayed at many shows, and the Victorian farmers south of the Murray River were going to have to pay £90 for this keenly awaited machine as against the £75 paid by their brothers north of the Murray River in free-trade New South Wales. This difference of £15 in the price of such an important item was very obvious to the farmers along the Murray River and was also emphasized by the importers of the machine.[41]

By mid-1879, with higher tariffs impending and the National Reform and Protection League and other pressure groups fostering various sectional interests, a group of farmers in north-central Victoria, close to the Murray River border, began to organize support for a revision of the tariff, particularly on reapers and binders, and generally to further the farmers' interests politically. With reference to the American Granger movement, the *Weekly Times* came out strongly in support of them, and in July and August, as new duties were being discussed in parliament, a number of farmers' unions were formed in the country districts.[42] The movement spread rapidly and on 8 October 1879 a farmers' conference was held in Melbourne at which thirty-six unions were represented. At this meeting the Victorian Farmers' Union was officially formed and a deputation sent to the Attorney-General.[43]

Almost immediately the farmers were successful and the duty was removed from reapers and binders.[44] Extensive publicity was given to these events by the *Weekly Times* and, following a move for the union to establish its own weekly newspaper, the *Weekly Times* was appointed to be the official organ of the union.[45] The newspaper itself greatly expanded its rural section and proceeded to publish detailed reports of the branch union meetings. For the remainder of the year and well into 1880 each weekly issue brought news of the formation of new local farmers' unions, many of which adopted the standard constitution of the Rochester Farmers' Union (the inaugural union) and affiliated with the central body.

The farmers in the Port Phillip region were caught up in the general momentum of the union movement and, whereas at the Melbourne meeting on 8 October 1879 only the Mornington Farmers' Union had been represented, by the beginning of 1880 a further six farmers' unions had been formed. But already the most urgent need had been met—the duty on reapers and binders had been removed—and the deliberations of the farmers were becoming less specific and less objective. With the major aim achieved, the union movement was to fade almost as quickly as it had arisen.[46] But the new generation of farmers had discovered that united they could exert a political influence and improve their lot, and no longer could the leader of the government ask with impunity, 'What can men who follow the plough know of politics?'[47]

The foregoing outline suggests certain tentative conclusions, although it must be emphasized that no more than a brief survey of these colonial-wide matters can be encompassed in a specifically regional study such as this. During the latter half of the 1850s the Port Phillip Farmers' Society predominated in official and influential circles. This society was particularly impressed by the then fashionable high farming of Great Britain and hoped, by means of experiments and careful observations, to test its suitability to local Victorian conditions. From this basis it was then hoped to go on and devise a farming system suited to the new environment. In this scientific approach the society had ample precedent in England in the work at Rothamstead and in the various reports published in the Journal of the Royal Agricultural Society, and of these the members of the Port Phillip Farmers' Society were very much aware. To further its objectives the society persuaded the government to provide grants-in-aid to agricultural societies, to establish an experimental farm and then to establish a Board of Agriculture.

But at the beginning of the 1860s the acclimatizers (both members of the Acclimatisation Society and its sympathizers) ousted the more practical people from their positions of power, as shown most dramatically in the Experimental Farm committee. This new influence was pervasive, being also revealed in the notes for the London International Exhibition, and in the novel industries legislation and grants-in-aid. Conversely, agriculture as it was being practised was ignored. There was money to import llamas but not for distressed farmers to buy seed wheat. Thus began a period of estrangement between the majority of influential parliamentarians and their associates on the one hand, and the practical farmers on the other hand.

Careful observation and trial, the corner-stones of sound agricultural advancement, were thrown to the winds by the acclimatizers who replaced them with their theories and ideas, conceived in sympathy with their British counterparts but without regard for reality. With the condemnation, in unmeasured terms, of the cropping, draining and subsoiling trials and their substitution by olives, tea and coffee plants, scientific agriculture was put in a cupboard for two decades, not to be aired again officially until the 1880s. Certainly the acclimatizers introduced new plants, animals and birds, but with no thought for or investigation into their place in the local environment. It was only after rabbits and sparrows had become pests in the 1870s that there was any serious opposition to these acclimatization activities.

The influential parliamentarians and their associates not only preferred to ignore agriculture as actually practised in Victoria, banished scientific agricultural investigations and imported exotic plants, animals and birds with gay abandon, but concurrently passed vital land legislation and planned the future agricultural development of the greater part of Victoria. That Victorian agriculture developed at all during the sixties and seventies is both remarkable and a tribute to the tenacity and ability of the men who directed the plough. For even during the seventies when the acclimatization influence was waning, the predominant official view was almost totally derivative. The new Department of Agriculture proceeded to collect information from other countries and distribute it among the farmers. It was only after some years of activity by the Secretary for Agriculture that finally a move was made to institute local trials and seek knowledge closer to home.

At any time in a country's rural development a balance needs to be struck between looking to the practices of other countries and developing local practices in response to the particular local situation. During the period to 1880 at Port Phillip a large proportion of the population was immigrant and there had been a considerable infusion of overseas experience. In order to maintain the balance, local methods and systems of farming had to be developed in response to the local environment. This the ordinary farmers slowly did, often at great cost and with many seeking an escape in the cities, in the new land selection areas (although here too the problem eventually had to be faced) or even in the bottle. As discussed in chapter 6, it was the local practical farmers who persevered and, with the assistance of men like Josiah Mitchell and Abraham Lincolne, developed a viable and integrated system of agriculture, a system heavily dependent on such things as simple rye-grass pastures, sheep grazing, and numerous combinations of enterprises specially adapted to specific locations, many of which had been ignored or frowned upon by the 'experts'. Between 1861 and 1881 the rural population of the Port Phillip region had increased by about 8000 to 66 000, and the urban population by 136 000 to 282 000. Yet by 1881 through the gradual rationalization of farming and the improvement of farming methods the farmers in the region were able to produce much of the fruit, vegetables, milk, butter, eggs, pork, hay and other perishable or bulky items required by the urban population. All this bore witness to the success of those who had persevered in the Port Phillip region, those who after many years of careful observation and trial had developed viable farming systems.

Conclusion

During a period of general prosperity within the Australian colonies in the 1830s, a commercialized grazing settlement was established at Port Phillip. Economic prosperity mushroomed into an economic boom: the sheepmen quickly explored and occupied large areas of grazing land and the new town of Melbourne arose as the commercial and administrative base for the pastoral expansion. Then came the Australia-wide depression of 1841–3 and rural expansion and urban growth came to a halt. Thereafter at Port Phillip a period of gradual readjustment set in during which the grazing industry progressively adapted its activities to the shortage of labour, to the demands of the London wool market, and after a time to the changes in the natural environment brought about by the intrusion of the sheep. Flock sizes were increased and greater efforts were made to improve the preparation of the wool clips, although insecurity of tenure was a serious deterrent to capital investment in fixed improvements for such things as wool-washing. Cropping on the other hand had developed separately from grazing in response to socio-cultural pressures, the circumstances of the land system and the prevailing farming techniques, and had made very little progress during the forties. Heavily dependent on wheat production for the limited local market, and faced with competition from imported wheat and flour, this type of farming had developed as the poor man's occupation on small areas of land, and continued to be so, reinforced by economic and social pressures.

After 1849 the grazier gained more security in the land. Ultimately this came in the form of a freehold title, but the cost of obtaining this title was so great that many of the smaller graziers were forced to give up grazing within the region. Under the renewed land-boom conditions in the fifties, ownership of the land was transferred to the speculators, the wealthiest graziers, and the prospective small cropping farmers. Grazing thereafter was consolidated on freehold land and on the remaining Crown leasehold which was gradually converted to freehold. A few of the grazing properties became much larger, covering tens of thousands of acres in the driest parts of the region, while in the remainder of the region the grazing properties became smaller and production had to be intensified to maintain a reasonable income.

The boom conditions, which had affected the land market so seriously, had been caused by the great rush of people to the colony after gold was discovered in 1851. Very quickly the population within the Port Phillip region had doubled, then tripled, and by 1861 it had almost quadrupled. In 1871 it had multiplied more than five times and in 1881 was almost six-and-a-half times greater than in 1851. The major part of this population growth occurred in the urban centre of Melbourne, but wherever it occurred the people and their horses had to be fed. With the first large influx of people, food and fodder prices soared and cropping revived and expanded, although for the time being it had changed little in technique. With social and political overtones, propaganda for small farms and wheat production increased and many immigrants borrowed money to buy small farms or lease farms from private individuals at boom rentals. By 1861 there were 5561 farms within the Port Phillip region. The minority were grazing properties; the majority were cropping holdings where the main and often sole crop was wheat. Many of the cultivators were inexperienced farmers with no capital trying to farm tiny areas of land, and by 1861 many, having stretched their resources too far, were also impoverished. The gold-rush boom had eased and prices were falling. With the early sixties came rust and caterpillar infestations in the crops, excessively wet seasons and droughts, and much land, too, had been over-cropped. As more and more wheat was imported and the northern wheat areas were developed, wheat growing on the small farms was abandoned and many people were forced to leave these farms.

The ensuing period, from the mid-sixties to 1880, was one of gradual rehabilitation of the older farming areas, during which the farmers came to terms with their natural and economic environments, combined cropping and grazing and created a viable, integrated, ecological system encompassing man and his surroundings.

These latter changes were complex, since they formed an integral part of rural community development, a development that was being shaped by various national, religious, social and economic forces stemming from the cultural background of the immigrants concerned. Added to these pressures were the actions of uninformed but enthusiastic government and community leaders pressing for rural development in directions antagonistic to the major trends on the farms. At the individual farm level, too, various forces were at work influencing the decisions of the farmers. Depopulation, following the small-farm crisis of the early sixties, had added to the problems in the most impoverished areas by tending to create a self-perpetuating system of low incomes, low education, poor farming ability and aged communities.

Opportunities for employment elsewhere in the colony did, however, lead to movement out of these areas which alleviated this problem and allowed for a gradual restructuring and rehabilitation of the farms in them. While elsewhere, particularly in the east of the region, a steady development occurred, carried forward by farmers catering specifically for the expanding Melbourne market and more alive to the realities of commercial farming than many of their predecessors. By 1880 the more successful of the farming families were well established on freehold farms. They lived in comfortable homes and increasingly identified themselves with the surrounding community and countryside. Their children knew no other land.

The sanctity of wheat growing—still professed in the city and new wheat areas—had been replaced by a respect for sown pastures, sheep, dairy cows, hay, potatoes, onions and various other crops. Not scattered haphazardly across the region, but discerningly grazed and grown where climate, soil and terrain dictated that they could be produced to best advantage, and where transport and markets endorsed the economic sense of so doing. As if to emphasize these variations, the pattern of farms varied across the countryside. Small farms close together lent a settled appearance to the landscape where intensive forms of farming, such as market gardening, had been developed, while on the dry, open, wind-swept plains a fence, or a flock of sheep, alone intruded upon the scene and suggested the existence of a large pastoral property.

In reviewing the course of rural development in the Port Phillip region, the one underlying influence that stands out is the cultural and agricultural background of the people concerned. This dictated the farming systems, and the types of crops and livestock introduced, the technology, the economic environment and the hopes and ambitions of the people. Rural development then became a complex process of adaptation of this given culture and agriculture to the new environment.

Appendix
Statistical Tables

Appendix

Table 1
Birth-places of the Rural People

Division	Year	Victoria		Other Australian and New Zealand		England		Scotland	
	(1800s)	Persons	Percentage	Persons	Percentage	Persons	Percentage	Persons	Percentage
Bellarine	54	489	21·4	62	2·7	931	40·7	323	14·1
	61	1 713	35·6	124	2·6	1 536	31·9	472	9·8
	71	2 566	53·9	113	2·4	1 163	24·4	274	5·8
	81	3 372	63·5	154	2·9	968	18·2	225	4·2
Barrabool	54	613	27·7	89	4·0	646	29·2	182	8·2
	61	2 306	36·3	182	2·9	1 769	27·8	562	8·8
	71	3 146	55·6	123	2·2	1 070	18·9	302	5·4
	81	2 726	63·7	130	3·1	616	14·4	216	5·1
Bannockburn	54	277	23·5	34	2·9	360	30·6	192	16·3
	61	1 908	34·2	130	2·3	1 459	26·2	829	14·9
	71	3 021	56·0	116	2·1	834	15·5	507	9·4
	81	2 802	63·6	107	2·4	564	12·8	346	7·8
Bacchus Marsh	54	237	20·5	58	5·0	352	30·4	204	17·6
	61	626	36·1	49	2·8	381	22·0	289	16·7
	71	1 327	54·5	81	3·3	317	13·0	262	10·7
	81	1 502	67·0	43	1·9	215	9·6	176	7·8
Werribee	54	64	19·9	8	2·5	93	29·0	83	25·9
	61	282	32·8	14	1·6	237	27·6	144	16·8
	71	702	47·6	47	3·2	273	18·5	135	9·1
	81	918	63·0	45	3·1	177	12·2	97	6·7
Sunbury	54	—	—	—	—	—	—	—	—
	61	1 982	27·3	236	3·2	1 841	25·4	1 056	14·5
	71	2 795	52·1	176	3·3	789	14·7	413	7·7
	81	2 665	55·4	177	3·7	639	13·3	331	6·9
Plenty	54	2 087	20·3	314	3·1	3 898	37·9	1 621	15·7
	61	4 988	30·5	383	2·4	4 857	29·7	1 862	11·3
	71	8 386	45·9	481	2·6	4 018	22·0	1 539	8·4
	81	9 810	57·9	588	3·5	2 904	17·1	920	5·4
Lilydale	54	225	27·2	20	2·4	307	37·0	110	13·3
	61	1 086	34·6	62	2·0	895	28·6	231	7·4
	71	2 281	50·3	108	2·4	945	20·8	242	5·3
	81	3 521	62·0	177	3·1	896	15·8	227	4·0
Oakleigh	54	—	—	—	—	—	—	—	—
	61	2 537	32·9	163	2·1	2 658	34·5	612	8·0
	71	4 677	49·3	256	2·7	2 268	23·9	603	6·4
	81	7 539	59·6	445	3·5	2 407	19·0	586	4·6
Berwick	54	109	22·0	23	4·6	165	33·3	52	10·5
	61	890	38·6	56	2·4	488	21·1	249	10·8
	71	1 847	52·2	136	3·9	614	17·4	229	6·5
	81	2 936	60·0	198	4·0	706	14·4	257	5·2
Mornington	54	80	19·3	29	7·0	152	36·7	44	10·6
	61	544	30·2	69	3·8	632	35·1	231	12·9
	71	1 406	48·4	96	3·3	693	23·8	266	9·1
	81	2 289	60·5	174	4·6	621	16·4	258	6·8
Total	54†	4 181	21·8	637	3·3	6 904	36·0	2 811	14·7
	61	18 862	32·6	1 468	2·5	16 753	28·9	6 537	11·3
	71	32 154	50·4	1 733	2·7	12 984	20·3	4 772	7·5
	81	40 080	60·3	2 238	3·4	10 713	16·1	3 639	5·5

* Includes Gorong parish to the west
† Excluding Sunbury and Oakleigh divisions

Ireland		Germany		Other European		Other countries, at sea, unspecified		Total
Persons	Percentage	Persons	Percentage	Persons	Percentage	Persons	Percentage	
413	18·1	13	0·6	24	1·0	32	1·4	2 287
745	15·5	30	0·6	65	1·3	132	2·7	4 817
521	11·0	13	0·3	45	0·9	61	1·3	4 756
476	9·0	18	0·3	42	0·8	59	1·1	5 314
492	22·3	133	6·0	28	1·3	29	1·3	2 212
1 029	16·2	327	5·2	95	1·5	85	1·3	6 355
578	10·2	287	5·1	115	2·0	35	0·6	5 656
317	7·4	164	3·8	53	1·2	56	1·3	4 278
277	23·5	10	0·8	13	1·1	15	1·3	1 178
1 037	18·6	30	0·5	97	1·8	83	1·5	5 573
731	13·6	26	0·5	95	1·8	60	1·1	5 390
474	10·8	12	0·3	75	1·7	28	0·6	4 408
236	20·4	7	0·6	22	1·9	41	3·6	1 157*
330	19·0	6	0·3	18	1·0	36	2·1	1 735‡
397	16·3	12	0·5	14	0·6	27	1·1	2 437
268	11·9	6	0·3	4	0·2	29	1·3	2 243
49	15·3	4	1·2	2	0·6	18	5·6	321
162	18·9	3	0·3	4	0·5	13	1·5	859
277	18·8	5	0·3	18	1·2	19	1·3	1 476
194	13·3	4	0·3	11	0·7	10	0·7	1 456
—	—	—	—	—	—	—	—	—
1 880	25·9	21	0·3	71	1·0	175	2·4	7 262
921	17·2	33	0·6	53	1·0	181	3·4	5 361
852	17·7	40	0·8	64	1·3	44	0·9	4 812
1 879	18·2	178	1·7	136	1·3	186	1·8	10 299
3 310	20·2	392	2·4	213	1·3	366	2·2	16 371
2 910	15·9	380	2·1	196	1·1	356	2·0	18 266
1 929	11·4	285	1·7	162	1·0	341	2·0	16 939
104	12·6	34	4·1	11	1·3	18	2·1	829
585	18·7	117	3·7	94	3·0	62	2·0	3 132‡
647	14·2	112	2·5	117	2·6	86	1·9	4 538
541	9·5	118	2·1	103	1·8	95	1·7	5 678
—	—	—	—	—	—	—	—	—
1 350	17·5	148	1·9	110	1·4	130	1·7	7 708
1 318	13·9	132	1·4	110	1·2	116	1·2	9 480
1 242	9·8	110	0·9	139	1·1	186	1·5	12 654
84	16·9	22	4·4	10	2·0	31	6·3	496
446	19·3	123	5·3	27	1·2	29	1·3	2 308‡
502	14·2	131	3·7	49	1·2	32	0·9	3 540
530	10·8	117	2·4	76	1·6	77	1·6	4 897
92	22·2	2	0·5	11	2·7	4	1·0	414
221	12·3	19	1·1	23	1·3	60	3·3	1 799‡
311	10·7	15	0·5	58	2·0	63	2·2	2 908
257	6·8	26	0·7	87	2·3	73	1·9	3 785
3 626	18·9	403	2·1	257	1·3	374	1·9	19 193
11 095	19·2	1 216	2·1	817	1·4	1 171	2·0	57 919‡
9 113	14·3	1 146	1·8	870	1·4	1 036	1·6	63 808
7 080	10·6	900	1·4	816	1·2	998	1·5	66 464

‡ These totals differ from those in table 2 because the results for some sparsely populated parishes were grouped together in the census report on birth-places

Sources: Censuses, 1854, 1861, 1871, 1881, Birth-places

Table 2
Total Population of the Port Phillip Region, 1854–1881

Division	1854			1857			1861			1871			1881		
	Males	Females	Persons	Males	Females	Persons	Males	Females	Persons	Males	Females	Persons	Males	Females	Persons
Bellarine	1 281	1 006	2 287	2 201	1 880	4 081	2 583	2 234	4 817	2 456	2 300	4 756	2 696	2 618	5 314
Barrabool	1 239	973	2 212	3 081	2 463	5 544	3 450	2 905	6 355	2 972	2 684	5 656	2 213	2 065	4 278
Bannockburn	698	480	1 178	2 187	1 538	3 725	3 138	2 435	5 573	2 841	2 549	5 390	2 254	2 154	4 408
Bacchus Marsh	—	—	1 157*	834	540	1 374	1 044	753	1 797	1 331	1 106	2 437	1 216	1 027	2 243
Werribee	—	—	321	520	284	804	493	366	859	868	608	1 476	780	676	1 456
Sunbury	—	—	4 116	3 000	1 871	4 871	4 310	2 952	7 262	3 202	2 159	5 361	2 515	2 297	4 812
Plenty West	—	—	9 303	7 564	5 099	12 663	8 050	5 803	13 853	8 166	6 388	14 554	7 315	6 069	13 384
Plenty East	569	427	996	1 159	820	1 979	1 496	1 022	2 518	2 112	1 600	3 712	1 912	1 643	3 555
Total	—	—	10 299	8 723	5 919	14 642	9 546	6 825	16 371	10 278	7 988	18 266	9 227	7 712	16 939
Lilydale	497	332	829	1 236	838	2 074	1 833	1 324	3 157	2 593	1 945	4 538	3 126	2 552	5 678
Oakleigh	—	—	4 677	2 976	2 143	5 119	4 151	3 557	7 708	4 951	4 529	9 480	6 437	6 217	12 654
Berwick	305	191	496	882	569	1 451	1 319	990	2 309	1 957	1 583	3 540	2 813	2 084	4 897
Mornington	254	160	414	665	342	1 007	1 036	737	1 773	1 614	1 294	2 908	1 974	1 811	3 785
Total rural	—	—	27 986	26 305	18 387	44 692	32 903	25 078	57 981	35 063	28 745	63 808	35 251	31 213	66 464
Geelong	10 500	8 579	19 079	10 525	10 537	21 062	10 092	10 827	20 919	9 202	10 573	19 775	8 912	10 296	19 208
Melbourne	48 069	34 361	82 430	55 158	48 830	103 988	63 554	61 307	124 861	94 788	96 661	191 449	127 492	134 897	262 389
Total urban	58 569	42 940	101 509	65 683	59 367	125 050	73 646	72 134	145 780	103 990	107 234	211 224	136 404	145 193	281 597
Grand Total	—	—	129 495	91 988	77 754	169 742	106 549	97 212	203 761	139 053	135 979	275 032	171 655	176 406	348 061

* Includes Gorong parish to the west
Sources: Censuses, 1854, 1857, 1861, 1871, 1881, Inhabitants, Religions, Occupations

Table 3
Occupations of Males in the Rural Divisions, 1861

Agricultural			
Farmers			
pastoral	128		
cultivating	4 471	4 599	
Employees			
pastoral	408		
cultivating	6 517	6 925	11 524
Occupations dependent on agriculture			
Storekeepers, butchers, bakers, implement makers, etc.	2 777		
General labourers, wood-splitters, and carters, etc.	1 597	4 374	
Other occupations			
Quarrying	1 397		
Gold-mining	595		
Government, professions, and independent means	820		
Masons, builders, cabinet makers, inn keepers, tailors, shoemakers, domestic servants, persons engaged in passenger traffic, other occupations	2 128		
Unemployed (not stated)	606		
Prisoners and patients	1 431	6 977	11 351
Under 15 and scholars			10 028
Total			32 903

Source: Census, 1861, Occupations

Table 4
Area Sown to Various Crops, 1856–7, 1860–1, 1870–1 and 1880–1 (acres)

Division and year	Wheat†	Oats†	Barley†	Potatoes‡	Hay	Maize†	Rye and bere†	Peas, beans, millet and sorghum †	Turnips	Mangels	Beet, carrots, parsnips and cabbage
Bellarine											
1856–7	7 403	2 190	247	680	1 401	—	*	*	45	20	—
60–1	7 930	2 290	238	645	2 516	4	2	55	12	115	26
70–1	2 486	332	318	657	3 160	—	12	535	2	53	13
80–1	753	271	531	957	3 511	—	15	1 208	6	51	73
Barrabool											
1856–7	8 674	2 742	157	1 277	4 204	—	*	*	13	23	8
60–1	11 606	4 270	275	756	4 807	51	3	72	22	145	44
70–1	3 937	943	484	367	5 743	—	59	1 155	—	51	15
80–1	870	701	210	327	5 756	5	6	1 105	3	66	7
Bannockburn											
1856–7	4 237	1 764	201	706	1 923	—	*	*	21	9	21
60–1	5 925	3 454	380	272	3 076	32	2	31	8	71	41
70–1	2 956	847	651	114	5 975	17	7	30	6	18	9
80–1	952	410	407	98	5 567	5	2	322	3	37	3
Bacchus Marsh											
1856–7	1 561	263	38	83	291	1	*	*	2	—	—
60–1	4 231	1 331	222	142	703	—	—	4	5	6	5
70–1	3 315	430	2 614	114	585	—	7	13	—	8	1
80–1	670	525	972	58	1 099	18	2	130	—	11	10
Werribee											
1856–7	601	264	12	55	226	1	*	*	—	—	—
60–1	451	696	65	43	986	6	—	15	1	36	2
70–1	216	136	153	13	3 782	—	3	—	—	3	—
80–1	92	97	133	8	4 312	2	—	20	—	4	—
Sunbury											
1856–7	6 037	1 119	116	516	7 008	20	*	*	8	1	—
60–1	4 819	3 134	247	305	8 936	19	—	34	10	61	12
70–1	1 424	959	382	151	7 388	14	—	17	1	9	1
80–1	255	610	240	79	5 486	—	1	117	4	5	—
Plenty											
1856–7	15 649	6 209	590	1 846	13 507	118	*	*	139	37	1
60–1	11 886	5 003	185	1 841	11 530	38	1	37	26	94	23
70–1	1 083	926	60	986	14 650	7	5	148	5	69	6
80–1	322	1 097	205	775	13 702	52	39	1 112	15	187	4
Lilydale											
1856–7	1 092	259	15	637	872	—	*	*	6	—	—
60–1	1 243	641	17	889	1 070	9	—	8	7	10	3
70–1	79	814	6	314	1 125	—	2	18	14	45	47
80–1	43	507	18	426	1 916	3	26	199	14	223	5
Oakleigh											
1856–7	866	169	68	1 013	2 297	3	*	*	103	—	1
60–1	597	416	136	1 173	2 448	17	10	58	64	122	130
70–1	10	29	7	921	1 440	2	20	24	9	68	7
80–1	8	37	37	933	1 728	1	20	87	52	105	46
Berwick											
1856–7	1 577	595	13	286	16	2	*	*	—	—	—
60–1	2 582	1 145	18	404	637	22	11	35	4	10	1
70–1	170	470	13	652	625	10	6	38	7	45	6
80–1	48	645	68	640	1 803	25	13	259	23	43	5
Mornington											
1856–7	480	232	4	134	73	3	*	*	6	12	—
60–1	507	220	31	120	237	21	—	3	4	22	1
70–1	63	533	66	303	509	4	5	72	3	8	—
80–1	31	66	10	210	995	16	10	128	20	34	3
Region total											
1856–7	48 177	15 806	1 461	7 233	31 818	148	*	*	343	102	31
60–1	51 777	22 600	1 814	6 590	36 946	219	29	352	163	692	288
70–1	15 739	6 419	4 754	4 592	44 982	54	126	2 050	47	377	105
80–1	4 044	4 966	2 831	4 511	45 875	127	134	4 687	140	766	156

* Not recorded separately
† For grain

Onions	Green forage	Lucerne, pasture legumes and grasses	Grass and clover seed	Vines	Tobacco	Hops	Orchard	Garden	Other	Fallow	Total cultivated area
1	67	7	*	5	—	*	*	2	*	*	12 068
*	135	185	*	43	—	*	34	179	64	898	15 371
210	18	1 277	*	58	—	*	32	95	—	89	9 347
835	68	1 420	1	6	—	—	86	122	8	197	10 119
7	46	40	*	156	—	*	*	46	*	*	17 393
*	458	270	*	306	—	*	85	281	29	479	23 959
—	131	5 128	*	490	1	*	406	544	13	739	20 206
1	194	3 928	6	271	—	—	383	236	11	362	14 448
6	59	10	*	40	11	*	*	4	*	*	9 012
*	227	78	*	163	—	*	78	213	45	983	15 079
3	2	240	*	399	4	*	129	138	—	696	12 241
24	34	982	21	196	—	—	274	138	5	619	10 099
—	2	—	*	—	—	*	*	—	*	*	2 241
*	199	434	*	6	2	*	13	40	5	118	7 466
—	3	1 010	*	13	—	*	6	11	25	60	8 215
3	119	928	33	7	—	—	9	14	8	8	4 624
—	7	—	*	1	—	*	*	2	*	*	1 169
*	115	81	*	3	—	*	7	34	2	315	2 858
—	18	522	*	9	—	*	6	13	—	997	5 871
—	1 808	2 530	5	3	—	—	5	37	—	1 235	10 291
—	124	21	*	—	—	*	*	92	*	*	15 062
*	385	1 844	*	45	1	*	35	186	33	830	20 936
6	6	2 727	*	328	—	*	117	75	17	1 998	15 620
2	137	1 759	—	232	—	—	76	80	10	994	10 087
—	270	26	*	60	—	*	*	551	*	*	39 003
*	955	1 127	*	121	—	*	336	685	58	2 450	36 396
6	508	2 644	*	118	—	*	374	711	2	1 284	23 592
16	474	9 066	1	113	20	1	539	781	35	1 477	30 033
—	13	—	*	—	—	*	*	9	*	*	2 903
*	156	232	*	68	—	*	58	219	33	645	5 308
1	99	1 595	*	419	1	*	413	416	—	564	5 972
3	131	3 315	69	462	—	—	1 147	547	173	1 149	10 376
3	242	1	*	12	—	*	*	687	*	*	5 465
*	599	247	*	121	—	*	355	730	265	1 530	9 018
11	232	647	*	216	—	*	693	2 769	—	696	7 801
52	263	1 321	1	33	10	—	1 011	3 791	45	892	10 473
—	—	—	*	—	—	*	*	—	*	*	2 489
*	81	382	*	16	—	*	16	110	42	882	6 398
—	190	4 994	*	13	—	*	33	37	—	887	8 196
—	366	5 065	85	8	—	1	257	138	40	746	10 278
—	—	—	*	—	—	*	*	—	*	*	944
*	47	40	*	17	—	*	20	44	7	148	1 489
—	63	1 292	*	46	—	*	135	51	—	76	3 229
—	74	3 873	5	7	—	—	549	95	6	707	6 839
17	830	105	*	274	11	*	*	1 393	*	*	107 749
*	3 357	4 920	*	909	3	*	1 037	2 721	583	9 278	144 278
237	1 270	22 076	*	2 109	6	*	2 344	4 860	57	8 086	120 290
936	3 668	34 187	227	1 338	30	2	4 336	5 979	341	8 386	127 667

‡ Exclusive of those in market and kitchen gardens
Sources: Agric. Stat., 1856, 1860, 1870, 1880

Table 5
Percentage of Males Aged 15–39, 40 and Older, Who Could Both Read and Write in 1854, 1871 and 1881

County or division and year	15–39 years			40+ years		
	Read and write	Total	Percentage	Read and write	Total	Percentage
1854						
Bourke						
Melbourne	19 290	20 781	92·8	3 810	4 358	87·4
beyond Melbourne	13 197	15 017	87·9	3 326	4 182	79·5
Grant						
Geelong	5 183	5 950	87·1	1 306	1 678	77·8
beyond Geelong	4 249	5 233	81·2	886	1 256	70·5
Evelyn	270	322	83·9	103	135	76·3
Mornington	408	504	81·0	101	149	67·8
1871						
Bellarine	650	744	87·4	470	586	80·2
Barrabool	848	949	89·4	510	657	76·8
Bannockburn	817	918	89·0	484	596	81·2
Bacchus Marsh	402	438	91·8	242	287	84·3
Werribee	338	376	89·9	138	162	85·1
Sunbury	874	962	90·9	468	572	81·8
Plenty	3 269	3 708*	88·2	1 918	2 367*	81·0
Lilydale	703	812*	86·6	395	493*	80·1
Oakleigh	1 583	1 724	91·8	999	1 166	85·7
Berwick	621	709	87·6	380	441	86·2
Mornington	554	614	90·2	338	389	86·9
Geelong	2 485	2 661	93·4	1 954	2 233	87·5
Melbourne	33 850	35 533	95·3	19 337	20 909	92·5
1881						
Bellarine	919	974	94·4	560	682	82·1
Barrabool	709	753	94·2	464	575	80·7
Bannockburn	737	779	94·6	487	576	84·4
Bacchus Marsh	374	401	93·3	260	308	84·4
Werribee	273	284	96·1	165	191	86·4
Sunbury	869	948	91·7	585	712	82·2
Plenty	3 318	3 564	93·1	2 170	2 619	82·9
Lilydale	1 029	1 119	92·0	671	799	84·0
Oakleigh	2 338	2 424	96·5	1 450	1 603	90·5
Berwick	1 057	1 136	93·0	591	685	86·3
Mornington	633	663	95·5	423	521	81·2
Geelong	2 954	3 090	95·6	2 021	2 396	84·3
Melbourne	50 137	51 460	97·4	28 234	30 386	92·9

* Education statistics were published in less detail than other 1871 census statistics and these figures exclude some people included in other tables

Sources: Censuses, 1854, 1871, 1881, Education

Table 6
Livestock on Occupied Farm Land, 1856–7, 1859–60, 1880–1, and Total Livestock, 2 April 1871

Division and year	No. of owners	Horses	Cattle			Sheep	Pigs	Goats
			Milch	Other	Total			
Bellarine								
1856–7	378	1 247	—	—	3 923	970	2 720	*
59–60	490	1 550	—	—	5 224	359	2 631	*
71	699	1 632	2 254	2 759	5 013	13 179	2 458	314
80–1	728	1 783	2 303	3 435	5 738	27 284	2 912	233
Barrabool								
1856–7	571	1 960	—	—	7 895	15 976	3 358	*
59–60	718	2 266	—	—	6 698	18 802	2 301	*
71	906	2 781	3 887	4 883	8 770	31 540	3 327	279
80–1	734	2 032	3 640	4 982	8 622	73 653	2 921	73
Bannockburn								
1856–7	457	1 436	—	—	8 650	60 036	3 023	*
59–60	544	1 476	—	—	8 094	60 625	1 737	*
71	800	2 359	4 415	7 254	11 669	110 071	2 645	277
80–1	667	2 134	4 308	6 657	10 965	116 925	3 267	104
Bacchus Marsh								
1856–7	75	283	—	—	2 234	0	397	*
59–60	137	622	—	—	3 094	6 205	504	*
71	364	1 287	1 921	3 533	5 454	15 324	1 429	268
80–1	323	1 200	3 677	3 943	7 620	14 378	2 190	60
Werribee								
1856–7	64	311	—	—	3 937	34 120	470	*
59–60	95	408	—	—	4 115	64 976	429	*
71	203	956	1 572	3 326	4 898	91 658	825	220
80–1	216	1 015	1 809	4 264	6 073	86 157	1 305	74
Sunbury								
1856–7	457	1 809	—	—	12 379	121 817	3 380	*
59–60	491	2 203	—	—	11 933	75 082	2 433	*
71	687	2 526	4 962	9 032	13 994	218 234	3 383	711
80–1	631	2 813	4 865	9 419	14 284	116 752	2 937	199
Plenty								
1856–7	899	3 881	—	—	22 135	4 013	5 438	*
59–60	1 167	4 675	—	—	20 972	16 059	4 172	*
71	2 331	7 466	15 742	19 714	35 456	40 203	7 013	1 905
80–1	2 124	6 808	15 684	18 239	33 923	58 902	6 245	1 220
Lilydale								
1856–7	227	938	—	—	2 503	0	1 039	*
59–60	300	1 151	—	—	7 078	1 900	1 053	*
71	609	2 094	2 917	4 632	7 549	3 529	1 303	321
80–1	996	2 415	4 258	7 437	11 695	9 082	2 104	159
Oakleigh								
1856–7	701	1 730	—	—	4 745	100	3 123	*
59–60	893	2 188	—	—	5 870	77	2 921	*
71	1 499	3 341	4 028	3 569	7 597	5 027	4 127	769
80–1	1 380	3 562	4 846	4 346	9 192	13 105	4 654	291
Berwick								
1856–7	97	962	—	—	4 212	1 600	680	*
59–60	281	2 769	—	—	15 438	2 597	918	*
71	566	4 481	5 527	14 879	20 406	10 994	2 179	176
80–1	785	4 935	7 279	14 870	22 149	30 777	3 064	99
Mornington								
1856–7	51	455	—	—	1 804	0	299	*
59–60	109	892	—	—	3 952	28	391	*
71	475	3 016	1 830	5 369	7 199	27 057	952	238
80–1	588	3 069	2 287	6 203	8 490	1 083	57	5
Geelong								
1871	1 300	1 131	908	434	1 342	2 992	932	890
Melbourne								
1871	7 912	10 512	5 484	2 421	7 905	11 637	5 213	4 495

* Not recorded
Sources: Agric. Stat., 1856, 1859, 1880; Census, 1871

Table 7
Total Number of Holdings, 1857–1881

Year (31 March)	Bellarine	Barrabool	Bannockburn	Bacchus Marsh	Werribee	Sunbury	Plenty	Lilydale	Oakleigh	Berwick	Mornington	Total
1857	378	583	459	79	65	461	899	245	801	101	55	4126
1858	449	701	589	74	76	480	1052	202	925	129	85	4762
1859	494	768	627	147	93	481	992	214	1027	126	76	5045
1860	508	756	591	156	110	538	1280	316	953	303	114	5625
1861	470	748	448	168	98	570	1367	380	843	335	134	5561
1862	484	833	514	158	95	507	1388	421	874	352	152	5778
1863	474	798	503	181	111	512	1436	438	981	363	205	6002
1864	512	768	474	195	103	552	1493	397	951	352	230	6027
1865	514	827	466	175	100	524	1395	435	942	359	217	5954
1866	455	814	568	206	121	581	1395	449	1200	360	265	6414
1867	422	805	527	242	117	561	1499	475	1349	345	250	6592
1868	—	—	—	—	—	—	—	—	—	—	—	—
1869	—	—	—	—	—	—	—	—	—	—	—	—
1870	487	851	618	265	137	363	1291	484	1021	405	313	6235
1871	494	759	602	263	141	461	1373	469	1063	422	337	6384
1872	500	750	591	254	150	471	1408	536	1011	437	357	6465
1873	489	735	584	248	148	495	1433	546	1050	464	358	6550
1874	506	716	594	244	147	514	1351	592	1067	462	356	6549
1875	488	651	589	244	149	479	1345	656	1078	464	427	6570
1876	484	625	561	250	148	487	1231	678	1051	473	437	6425
1877	475	603	561	259	148	498	1247	674	1095	535	455	6550
1878	505	582	533	259	153	469	1275	722	1119	552	459	6628
1879	515	607	507	258	164	457	1300	772	1084	607	519	6790
1880	517	588	492	251	167	452	1318	811	1058	608	538	6800
1881	505	534	474	224	154	377	1248	772	1074	649	421	6432

Source: Agric. Stat., 1856–80

Table 8
Total Area of Land Occupied, 1857–1881 (thousands of acres)

Year (31 March)	Bellarine	Barrabool	Bannockburn	Bacchus Marsh	Werribee	Sunbury	Plenty	Lilydale	Oakleigh	Berwick	Mornington	Total
1857	36	87	136	11	58	166	158	29	29	29	18	757
1858	43	98	140	8	74	165	178	29	40	53	25	853
1859	47	100	150	23	80	159	202	28	43	57	24	913
1860	44	97	140	33	97	180	215	49	41	100	33	1029
1861	41	93	120	50	118	194	209	62	38	114	36	1075
1862	43	109	153	51	118	181	243	67	48	110	40	1163
1863	45	138	132	39	146	189	242	50	40	134	50	1205
1864	53	84*	62*	27*	60*	192	228	43	36	96	51	932*
1865	50	104	118	32	133	196	219	43	46	98	40	1079
1866	47	110	159	34	145	197	227	43	55	98	54	1169
1867	60	106	163	41	114	198	240	57	51	102	51	1183
1868	—	—	—	—	—	—	—	—	—	—	—	—
1869	—	—	—	—	—	—	—	—	—	—	—	—
1870	63	126	198	43	152	243	232	60	50	154	85	1406
1871	59	109	193	47	156	251	259	56	52	156	80	1418
1872	60	118	190	45	191	197	255	65	50	158	89	1418
1873	65	111	193	58	187	202	267	73	55	177	87	1475
1874	68	108	219	46	162	204	272	77	59	169	85	1469
1875	66	106	222	51	178	229	272	87	58	166	111	1546
1876	64	110	226	51	169	216	275	88	59	178	109	1545
1877	65	108	226	51	153	215	283	93	60	183	114	1551
1878	68	108	228	52	180	212	279	101	63	200	118	1609
1879	67	117	229	51	168	212	285	105	63	203	122	1622
1880	68	114	228	51	186	185	270	109	65	215	130	1621
1881	67	124	218	56	167	185	312	111	69	231	121	1661

* This deficit seems to be due to the erroneous exclusion of land from the parish returns for County Grant and its inclusion under a new heading 'Stations'
Source: Agric. Stat., 1856–80

Table 9
Total Area of Freehold Land Rented, 1861–1867 and 1879–1881 (thousands of acres)

Year (31 March)	Bellarine	Barrabool	Bannockburn	Bacchus Marsh	Werribee	Sunbury	Plenty	Lilydale	Oakleigh	Berwick	Mornington	Total
1861	18	30	21	10	5	75	102	21	10	30	3	325
1862	17	40	33	9	18	38	103	27	9	24	3	321
1863	23	53	49	10	13	38	119	17	11	28	8	369
1864	27	33	12	10	14	40	121	9	5	37	6	314
1865	26	41	49	9	47	40	102	15	13	33	5	380
1866	31	38	45	12	26	45	110	15	12	43	6	383
1867	37	43	48	9	65	33	119	20	9	46	9	438
						Not available						
1879	30	41	79	12	16	37	109	16	14	47	23	424
1880	27	46	72	11	20	42	109	19	12	44	20	422
1881	26	39	72	12	17	44	127	19	16	57	22	451

Source: Agric. Stat., 1860–6, 1878–80

Abbreviations

Agric. Stat.	Agricultural and Livestock Statistics for the Year Ending 31 March (Victoria)
C.C.P.	P. L. Brown (ed.), *Clyde Company Papers*
H.R.A.	*Historical Records of Australia*
Stat.	Statistics of the Colony of Victoria for the Year
Vict. Hist. Mag.	*Victorian Historical Magazine*
V.P.P.	*Votes and Proceedings of the Legislative Assembly of Victoria* and *Papers Presented to Parliament by Command*
V. & P., L.C. N.S.W.	*Votes and Proceedings*, Legislative Council of New South *Wales*
V. & P., L.C. Vic.	*Votes and Proceedings*, Legislative Council of Victoria

Note on Agricultural Statistics

Agricultural statistics were collected for the year ending 31 March so that harvest yields during the summer could be included with sowing data for the previous calendar year.

From 1856–7 to 1866–7 the statistics were published as a separate Parliamentary Paper each year under the title 'Agricultural and Livestock Statistics for the Year Ending 31 March . . .', and reports of the collectors of statistics were often included. Thus '. . . Year Ending 31 March 1862', for example, would relate to acreages cultivated, sown to pasture, etc. in 1861 and harvest results for November 1861 to March 1862, and comments of the collectors of statistics would have been written in April–July 1862. Throughout this book reference is given to these statistics as Agric. Stat., 1861.

Agricultural statistics for the years 1867–8 and 1868–9 were only published on a county basis and could not be used for this work.

From 1869–70 onwards the agricultural statistics were included in what became the Statistical Register of Victoria. They were published in the Parliamentary Papers as the 'Production' section of the annual series titled 'Statistics of the Colony of Victoria for the Year . . .' Most of the statistics in the other sections were for the year ending 31 December. Therefore the Parliamentary Paper titled 'Statistics of the Colony of Victoria for the Year 1872, Production', for example, contained the agricultural statistics for the year ending 31 March 1873. This series was without collectors' comments and was collected on a municipal rather than a parish basis. Throughout this book these statistics have been referred to as Agric. Stat., 1872; they are comparable with the other statistics referred to as Stat., 1872.

Notes

1: THE PORT PHILLIP REGION

[1] For a more detailed description of these early voyages see Boys, *First Years at Port Phillip 1834–1842*, pp. 1–36.

[2] First Survey and Settlement of Port Phillip, *V.P.P.*, 1878, vol. 1, no. C15, p. 15.

[3] Bland (ed.), *Journey of Discovery to Port Phillip, New South Wales, in 1824 and 1825. By W. H. Hovell and H. Hume, Esquires*, p. 70.

[4] Northcote, *Atlas of Australian Soils: explanatory data for sheet 2*; Leeper, *Soils of Victoria*, pp. 1–8.

[5] First Survey and Settlement of Port Phillip, op. cit.

[6] Darke, Survey of Present and Proposed Lines of Road and the Coast between Melbourne and Geelong, 1841 (MS. map).

[7] Brown (ed.), *The Narrative of George Russell of Golf Hill*, p. 86.

[8] 'The length of the growing season in Australia as determined by the effectiveness of the rainfall', *Proceedings of the South Australian Branch of the Royal Geographical Society of Australasia*, vol. 50 (1949), pp. 42–6.

[9] *H.R.A.*, ser. 1, vol. 25, p. 431.

2: SETTLEMENT

[1] Thomas Winter to Mr Swanston, *c.* 1837, in Bride (ed.), *Letters from Victorian Pioneers*, pp. 275–6. Detailed accounts of these events are available in Boys, *First Years at Port Phillip 1834–1842*, pp. 1–58, and Brown (ed.), *The Narrative of George Russell of Golf Hill*, pp. 92–9.

[2] Census of New South Wales, 9 Nov. 1836.

[3] Ibid.

[4] Lonsdale to Bourke, 1 Feb. 1837, Police Magistrate's Correspondence, 36/1–36/45.

[5] The settlement of John Batman in Port Phillip from his own journal, Clark, *Select Documents in Australian History 1788–1850*, p. 92.

[6] 14 June 1837, *H.R.A.*, ser. 1, vol. 18, pp. 780–1.

[7] Census of New South Wales, March 1841.

[8] Mansfield, *Analytical View of the Census of New South Wales for the Year 1846*, pp. 9, 14.

[9] Lonsdale to Thomson, 6 Nov. 1838, Colonial Secretary's Correspondence, 4/2423.3.

[10] Orwin and Whetham, *History of British Agriculture 1846–1914*, p. 82.

[11] Ibid., p. 78.

[12] *H.R.A.*, ser. 1, vol. 18, pp. 154, 811–12.

[13] Endorsement on various letters, Colonial Secretary's Correspondence, 4/2334.5.

[14] Endorsement by V. D. Thomson on W. Wood to Surveyor-General, 10 Sept. 1836, Colonial Secretary's Correspondence, 4/2334.5.

[15] Lonsdale to Thomson, 16 June 1838, Colonial Secretary's Correspondence, 4/2423.3.

[16] P. Snodgrass to Colonial Secretary, 23 June 1838, Colonial Secretary's Correspondence, 4/2393.2.

[17] Unless otherwise indicated, a copy of all the Acts and regulations referred to in this section will be found in the Return to Address, *V. & P.*, L.C. N.S.W., 1847, vol. 1, pp. 633–719.

[18] Proclamation, 21 May 1839.

[19] *Port Phillip Gazette*, 2 Feb. 1839.

[20] Endorsement by G. G. (George Gipps), dated 25 Dec., on La Trobe to Colonial Secretary, 6 Dec. 1842, Colonial Secretary's Correspondence, 4/2564.

[21] *Port Phillip Government Gazette*, 21 Nov. 1848, 10 Oct. 1849.

[22] Roberts, *The Squatting Age in Australia 1835–1847*; Burroughs, *Britain and Australia 1831–*

1855; Buckley, 'Gipps and the graziers of New South Wales, 1841–1846', parts 1 and 2, in Eastwood and Smith (eds), *Historical Studies, Australia and New Zealand, Selected Articles*, pp. 57–102; Dyster, 'Support for the squatters, 1844', *Journal of the Royal Australian Historical Society*, vol. 51 (1965), pp. 41–59.

23 Brown (ed.), *The Narrative of George Russell of Golf Hill*, pp. 106–7, 157; *C.C.P.*, vol. 2, pp. 123–4.

24 Brown (ed.), op. cit., p. 179; Phillip Russell to George Russell, 11 Jan. 1838, *C.C.P.*, vol. 2, pp. 130–2; *C.C.P.*, vol. 4, p. 594, appendix 1.

25 Brown (ed.), op. cit., pp. 176, 213–14; Batey, The Pioneers of the Sunbury District (MS.), pp. 30–2; Men Engaged by the Clyde Company 1839–1842, *C.C.P.*, vol. 2, pp. 182–3.

26 George Russell to William Cross, May 1839, *C.C.P.*, vol. 2, p. 219.

27 Returns, Clyde Co., 1839, *C.C.P.*, vol. 2, p. 320; Returns, Clyde Co., 1 July to 31 Dec. 1840, *C.C.P.*, vol. 3, pp. 8–9.

28 Miss Anne Drysdale's Diary, 12, 15 Oct. 1841, *C.C.P.*, vol. 3, pp. 115–16.

29 Batey, The Pioneers of the Sunbury District (MS.), p. 204; Howitt, *Land, Labour, and Gold; or, Two Years in Victoria*, vol. 1, p. 131; Men Engaged by the Clyde Company 1839–1842, *C.C.P.*, vol. 2, pp. 182–3; *C.C.P.*, vol. 2, pp. 415–16, appendix 2.

30 Miss Anne Drysdale's Diary, 22 Oct. 1841, *C.C.P.*, vol. 3, p. 117.

31 *Port Phillip Gazette*, 24 Nov. 1838; Batey, The Pioneers of the Sunbury District (MS.), pp. 27–8.

32 George Russell to William Cross, 10 Sept. 1842, *C.C.P.*, vol. 3, pp. 240–1; John Cotton to William Cotton, Nov., Dec. 1846, in Mackaness (ed.), *The Correspondence of John Cotton*; *C.C.P.*, vol. 4, pp. 593–4, appendix 1.

33 *Port Phillip Gazette*, 3 Nov. 1838.

34 Report of the Resources of the Colony of Victoria, *Transactions of the Philosophical Institute of Victoria*, vol. 4 (1859), p. 65.

35 *Port Phillip Gazette*, 2 Mar., 17 Apr. 1839.

36 *Port Phillip Gazette*, 17 Apr. 1839.

37 Cox, *The Evolution of the Australian Merino*, p. 34.

38 Brown, *Sheep Breeding in Australia*, p. 188.

39 George Russell to John Aitken, 5 Oct. 1840, *C.C.P.*, vol. 2, p. 389.

40 Bells and Buchanan to George Russell, 25 Oct. 1844, *C.C.P.*, vol. 3, p. 455.

41 Returns, Clyde Co., 1 July to 31 Dec. 1840, *C.C.P.*, vol. 3, p. 9.

42 Report of the Resources of the Colony of Victoria, *Transactions of the Philosophical Institute of Victoria*, vol. 4 (1859), p. 64; Annual Report, *Transactions of the Port Phillip Farmers' Society*, 1856–7, p. 11; William Russell to relatives in Scotland, 28 Aug. 1839, *C.C.P.*, vol. 2, p. 248; *C.C.P.*, vol. 3, p. 14, n. 1; William Russell to George Russell, 8 July 1841, *C.C.P.*, vol. 3, p. 65.

43 *Port Phillip Gazette*, 3, 20 July 1839.

44 *C.C.P.*, vol. 3, p. 287; John Cotton to William Cotton, 2 Sept. 1843, in Mackaness (ed.), *The Correspondence of John Cotton.*

45 Butlin, *Foundations of the Australian Monetary System 1788–1851*, p. 316.

46 Hayter, *Victorian Year Book for 1881–2*, endpaper no. 1; Roberts, *The Squatting Age in Australia 1835–1847*, pp. 225–8.

47 Butlin, op. cit., pp. 318–19; Macmillan, *The Debtor's War*, pp. 36–7, 61–3.

48 Census, 1836; Census, 1841; parish maps; Billis and Kenyon, *Pastoral Pioneers of Port Phillip*; Brown (ed.), *The Narrative of George Russell of Golf Hill*; Bride (ed.), *Letters from Victorian Pioneers*; Batey, The Pioneers of the Sunbury District (MS.).

49 Roberts, op. cit., p. 246; Brown (ed.), op. cit., pp. 204–5, 208; John Cotton to William Cotton, Apr. 1844, in Mackaness (ed.), op. cit.

50 New South Wales Statistical Returns, 1835–1844, *V. & P.*, L.C. N.S.W., 1845, p. 402.

51 Batey, The Pioneers of the Sunbury District (MS.), p. 214.

52 George Russell to William Cross, 1 Sept. 1841, *C.C.P.*, vol. 3, p. 87.

53 John Cotton to William Cotton, Oct. 1845, in Mackaness (ed.), op. cit.

54 George Russell to J. and A. Dennistoun, 15 Aug. 1848, *C.C.P.*, vol. 4, pp. 319–20.

55 George Russell to William Lewis, 9 Apr. 1852, *C.C.P.*, vol. 5, p. 234.

56 George Russell to William Lewis, 2 Mar. 1853, *C.C.P.*, vol. 5, p. 436.

57 George Russell to J. and A. Dennistoun, 3 Oct. 1853, *C.C.P.*, vol. 5, p. 527.

58 Batey, The Pioneers of the Sunbury District (MS.), pp. 10, 16, 28, 32, 41–2, 407, 459; *Port Phillip Government Gazette*, Extraordinary, 16 June 1849.

59 *H.R.A.*, ser. 1, vol. 16, p. 865, n. 116.

60 See note 17.

61 La Trobe to Colonial Secretary, 28 Jan. 1842, Chief Secretary's Correspondence, 42/118,

Letters Outwards 1 July 1841 to 9 Nov. 1842; Settled Districts of Melbourne, 1854? (MS. map).

62 The regulations of 10 Feb. 1842 as published in the *New South Wales Government Gazette* (the *Port Phillip Government Notes* were not published until 1843), simply reinstated the system of auction in operation before 5 Dec. 1840, and stated that the upset price was never to be less than 12s per acre. But in a private dispatch to Governor Gipps, Lord Stanley stipulated that in the Port Phillip District the upset price at auction was never to be less than 20s per acre (Stanley to Gipps, 18 Oct. 1841, *H.R.A.*, ser. 1, vol. 21, p. 559).

63 24 Vict., no. 117. But during the 1850s additional Orders in Council and regulations provided for the purchase of land both within and beyond the settled districts (see chapter 3).

64 George Russell to William Cross, 5 Mar. 1840, *C.C.P.*, vol. 2, p. 316.

65 Hayter, *Victorian Year Book for 1881–2*, endpaper no. 1.

66 Select Committee on Immigration, Minutes of Evidence, *V. & P.*, L.C. N.S.W., 1845, pp. 616–17; ibid., 1847, vol. 2, p. 280.

67 George Russell to William Cross, 18 Mar. 1844, *C.C.P.*, vol. 3, p. 388; Memoranda, *C.C.P.*, vol. 4, pp. 515–18; George Russell to J. and A. Dennistoun, 8 Sept. 1847, 19 Feb. 1849, 16 Feb. 1850, *C.C.P.*, vol. 4, pp. 213, 372–3, 465–6.

68 'Melbourne Prices Current', *Port Phillip Gazette*, 1839.

69 Select Committee on Immigration, Minutes of Evidence, 1845, op. cit., p. 617; *Port Phillip Herald*, 2 Mar. 1847; *Weekly Times*, 13 Mar. 1875.

70 Select Committee on Immigration, Minutes of Evidence, 1845, op. cit., p. 616.

71 Farm Day Book (MS.).

72 Memoranda, George Russell and William Lewis, *C.C.P.*, vol. 4, pp. 515–18.

73 Lang, *Port-Phillip*, p. 101.

74 *Port Phillip Herald*, 10 Apr. 1840.

75 *Port Phillip Herald*, 28 Feb. 1843.

76 Statistics of the Port Phillip District, 1850, *V. & P.*, L.C. Vic., 1851–2, p. 399.

77 *Royal Commission on the Wheat, Flour and Bread Industries*, Fourth Report (Canberra, 1936), p. 25.

78 Dunsdorfs, *The Australian Wheat-Growing Industry 1788–1948*, p. 59.

79 *Melbourne Morning Herald and General Daily Advertiser*, 13 Feb. 1851.

80 Agric. Stat., 1858, preliminary notes. But this was not a simple relationship; the whole question of assisted immigration was linked closely with land policy.

81 Agric. Stat., 1858, preliminary notes; Census of Victoria, 2 March 1851, *V. & P.*, L.C. Vic., 1851–2, p. 292.

3: TRANSITION

1 p. 331. See also Burroughs, *Britain and Australia, 1831–1855*, p. 323.

2 *Port Phillip Government Gazette*, 12 Apr., 29 Nov. 1848, 10 Oct. 1849.

3 Ibid., 10 Oct., 1849.

4 Ibid., 7 Aug. 1850.

5 George Russell to J. and A. Dennistoun, 16 Feb. 1850, *C.C.P.*, vol. 4, p. 466.

6 *Victoria Government Gazette*, 1851, pp. 839–40.

7 Peck, *Memoirs of a Stockman*, p. 86; Howitt, *Land, Labour, and Gold; or, Two Years in Victoria*, vol. 2, pp. 128–9.

8 Kiddle, *Men of Yesterday*, p. 25; Peck, op. cit., p. 86.

9 Bride (ed.), *Letters from Victorian Pioneers*, pp. 165–7.

10 Lang, *Port-Phillip*, p. 105.

11 Bride (ed.), op. cit., pp. 165–7.

12 La Trobe to Clarke, 30 Oct. 1850, 15 Jan. 1851, La Trobe to John Aitken, et al., 22 Nov. 1850, Letterbooks, Land Branch, Local, Letters Out, Series 'A', Chief Secretary's Correspondence; Settled Districts of Melbourne, 1854? (MS. map).

13 La Trobe to Clarke, 15 Jan. 1851, Letterbooks, Land Branch, Local, Letters Out, Series 'A', Chief Secretary's Correspondence.

14 Ibid., 18 Mar. 1851.

15 Ibid., 6, 21 May 1851.

16 Lonsdale to Clarke, 18 Feb. 1853, Letterbooks, Land Branch, Local, Letters Out, Re Land Applications, July 1851 to Nov. 1853, Chief Secretary's Correspondence.

17 The full title at this time was *Melbourne Morning Herald and General Daily Advertiser.*

18 They did send a memorial to the governor but to no avail (La Trobe to John Aitken, et al., 22 Nov. 1850).

19 Crown Lands' Sale and Leases, *V. & P.*, L.C. Vic., 1854–5, vol. 3, no. C8a, p. 12.

[20] La Trobe to Clarke, 30 Oct. 1850, 3 Jan. 1851, Letterbooks, Land Branch, Local, Chief Secretary's Correspondence.
[21] Batey, Further Notes on Early Days on the Keilor and Werribee Plains (MS.), p. 7.
[22] Return of Occupiers of Crown Lands Etc., n.d., Letterbook, Land Board, Letters 1841–47, Reserves 1850–51, Etc., Chief Secretary's Correspondence, p. 22.
[23] Howard and Philip, The History and Settlement of the Bulla District (thesis), p. 45; Batey, The Pioneers of the Sunbury District (MS.), pp. 22, 39–42, 136–8, 148, 285.
[24] Batey, ibid., pp. 136–8, 148; Batey, Further Notes (MS.), p. 8.
[25] Batey, The Pioneers (MS.), pp. 41, 285.
[26] Waste Lands 1852, *V. & P.*, L.C. Vic., 1852–3, vol. 2, no. 7, p. 15.
[27] George Russell to J. and A. Dennistoun, 3 Oct. 1853, *C.C.P.*, vol. 5, pp. 525–6.
[28] *Port Phillip Government Gazette*, 16 June 1849.
[29] Derrimut parish map, County Bourke, 1949.
[30] The 19 June 1850 Order in Council under the 1846 Land Act, and the New South Wales regulations of 28 June 1850 under the 1847 Order in Council, provided for sale of land beyond the settled districts to the holders of licensed runs, but at Port Phillip, for the time being, this was limited to the sale of pre-emptive right homestead sections only. See Serle, *The Golden Age*, pp. 130–6.
[31] *Port Phillip Government Gazette*, 22 Mar., 16 June, 21 July, 17 Oct. 1849; Valuation of Crown Lands under Pre-emptive Right, *V. & P.*, L.C. Vic., 1854–5, vol. 3, no. C26a; parish maps of the twenty-one parishes, various dates.
[32] Valuation of Crown Lands under Pre-emptive Right, op. cit.; Crown Lands' Sale and Leases, *V. & P.*, L.C. Vic., 1854–5, vol. 3, no. C8a, pp. 10–12; 'Land Tax Register and Valuation for Victoria', *Victoria Government Gazette*, 1880, pp. 2937–62.
[33] This land remained in rural use; the encroachment of the city was not a major factor in these cases.
[34] Census of Victoria, 2 March 1851, *V. & P.*, L.C. Vic., 1851–2, p. 207.
[35] Census, 1854, Ages.
[36] Serle, *The Golden Age,* chs 1 and 2. The only gold found in the Port Phillip region was in very poor deposits in mountainous timbered country in the Plenty and Lilydale divisions.
[37] Batey, The Pioneers (MS.), pp. 184, 199.
[38] Bennett, *Christison of Lammermoor*, p. 35.
[39] George Russell to J. and A. Dennistoun, 3 Oct. 1853, *C.C.P.,* vol. 5, p. 524–5.
[40] Ibid., p. 525.
[41] Batey, The Pioneers (MS.), pp. 199, 209.
[42] George Russell to J. and A. Dennistoun, 3 Oct. 1853, *C.C.P.*, vol. 5, p. 526.
[43] John Learmonth to William Lewis, 24 June 1853, *C.C.P.*, vol. 5, p. 478.
[44] James Riley to William Lewis, 23 July 1853, *C.C.P.*, vol. 5, p. 494.
[45] Dennistoun Bros & Co. to George Russell, 22 Nov. 1853, *C.C.P.*, vol. 5, p. 554, 3 Dec. 1853, *C.C.P.*, vol. 5, p. 578.
[46] 'Summary of the Agricultural Statistics of Victoria from 1836 to 1881–2 Inclusive' in Hayter, *Victorian Year Book for 1881–2*, endpaper no. 2.
[47] Pollitt, *An Historical Record of Melton*, p. 20.
[48] Condon, Point Cooke (thesis), chs 2 and 3; Bride (ed.), *Letters from Victorian Pioneers*, pp. 233–8; Billis and Kenyon, *Pastoral Pioneers of Port Phillip*, pp. 32–3; Stock Returns, Bourke District, 1851, Chief Secretary's Correspondence; *Werribee Shire Banner*, 22, 29 Mar. 1962; Land Sale by Public Auction, Country and Suburban Land, 1849–51, Registers, Lands and Survey Department.
[49] Flynn, History of Braybrook District (typescript).
[50] George Russell to Dennistoun Bros & Co., 29 Nov. 1853, *C.C.P.*, vol. 5, p. 555.
[51] George Russell to Walter Chisholm, 17 Dec. 1853, *C.C.P.*, vol. 5, p. 581.
[52] Tullamarine parish map, County Bourke, 1958; Agric. Stat. 1856–60.
[53] Mingay, 'The agricultural revolution in English history: a reconsideration' in Minchinton (ed.), *Essays in Agrarian History*, vol. 2, p. 18.
[54] 27 Sept. 1879; see also Waterson, *Squatter, Selector and Storekeeper*, p. 101.
[55] Drummond and Wilbraham, *The Englishman's Food*, pp. 327–42.

4: COMMUNITY DEVELOPMENT

[1] Lang, *Port-Phillip*, p. 335.
[2] 27 Oct. 1838.
[3] 1 May 1852.
[4] Kiddle, *Men of Yesterday*, p. 217.
[5] This is based on religious affiliation as recorded in the 1841 census; see note 18 below.

6 'The coming of the Irish to Victoria', *Historical Studies, Australia and New Zealand*, vol. 12 (1965), pp. 68, 84, 68n.
7 *Men of Yesterday*, p. 14 and ch. 2, n. 1.
8 Jordan, A Geographical Appraisal of the Significance of German Settlement in Nineteenth Century Texas Agriculture (thesis), pp. 290–2.
9 Agric. Stat., 1860.
10 Lyng, *Non-Britishers in Australia*, pp. 34, 43–4.
11 Peel, 'Viticulture at Geelong and Lillydale', *Vict. Hist. Mag.*, vol. 36 (1965), pp. 154–73.
12 Select Committee on Chinese Immigration, Report with Evidence, *V. & P.*, L.C. Vic., 1856–7, no. D19, p. 11; Serle, *The Golden Age*, p. 332.
13 de Castella, 'Early Victorian wine-growing', *Vict. Hist. Mag.*, vol. 19 (1941–2), pp. 140–54.
14 Whitworth, *Baillieres Victorian Gazetteer*, 1879, pp. 113, 354.
15 Inglis, 'Religious behaviour' in Davies and Encel (eds), *Australian Society*, p. 51.
16 Personal observation (the author is a member of one of the farming families of the region); see also Oeser and Emery, *Social Structure and Personality in a Rural Community*, pp. 11–12.
17 Kendall, *Farming Memoirs of a West Country Yeoman*, pp. 56–7.
18 Census, 1861, Birth-places, Religions; Presbyterians on Scottish, $r^2 = 0{\cdot}983$, $P<0{\cdot}01$; Catholics on Irish, $r^2 = 0{\cdot}986$, $P<0{\cdot}01$; Snedecor and Cochran, *Statistical Methods*, p. 176.

5: THE FARMERS

1 Serle, *The Golden Age*, p. 85.
2 Agric. Stat. (Reports), 1858, p. 66.
3 Censuses, 1861, 1871, 1881, Birthplaces.
4 Agric. Stat. (Reports), 1861–6.
5 Bićanić, 'Lack of institutional flexibility in agriculture' in *Proceedings of the Tenth International Conference of Agricultural Economics*, pp. 159–61.
6 Jeeves, 'The relation of the assimilation of new information to increasing age, in *Reviews, Papers and Reports*, pp. 286–7.
7 George Russell to William Lewis, 9 Oct. 1850, *C.C.P.*, vol. 4, p. 559; *Weekly Times*, 15 Feb. 1879.
8 Diary, 1870, p. 2.
9 Felstehausen, 'Economic knowledge, participation and farmer decision making in a developed and under-developed country', *International Journal of Agrarian Affairs*, vol. 5 (1968), pp. 269–70.
10 The Pioneers of the Sunbury District (MS.), p. 407.
11 Callaghan and Millington, *The Wheat Industry in Australia*, p. 450.
12 Census, 1851, p. 207.

6: PRODUCTION

1 Agric. Stat. (Reports), 1856, p. 48.
2 Hayter, *Victorian Year Book for 1881–2*, endpapers.
3 Registrar-General's Report, Agric. Stat., 1857, p. 8.
4 *Melbourne Morning Herald*, 6 Feb. 1853, 2 Apr. 1854.
5 Agric. Stat. (Reports), 1858, pp. 62, 66; Stat., 1864., Interchange.
6 *Port Phillip Herald*, 11 Jan. 1848; *Geelong Advertiser*, 2 Jan. 1864. The 'customary rations' remained constant over a long period.
7 Agric. Stat. (Reports), 1858, p. 64; *Victorian Agricultural and Horticultural Gazette*, 21 Mar. 1857.
8 Stat., 1864, Interchange.
9 Serle, *The Golden Age*, p. 289.
10 *Melbourne Leader*, 22 May 1858.
11 Ibid., 11 Feb. 1860.
12 Agric. Stat. (Reports), 1864, p. 89.
13 The results of Clarke and Marshall's experiments are described in Callaghan and Millington, *The Wheat Industry in Australia*, pp. 76, 86.
14 Report on Experimental Farm, near Melbourne, Agric. Stat. (Reports), 1858, p. 60.
15 Experimental Farm, First Annual Report of the Director, *V.P.P.*, 1859-60, vol. 3, no. 14, pp. 4, 12.
16 Agric. Stat. (Reports), 1862, p. 93.
17 Agric. Stat. (Reports), 1864, p. 90.
18 Callaghan and Millington, *The Wheat Industry in Australia*, pp. 282–3.
19 Agric. Stat. (Reports), 1864, p. 90. The benefits of early sowing have been verified by more

recent research (Callaghan and Millington, op. cit., p. 283). For the history of rust occurrence and control on a world-wide basis see Large, *The Advance of the Fungi*, ch. 22.

20 White Tuscan was included here as a more susceptible variety, but this appears to have been an error (for white velvet?), since in a preliminary report it was named as a more resistant variety and other observers verified its relative resistance.

21 Sixth Annual Report Presented by the Council to the Board of Agriculture, *V.P.P.*, 1864–5, vol. 4, no. 76, pp. 18-19.

22 Agric. Stat. (Reports), 1866, p. 89.

23 *Victorian Agricultural and Horticultural Gazette*, 21 Mar. 1857.

24 Ibid.

25 Agric. Stat. (Reports), 1861, p. 99.

26 Agric. Stat. (Reports), 1862, p. 94.

27 *Melbourne Leader,* 14 Jan. 1860.

28 Agric. Stat. (Reports), 1864, p. 90.

29 Agric. Stat. (Reports), 1862, pp. 100–1.

30 Dondlinger, *The Book of Wheat*, pp. 100–1; Napolitan, *Centenary of the Agricultural Census 1866 to 1966*, pp. 11, 17; Orwin and Whetham, *History of British Agriculture 1846–1914*, pp. 120, 241–2.

31 *Port Phillip Gazette*, 27 Oct. 1838.

32 'Melbourne Prices Current', *Port Phillip Gazette*, various dates, 1839; *Port Phillip Herald*, 24 Mar. 1840.

33 Agric. Stat. (Reports), 1865, p. 83.

34 Stat., 1862–5, Interchange.

35 Agric. Stat. (Reports), 1865, p. 83; see also Agricultural Machinery Returns, Agric. Stat., 1862–4.

36 Stat., 1872 and 1880, Production (Machinery in Operation).

37 *Victorian Agricultural and Horticultural Gazette*, 21 Mar. 1857.

38 *Weekly Times*, 16 Aug., 20 Sept., 29 Nov. 1879.

39 Agric. Stat. (Reports), 1856, p. 50.

40 Agric. Stat. (Reports), 1863, pp. 96–7.

41 Ibid., 1865, p. 84.

42 Ibid., 1864, p. 90.

43 *Melbourne Leader*, supplement, 23 Apr. 1881.

44 Seventh Annual Report Presented by the Council to the Board of Agriculture, *V.P.P.*, 1867, vol. 3, no. 10, pp. 21–2.

45 Johnston, Return Made to Government on 10 July 1868, when applying for Crown Grant (MS.), folded quarto sheets in Johnston papers; Johnston, Diary, 20 Sept. 1870.

46 *Weekly Times*, 3 Jan. 1880.

47 *Weekly Times*, 15 Mar. 1879; Department of Lands and Agriculture (Victoria), *Third Annual Report of the Secretary for Agriculture*, 1875, pp. 212–19.

48 *Australasian* (newspaper staff), *The Australasian Farmer*, Melbourne 1885, p. 163.

49 Ibid., pp. 161–3; von Mueller, *Select Extra-tropical Plants*, see under the various species.

50 *Weekly Times*, 5 June 1875, 9 Aug. 1879; Agric. Stat., 1880.

51 *Weekly Times*, 6 Mar. 1880.

52 Russell, *A History of Agricultural Science in Great Britain 1620–1954*, pp. 383–4; Fussell, *The English Dairy Farmer 1500–1900*, pp. 94, 111–12.

53 Morton, *The Farmer's Calendar*, p. 205.

54 Seventh Annual Report Presented by the Council to the Board of Agriculture, op. cit., p. 17; Second Annual Report, *V.P.P.*, 1861–2, vol. 3, no. 42, pp. 22–3.

55 Third Annual Report, *V.P.P.*, 1862–3, vol. 3, no. 7, p. 14.

56 Johnston, Return Made to Government on 10 July 1868 (MS.); Johnston, Diary, 18 Mar. 1865.

57 Fussell, *The English Dairy Farmer 1500–1900*, p. 112; see also *Melbourne Leader,* 8 Jan. 1870, for comments on the controversy about the relationship between the age of a ryegrass pasture and the perennial characteristics of the plants grown from its seed.

58 Seventh Annual Report Presented by the Council to the Board of Agriculture, op. cit., p. 17.

59 Personal communication from Victorian Government Botanist, 1967; George Russell to J. and A. Dennistoun, 3 Oct. 1853, *C.C.P.*, vol. 5, p. 523; *Port Phillip Herald,* 2 Sept. 1847.

60 *Third Annual Report of the Secretary for Agriculture*, 1875, p. 221.

61 Seventh Annual Report, *V.P.P.*, 1867, vol. 3, no. 10, p. 17.

62 Johnston, Diary, 16 May 1867.

63 *Third Annual Report of the Secretary for Agriculture*, 1875, pp. 213, 216, 219; Report of the Proceedings under the Land Act 1869, *V.P.P.*, 1878, vol. 2, no. 22, p. 13; Stat., 1877, Production.

64 Sixth Annual Report, *V.P.P.*, 1864–5, vol. 4, no. 76, p. 28; von Mueller, op. cit., p. 68.
65 Agric. Stat. (Reports), 1862, p. 96.
66 Second Annual Report, *V.P.P.*, 1861–2, vol. 3, no. 42, p. 23.
67 Seventh Annual Report, *V.P.P.*, 1867, vol. 3, no. 10, p. 17.
68 Wright, Stephenson & Co. Ltd, *A Guide to Better Pastures*, pp. 8–10.
69 *The Australasian Farmer*, pp. 91–9.
70 *Journal of the National Agricultural Society of Victoria*, June 1877, Mar., June 1880.
71 Ibid., June 1877.
72 Stat., 1877, Interchange.
73 *Journal of the National Agricultural Society of Victoria*, Nov. 1879.
74 Second Annual Report, *V.P.P.*, 1861–2, vol. 3, no. 42, p. 23; Third Annual Report, *V.P.P.*, 1862–3, vol. 3, no. 7, pp. 13, 14.
75 *Weekly Times*, 20 Nov. 1875.
76 Buxton, *The Riverina 1861–1891*, pp. 24–32, 250; *Weekly Times*, 28 Feb. 1880.
77 'Town-Herd Richmond', *Victoria Government Gazette*, 1859, p. 1335.
78 Agric. Stat. (Reports), 1858, p. 66.
79 'Rusticus', *How to Settle in Victoria*, pp. 10, 32; *Melbourne Leader*, 21 Aug. 1858.
80 Returns, Trade and Customs, 1860, *V.P.P.*, 1861–2, vol. 3, no. 2, pp. 9, 12, 17, 19.
81 Stat., 1862–80, Interchange.
82 Stat., 1864, Interchange; Agric. Stat. (Reports), 1858, p. 64; *Victorian Agricultural and Horticultural Gazette*, 21 Mar. 1857.
83 Annual Report 1856–7, *Transactions of the Port Phillip Farmers' Society*, 1857, p. 10.
84 *Victorian Agricultural and Horticultural Gazette*, 21 Mar. 1857.
85 Agric. Stat. (Reports), 1866, p. 91; see also *Dandenong Journal*, centenary issue, 22 Dec. 1965, p. 12.
86 de Pury, Diary, 4 Feb., 13 Feb. 1874, p. 1.
87 Royal Commission on Foot and Mouth Disease, Progress Report with Evidence, *V.P.P.*, 1872, vol. 3, no. 58, Evidence pp. 3–6, 24–33, 48.
88 Agric. Stat. (Reports), 1866, p. 91.
89 Agric. Stat. (Reports), 1864, p. 90.
90 *Weekly Times*, 24 Jan. 1880; in general for this section see reports from 'Our Travelling Reporter', *Weekly Times*, Dec. 1879 to Mar. 1880.
91 *Weekly Times*, 13 Dec. 1879, 3 Jan. 1880.
92 *Weekly Times*, 13, 30 Dec. 1879.
93 Agric. Stat. (Reports), 1863, p. 96.
94 Ibid., p. 93.
95 Agric. Stat. (Reports), 1866, p. 89.
96 Thomson, 'On diseases among stock' in Department of Lands and Agriculture (Victoria), *Second Annual Report of the Secretary for Agriculture*, 1874, pp. 150–1.
97 Stat., 1864, Interchange.
98 *How to Settle in Victoria*, p. 38.
99 Broughton and Walter, A General Survey of the Early Settlement and Architecture along the Maribyrnong between Bulla and Keilor (thesis); Wright, *The Live Stock Annual of Australia 1905*, pp. 257–60.
1 Wright, op. cit., p. 257.
2 Agric. Stat. (Reports), 1865, p. 84; Johnston, Diary, 9 Oct. 1868.
3 e.g. Robert McDougall's visit to the Booths at Warlaby, *Melbourne Leader*, 28 Jan. 1860.
4 Although its forerunner was at Mt Aitken in the same division; Riddell, 'Shorthorns' in *Third Annual Report of the Secretary for Agriculture*, 1875, pp. 177–9.
5 *Weekly Times*, 27 Feb., 13 Nov. 1875.
6 Ibid., 30 Oct. 1875.
7 Ibid., 23 Oct. 1875.
8 Billis and Kenyon, *Pastures New*, pp. 141–2.
9 *Weekly Times*, 12 Jan. 1878.
10 *Weekly Times*, 11 Jan. 1879.
11 *Weekly Times*, 26 July, 20 Sept. 1879.
12 Short and Carter, *An Analysis of the Records of the Registered Australian Merino Stud Flocks*, p. 11.
13 'Rusticus', *How to Settle in Victoria*, pp. 6, 32.
14 Agric. Stat., 1870–80; see next chapter.
15 *Weekly Times*, 17 Apr. 1875.
16 Agric. Stat., 1856.
17 *Weekly Times*, 9 Jan. 1875.

[18] Wattle Bark Board of Inquiry, Report with Evidence, *V.P.P.*, 1878, vol. 2, no. 36, pp. 6, 8, 51–4.
[19] *Victoria Government Gazette*, 1866, p. 1871; *Weekly Times*, 13 Mar., 17 Apr. 1875. The farmers on the north-west shore of the bay also took advantage of this type of fertilizer.
[20] *Weekly Times*, 13 Mar. 1875.
[21] Agric. Stat., 1878, 1879.
[22] Stat., 1879, Interchange.

7: LAND TENURE AND FARM SIZE

[1] 'Land Tax Register and Valuation for Victoria', *Victoria Government Gazette*, 1880, pp. 2937–63.
[2] Serle, *Dictionary of Australian Biography*, vol. 1, pp. 177–8; Peck, *Memoirs of a Stockman*, p. 87; Sutherland, *Victoria and Its Metropolis Past and Present*, vol. 2, p. 476.
[3] Williams, et al., *A History of Bacchus Marsh and Its Pioneers 1836–1936*, pp. 25–6, 156; Peck, op. cit., pp. 100–1.
[4] Sutherland, op. cit., vol. 1, p. 31, vol. 2, pp. 458–9; Austin, 'The Austin family in Australia', *Vict. Hist. Mag.*, vol. 36 (1965), pp. 78–96; *C.C.P.*, vol. 5, pp. 625–6; George Armytage to La Trobe, 6 Oct. 1853, in Bride (ed.), *Letters from Victorian Pioneers*, pp. 138-40.
[5] Billis and Kenyon, *Pastoral Pioneers of Port Phillip*, 'Glenmore' and 'Mooradoranook'; Williams, et al., op. cit., pp. 13, 153; Batey, The Pioneers of the Sunbury District (MS.), p. 349.
[6] Broughton and Walter, A General Survey of the Early Settlement and Architecture along the Maribyrnong between Bulla and Keilor (thesis); Sutherland, op. cit., vol. 2, p. 437.
[7] Sutherland, op. cit., vol. 2, p. 208.
[8] Various parish maps for sale of allotments listed in Land Tax Register; Ham, *Barrabool Shire Council, Jubilee, 1865–1915*, list of councillors.
[9] See Kiddle, *Men of Yesterday*.
[10] Clarke to La Trobe, 13 Sept. 1853, in Bride (ed.), *Letters from Victorian Pioneers*, p. 167.
[11] Agric. Stat. (Reports), 1858, pp. 65–6.
[12] Ibid.
[13] Agric. Stat. (Reports), 1861, p. 99.
[14] Ibid., p. 100; Bulla District Roads Board, Rate Book, 1863–5.
[15] Agric. Stat. (Reports), 1863, pp. 93–7, 1864, p. 92.
[16] Stat., 1869–79, Production, Leases of Farms from Private Individuals.
[17] Proclamation, Regulations for Farmers' Commons, *V.P.P.*, 1860–1, vol. 3, no. 69.
[18] Proclamation, Depasturing Sheep on Farmers' Commons Prohibited, *V.P.P.*, 1861–2, vol. 3, no. 34.
[19] Agric. Stat. (Reports), 1865, p. 84.
[20] Duffy, *Guide to the Land Law of Victoria*, p. 13; Immigration, Introduction of Vine-dressers, Etc. from Europe, *V.P.P.*, 1862–3, vol. 4, nos 60, 69, 79, 87.
[21] *Victoria Government Gazette*, 1862, pp. 1472, 1566–7, 1897, 2150–7, 2640.
[22] Agric. Stat. (Reports), 1865, p. 83.
[23] *Weekly Times*, 15 May 1875.
[24] Royal Commission on Foreign Industries and Forests, Progress Report, *V.P.P.*, 1871, vol. 3, no. 60, pp. 5, 6.

8: INSTITUTIONAL INFLUENCES

[1] Napolitan, *Centenary of the Agricultural Census 1866 to 1966*, pp. 1–2.
[2] For a discussion of this see Blainey, *The Tyranny of Distance*, pp. 228–35.
[3] Harrigan, *Victorian Railways to '62*, pp. 283–7.
[4] Patterson, *The Tariff in the Australian Colonies 1856–1900*, p. 58, chs 1, 2, 5.
[5] Ibid., ch. 11; Parnaby, The Economic and Political Development of Victoria 1877–1881 (thesis), ch. 12; Bartlett, 'The political orders of Victoria and New South Wales, 1856–1890', *Australian Economic History Review*, vol. 8 (1968), pp. 49–54.
[6] Intercolonial Conference, Report of Proceedings, *Journal of the Legislative Council of N.S.W.* 1872–3, vol. 22, no. C30, p. 2; Johnston, Diary, 19 Mar. 1876.
[7] *Port Phillip Government Gazette*, 13 May 1851; Le Souef, 'Acclimatisation in Victoria', *Vict. Hist. Mag.*, vol. 36 (1965), pp. 10, 20–1.
[8] International Exhibition 1862, London, Reports and Enclosures from the Commissioners, *V.P.P.*, 1862–3, vol. 4, no. 26, enclosure no. 1, p. 7. Similar views are also expressed in Story, 'Essay upon the agriculture of Victoria' in *The Victorian Government Prize Essays 1860*, pp. v–viii, 53–208.

[9] Encouragement of the Production of Flax and Silk, *V.P.P.*, 1875–6, vol. 3, no. 52; Beetroot Sugar, *V.P.P.*, 1875–6, vol. 3, no. 53.

[10] *Yeoman and Australian Acclimatiser*, 7 Dec. 1861, 24 May, 13 Sept. 1862.

[11] 7 Vict., no. 3 (N.S.W.); for a discussion of credit facilities for graziers see Barnard, *The Australian Wool Market 1840–1900*, pp. 116–25.

[12] 29 Vict., no. 280; *Victorian Hansard*, 1864–5, vol. 11, p. 250.

[13] *Victorian Hansard*, 1863–4, vol. 10, p. 370.

[14] *Victorian Hansard*, 1863–4, vol. 9, p. 205, vol. 10, p. 455.

[15] Barley, A History of Two Victorian Farmers' Organisations (thesis), p. 4.

[16] Annual Report, 1856–7, *Transactions of the Port Phillip Farmers' Society*, 1857, pp. 3–5, 14.

[17] Orwin and Whetham, *History of British Agriculture 1846–1914*, p. 29.

[18] Annual Report, 1856–7, op. cit., pp. 14–20; Lennon, Letterbook, 12 Apr. to 4 Sept. 1876, pp. 907–13.

[19] Annual Report, 1856–7, op. cit., pp. 39–42.

[20] Ibid., p. 8; Report, 1857, op. cit., pp. 13, 14.

[21] Annual Reports, 1857–8, 1858–9, op. cit.; Barley, A History of Two Victorian Farmers' Organisations (thesis), pp. 5, 6; 22 Vict., no. 83; First Annual Report Presented by the Council to the Board of Agriculture, *V.P.P.*, 1860–1, vol. 3, no. 1, p. 19; Select Committee on the Experimental Farm, Report with Evidence, *V.P.P.*, 1861–2, vol. 2, no. D57, p. 6.

[22] First Annual Report, *V.P.P.*, 1860–1, vol. 3, no. 1, pp. 3–8, 20–1, and subsequent reports.

[23] Eighth Annual Report Presented by the Council to the Board of Agriculture, *V.P.P.*, 1867, vol. 5, no. 8, pp. 14–15; Board of Agriculture, *V.P.P.*, 1869, vol. 2, no. C18; £13 510 and £9930 were granted in 1860 and 1861 respectively.

[24] Report on Experimental Farm, near Melbourne, Agric. Stat. (Reports), 1858, p. 60; Experimental Farm, First Annual Report of the Director, *V.P.P.*, 1859–60, vol. 3, no. 14, p. 3.

[25] First Annual Report, *V.P.P.*, 1860–1, vol. 3, no. 1, p. 14.

[26] Ibid., pp. 11, 16.

[27] Select Committee on Experimental Farm, Report with Evidence, *V.P.P.*, 1861–2, vol. 2, no. D57, p. 41.

[28] Second Annual Report Presented by the Council to the Board of Agriculture, *V.P.P.*, 1861–2, vol. 3, no. 42, p. 7; Third Annual Report, *V.P.P.*, 1862–3, vol. 3, no. 7, pp. 5, 12; Select Committee on Experimental Farm, Report with Evidence, op. cit.

[29] Fourth Annual Report, *V.P.P.*, 1862–3, pp. 5, 6; *Victorian Parliamentary Debates*, 1872, vol. 14, p. 918.

[30] *Victorian Parliamentary Debates*, 1866, vol. 2, pp. 92, 369–73. The board had been under attack from as early as 1861, see e.g. Third Report, 1862–3, p. 4, and Fourth Report, 1862–3, p. 5.

[31] *Victorian Parliamentary Debates*, 1867, vol. 4, p. 1759; 1869, vol. 9, pp. 2315–16, 2339–43; 1870, vol. 11, p. 169; 34 Vict., no. 380.

[32] *Victorian Parliamentary Debates*, 1872, vol. 14, pp. 804, 915–18.

[33] Ibid., p. 916.

[34] Ibid., pp. 915–18; ibid., 1872, vol. 15, pp. 1908–9; Department of Lands and Agriculture (Victoria), *First Annual Report of the Secretary for Agriculture*, 1873, appendix U, pp. 251–68.

[35] *Victoria Government Gazette*, 1872, p. 2144.

[36] *Victorian Parliamentary Debates*, 1876, vol. 25, pp. 1789–92.

[37] Experimental Farm at Dookie, *V.P.P.*, 1877–8, vol. 1, no. C11.

[38] *Victorian Parliamentary Debates*, 1867, vol. 25, p. 1790; 1879–80, vol. 31, p. 1517; Sutherland, *Victoria and Its Metropolis Past and Present*, vol. 2, p. 476.

[39] Ibid.; *Weekly Times*, 25 Jan., 28 June, 15 Nov. 1879.

[40] *Victorian Parliamentary Debates*, 1875–6, vol. 23, p. 2369.

[41] *Weekly Times*, 16 Nov. 1878, 16 Aug. 1879.

[42] 24 May, 5, 19 July, 9, 23 Aug. 1879.

[43] *Weekly Times*, 11 Oct. 1879.

[44] Ibid., 25 Oct., 13 Dec. 1879.

[45] 11 Oct., 8 Nov. 1879.

[46] Graham, *The Formation of the Australian Country Parties*, pp. 48–9, 67.

[47] Graham Berry, quoted in *Weekly Times*, 9 Aug. 1879.

Bibliography

OFFICIAL SOURCES

Colonial Secretary's Correspondence, 1836–49. Archives Office of New South Wales.

Lands and Survey Department (Victoria). Land Sale by Public Auction, Country and Suburban Land, 1849–1880. MS. Registers.

—— Run Plans, MS. Records.

Police Magistrate's and Chief Secretary's Correspondence 1836–56. Archives, State Library, Victoria.

Adamson, T. (ed.). *Acts and Ordinances in Force in Victoria.* 2 vols, Melbourne 1855–6.

Acts and Ordinances of Victoria, The. 1851 to 1855–6.

Acts of Parliament of Victoria. 1856–7 to 1880–1.

Department of Lands and Agriculture (Victoria). *Annual Report of the Secretary for Agriculture*, First to Third, 1872–3 to 1874–5. Melbourne, 1873–5.

Historical Records of Australia. Ser. 1, vols 16–26.

New South Wales Government Gazette. 1835–44.

Port Phillip Government Gazette. 1844–51.

Port Phillip Government Notes. 1843.

Royal Commission on the Wheat, Flour and Bread Industries, First, Second and Fourth Reports. Canberra, 1934–6.

Statutes of the United Kingdom of Great Britain and Ireland, The (Statutes at Large).

Victoria Government Gazette. 1851–81.

Victorian Hansard. 1856–65.

Victorian Parliamentary Debates. 1866–81.

Votes and Proceedings of the Legislative Assembly of Victoria, and *Papers Presented to Parliament by Command.* 1856–83.

Votes and Proceedings of the Legislative Council of New South Wales. 1835–51.

Votes and Proceedings of the Legislative Council of Victoria. 1851–6.

Censuses and Statistics

Agricultural and Livestock Statistics for the Year Ending 31 March (Victoria), 1857–67, including reports of the collectors of statistics. *V.P.P.*, 1857–67.

Census of New South Wales, 9 November 1836. MS. Returns, Port Phillip District, Police Magistrate's Correspondence, 36/1–36/45, Archives, State Library, Victoria.

Census of New South Wales, March 1841. MS. Household Returns and Abstracts, Port Phillip District, 4/1244 and 4/1248, Archives Office of New South Wales.

Censuses of Victoria

2 March 1851, *V. & P.* L.C. Vic., 1851–2.

26 April 1854, *V. & P.* L.C. Vic., 1854–5, 1855–6; *V.P.P.*, 1856–7.

29 March 1857, *V.P.P.*, 1857–8, 1858–9.

7 April 1861, *V.P.P.*, 1862–3, 1864, 1864–5.

2 April 1871, *V.P.P.*, 1872, 1873, 1874.

3 April 1881, *V.P.P.*, 1882–3, 1883, 1884.

Mansfield, R. *Analytical View of the Census of New South Wales for the Year 1846.* Sydney, 1847.
Statistical Returns, 1837–46. *V. & P.* L.C. N.S.W., 1847, no. 42.
Statistics of the Colony of Victoria for the Year (subsequently Statistical Register of Victoria) , *V. & P.* L.C. Vic., 1851–6; *V.P.P.*, 1858–83.

MAPS

Held in Central Plan Office, Lands and Survey Department, Victoria

County and parish maps, Counties Bourke, Evelyn, Grant and Mornington. Manuscript and published, various dates.
Darke, W. Survey of Present and Proposed Lines of Road and the Coast between Melbourne and Geelong, 1841 (MS.), no. P4, 1066, 109.
—— Werribee River and Its Tributaries, 1839–40 (MS.), no. P39, 1010.
Hoddle, R. General Plan of Port Phillip—Campaspe River, 1839 (MS.), no. 117.
—— Port Phillip, 1840 (MS.), no. 113.
Rough Skeleton Map Showing All Existing Shires and Road Districts in Victoria, 22 May 1867 (MS.).
Settled Districts of Melbourne, 1854 (?), (MS.), H12380, Land S, Cd 7.

Other

Bailliere, F. F. *The County Atlas of the Colony of Victoria.* Melbourne, 1866.
Bureau of Meteorology (Australia). *Monthly Evaporation in Australia.* Map series. Melbourne, 1963.
Central Planning Authority (Victoria). *Resources Survey, Central Highlands Region.* Map no. 1, Melbourne, 1956.
Department of Mines (Victoria). *Geological Map of Victoria.* Melbourne, 1963.
Ham, T. *A Map of Australia Felix.* Melbourne, 1847.
—— *Map of the Purchased & Measured Lands, Counties, Parishes, &c. &c. of the Melbourne & Geelong Districts.* Melbourne, 1849.
—— *Map of the Settled District of 25 Miles Round Melbourne.* Melbourne, 1854.
Map of Municipal Boundaries, 1891, in Census of Victoria, 1891, *V.P.P.*, 1893, vol. 2, no. 9.
Military survey maps (published)
Series—1 mile = 1 inch, Ballan, 1933; Geelong, 1955; Melbourne, 1933; Meredith, 1953; Ringwood, 1922; Sunbury, 1938; Yan Yean, 1935.
Series—4 miles = 1 inch, Melbourne, 1943; Queenscliff, 2nd ed., n.d.
Northcote, K. H. *Atlas of Australian Soils.* C.S.I.R.O. Melbourne, 1962.
Whitehead's New Map of Victoria, 1881–2. Melbourne, 1882.

NEWSPAPERS AND OTHER PERIODICALS

Argus
Australasian
Church of England Messenger
Geelong Advertiser
Journal of the National Agricultural Society of Victoria
Melbourne Leader
Port Phillip Gazette
Port Phillip Herald which in 1849 became *Melbourne Morning Herald and General Daily Advertiser* and in 1855 the *Herald*
Victorian Agricultural and Horticultural Gazette
Victorian Farmers' Journal and Gardeners' Chronicle
Weekly Times
Yeoman and Australian Acclimatiser

MANUSCRIPTS AND TYPESCRIPTS

Batey, I. The Pioneers of the Sunbury District, 1907 (MS.). Box 26/2, La Trobe Library.
——— Further Notes on Early Days on the Keilor and Werribee Plains, n.d. (MS.). Box 26/1, La Trobe Library.
Bulla District Roads Board. Minute Book, 1862–71 (MS.). Bulla Shire Offices, Sunbury.
——— Rate Book, 1863–5 (MS.). Bulla Shire Offices, Sunbury.
de Pury, G. Diaries, 1874–81 (MS.). In possession of G. de Pury, Yeringburg, Coldstream.
Flynn, T. History of Braybrook District, 1906 (typescript). In possession of Imperial Chemical Industries of Australia and New Zealand Ltd, Melbourne, Mt Derrimut file.
Greig, W. Farm Day Book, Oct. 1840 to Feb. 1841 (MS.). B743, Mitchell Library.
Johnston, J. S. Diaries, 1864–80, and other papers (MS.). In possession of Lady Johnston, Melbourne, and University of Melbourne Archives.
Lennon, H. (agricultural implement and machine manufacturer). Letterbooks, 1876–7 (MS.). University of Melbourne Archives.
Melton Agricultural Society. Minute Books, 1863–76 (MS.). Melton Shire Offices, Melton.
Melton District Roads Board. Minute Books, 1862–76 (series incomplete), (MS.). Melton Shire Offices, Melton.
Mt Derrimut. Correspondence and other papers relating to Mt Derrimut. In possession of Imperial Chemical Industries of Australia and New Zealand Ltd, Melbourne, Mt Derrimut file.
Peel, C. H. Memoirs, 1956 (typescript). In author's possession.
Port Phillip Association. Papers, 1835–66 (typescript). M5119, Box 113/8, La Trobe Library.
Smith, M. Letter to her brothers in England, 9 Feb. 1857, Melbourne (MS.). In possession of Mr H. Muir, Christmas Hills.
Yeringburg. Workman's Time Books, 1883–4, 1893–4. In possession of G. de Pury, Yeringburg, Coldstream.

BOOKS AND ARTICLES

Acclimatisation Society of Victoria. *Annual Report*. First to Fourth, Melbourne, 1862, 1863, 1864, 1866. Victorian Pamphlets, vols 36, 60, La Trobe Library.
Austin, H. B. *The Merino: past, present and probable*. 2nd ed., Sydney, 1944.
Austin, R. A. 'The Austin family in Australia', *Victorian Historical Magazine*, vol. 36 (1965), pp. 78–96.
Australasian (newspaper staff). *The Australasian Farmer*. Melbourne, 1885.
Australian and New Zealand Association for the Advancement of Science. *Handbook for Victoria*. Melbourne, 1935.
Baker, C. J. *Sydney and Melbourne; with Remarks on the Present State and Future Prospects of New South Wales . . .* London, 1845.
Baldwin, J. G. 'A Soil Survey of the Shire of Whittlesea, Victoria', *Proceedings of the Royal Society of Victoria*, vol. 62 (1949), pp. 173–96.
Barnard, A. *The Australian Wool Market 1840–1900*. Melbourne, 1958.
Barnard, A. (ed.). *The Simple Fleece: studies in the Australian wool industry*. Melbourne, 1962.
Barrabool Shire Council. *Shire of Barrabool Centenary, 1865–1965*. Geelong, 1965.
Bartlett, G. R. 'The political orders of Victoria and New South Wales, 1856–1890'. *Australian Economic History Review*, vol. 8 (1968), pp. 49–54.
Bate, W. *A History of Brighton*. Melbourne, 1962.
Belperroud, J. and Pettavel, D. L. *The Vine, the Treatment of the Soil and How to Make Wine from Victorian Grapes*. Geelong, 1859.
Bennett, M. M. *Christison of Lammermoor*. 2nd ed., London, 1928.
Bićanić, R. 'Lack of institutional flexibility in agriculture', *Proceedings of the Tenth International Conference of Agricultural Economics*. London, 1960.

Bibliography

Billis, R. V. and Kenyon, A. S. *Pastures New: an account of the pastoral occupation of Port Phillip*. Melbourne, 1930.

—— *Pastoral Pioneers of Port Phillip*. Melbourne, 1932.

Blainey, G. *The Tyranny of Distance: how distance shaped Australia's history*. Melbourne, 1966.

Bland, W. (ed.). *Journey of Discovery to Port Phillip, New South Wales, in 1824 and 1825. By W. H. Hovell and H. Hume, Esquires*. 2nd ed., Sydney, 1837.

Bonwick, J. *Discovery and Settlement of Port Phillip*. Melbourne, 1856.

—— *John Batman, the Founder of Victoria*. 2nd ed., Melbourne, 1868.

Borrie, W. D. *Italians and Germans in Australia*. Melbourne, 1954.

Boys, R. D. *First Years at Port Phillip 1834–1842*. 2nd ed., Melbourne, 1959.

Bride, T. F. (ed.). *Letters from Victorian Pioneers*. Melbourne, 1898.

Brown, G. A. *Sheep Breeding in Australia*. Melbourne, 1880.

Brown, P. L. (ed.). *The Narrative of George Russell of Golf Hill*. London, 1935.

—— *Clyde Company Papers*. Prologue, 1821–35, vol. 2, 1836–40, vol. 3, 1841–5, vol. 4, 1846–50, vol. 5, 1851–3, vol. 6, 1854–8, London, 1941, 1952, 1958, 1959, 1963, 1968.

Brown, W. H. *The Farmers' Handbook*. 4th ed., Sydney, 1922.

Brownhill, W. R. *The History of Geelong and Corio Bay*. Geelong, 1955.

Buckley, K. 'Gipps and the graziers of New South Wales, 1841–1846', parts 1 and 2, in J. J. Eastwood and P. B. Smith (eds), *Historical Studies, Australia and New Zealand, Selected Articles*. Melbourne, 1964.

Bureau of Meteorology (Australia). *Rainfall Statistics, Victoria*. Melbourne, 1966.

—— *Results of Rainfall Observations Made in Victoria during 1840–1910*. Melbourne, 1911.

—— *Results of Rainfall Observations Made in Victoria* (supplementary volume). Melbourne, 1937.

Burroughs, P. 'The fixed price experiment in New South Wales, 1840–1841'. *Historical Studies, Australia and New Zealand*, vol. 12 (1966), pp. 389–404.

—— *Britain and Australia 1831–1855: a study in imperial relations and Crown lands administration*. London, 1967.

Butlin, N. G. *Investment in Australian Economic Development 1861–1900*. Cambridge, 1964.

Butlin, S. J. 'Charles Swanston and the Derwent Bank, 1827–50', *Historical Studies, Australia and New Zealand*, vol. 2 (1943), pp. 161–85.

—— *Foundations of the Australian Monetary System 1788–1851*. Melbourne, 1953.

Buxton, G. L. *The Riverina 1861–1891*. Melbourne, 1967.

Callaghan, A. R. and Millington, A. J. *The Wheat Industry in Australia*. Sydney, 1956.

Castella, H. de, *see* de Castella, H.

Chambers, J. D. and Mingay, G. E. *The Agricultural Revolution 1750–1880*. London, 1966.

Clark, C. M. H. *Select Documents in Australian History 1788–1850*. Sydney, 1950.

—— *Select Documents in Australian History 1851–1900*. Sydney, 1955.

Coghlan, T. A. *Labour and Industry in Australia*. 4 vols, London, 1918.

Coughlan, N. 'The coming of the Irish to Victoria', *Historical Studies, Australia and New Zealand*, vol. 12 (1965), pp. 68–86.

Cox, E. W. *The Evolution of the Australian Merino*. Sydney, 1936.

Curr, E. M. *Recollections of Squatting in Victoria*. 2nd ed., Melbourne, 1965.

de Castella, F. 'Early Victorian wine-growing', *Victorian Historical Magazine*, vol. 19 (1941–2), pp. 140–68.

—— 'Some pioneer Lillydale vignerons', *Victorian Historical Magazine*, vol. 20 (1943–4), pp. 51–68.

de Castella, H. *Les Squatters Australiens*. Paris, 1861.

—— *Notes d'un Vigneron Australien*. Melbourne, 1882.

—— *John Bull's Vineyard: Australian Sketches*. Melbourne, 1886.

Dondlinger, P. T. *The Book of Wheat: an economic history and practical manual of the wheat industry*. New York, 1908.

Drummond, J. C. and Wilbraham, A. *The Englishman's Food: a history of five centuries of English diet.* 2nd ed. (Readers Union Private edition), London, 1959.

Duffy, C. G. *Guide to the Land Law of Victoria.* Melbourne, 1862.

Dunsdorfs, E. *The Australian Wheat-Growing Industry 1788–1948.* Melbourne, 1956.

Dyster, B. 'Support for the squatters, 1844', *Journal of the Royal Australian Historical Society*, vol. 51 (1965), pp. 41–59.

Eblen, J. E. 'An analysis of nineteenth-century frontier populations', *Demography*, vol. 2 (1965), pp. 399–413.

Ewart, A. J. *The Weeds, Poison Plants, and Naturalized Aliens of Victoria.* Melbourne, 1909.

Felstehausen, H. 'Economic knowledge, participation and farmer decision making in a developed and under-developed country', *International Journal of Agrarian Affairs*, vol. 5 (1968), pp. 263–81.

Fenner, C. 'The physiography of the Werribee River area', *Proceedings of the Royal Society of Victoria*, vol. 31 (1918), pp. 176–313.

—— 'The Bacchus Marsh basin, *Proceedings of the Royal Society of Victoria*, vol. 37 (1925), pp. 144–69

Fitzpatrick, B. *The British Empire in Australia: an economic history 1834–1939.* Melbourne, 1941.

Foley, J. C. *Frost in the Australian Region.* Bureau of Meteorology bulletin no. 32, Melbourne, 1945.

—— *Droughts in Australia: review of records from earliest years of settlement to 1955.* Bureau of Meteorology bulletin no. 43, Melbourne, 1957.

Franklyn, H. M. *A Glance at Australia in 1880.* Melbourne, 1881.

Fussell, G. E. *The English Dairy Farmer 1500–1900.* London, 1966.

Graham, B. D. *The Formation of the Australian Country Parties.* Canberra, 1966.

Gunson, N. *The Good Country, Cranbourne Shire.* Melbourne, 1968.

Ham, W. *Barrabool Shire Council, Jubilee, 1865–1915.* Geelong, 1915.

Hammond, W. 'The early history of the Barrabool Hills', *Geelong Advertiser*, 17, 24 Dec. 1898, 7 Jan. 1899.

Harrigan, L. J. *Victorian Railways to '62.* Melbourne, 1962.

Hayter, H. H. *Victorian Year Book for the Year 1874.* Melbourne, 1875.

—— *Victorian Year Book for 1881–2.* Melbourne, 1882.

Holmes, L. C., Leeper, G. W. and Nicolls, K. D. 'Soil and land utilization survey of the country around Berwick', *Proceedings of the Royal Society of Victoria*, vol. 52 (1940), pp. 177–238.

Holt, A. J. *Wheat Farms of Victoria: a sociological survey.* Melbourne, 1947.

Hounam, C. E. *Evaporation in Australia.* Bureau of Meteorology bulletin no. 44, Melbourne, 1961.

Housman, W. *Cattle: breeds and management.* London, 1908.

Howitt, W. *Land, Labour, and Gold; or, Two Years in Victoria: with visits to Victoria and Van Diemen's Land.* 2 vols, London, 1855.

Humphreys, H. M. *Men of the Time in Australia.* Victorian Series. 2nd ed., Melbourne, 1882.

Inglis, K. S. 'Religious behaviour' in A. F. Davies and S. Encel (eds), *Australian Society: a sociological introduction.* Melbourne, 1965.

Jeeves, M. A. 'The relation of the assimilation of new information to increasing age', *Reviews, Papers and Reports.* Australian Agricultural Extension Conference 1962. Melbourne, 1963.

Joyce, A. *A Homestead History.* Melbourne, 1942.

Kelly, W. *Life in Victoria, or Victoria in 1853 and Victoria in 1858* . . . 2 vols, London, 1859.

Kelly, W. S. *Rural Development in South Australia.* Adelaide, 1962.

Kendall, S. G. *Farming Memoirs of a West Country Yeoman.* London, 1944.

Kerr, W. *Kerr's Melbourne Almanac and Port Phillip Directory for 1841.* Melbourne, 1841.

Kiddle, M. *Men of Yesterday: a social history of the Western District of Victoria 1834–1890*. Melbourne, 1961.
King, C. J. *An Outline of Closer Settlement in New South Wales: Part I, the sequence of the land laws 1788–1956*. Sydney, 1957.
Labilliere, F. P. *Early History of the Colony of Victoria*. 2 vols, London, 1878.
Lang, J. D. *Port-Phillip: or the colony of Victoria*. Glasgow, 1853.
Large, E. C. *The Advance of the Fungi*. London, 1940.
Le Souef, J. C. 'Acclimatisation in Victoria', *Victorian Historical Magazine*, vol. 36 (1965), pp. 8–29.
Ledger, G. *The Alpaca: its introduction into Australia and the probabilities of its acclimatisation there*. Melbourne, 1861.
Leeper, G. W. *Soils of Victoria*. Melbourne, 1964 (reprinted from *Victorian Year Book*, no. 78).
London International Exhibition of 1873 (Melbourne 1872–73). Official Record. Melbourne, 1873.
Lowe, E. J. *A Natural History of British Grasses*. London, 1871.
Lyng, T. *Non-Britishers in Australia*. Melbourne, 1935.
McAlpine, D. *The Smuts of Australia*. Melbourne, 1910.
McIntyre, A. J. *The Whittlesea District*. Whittlesea, 1947. Published privately by Whittlesea Agricultural Society.
Mackaness, G. (ed.). *The Correspondence of John Cotton, Victorian Pioneer, 1842–1849*. Australian Historical Monographs, nos 26–8, being pts 1–3, privately printed, 1953.
Macmillan, D. S. *The Debtor's War: Scottish capitalists and the economic crisis in Australia 1841–1846*. Melbourne, 1960.
Meinig, D. W. *On the Margins of the Good Earth*. London, 1963.
Minchinton, W. E. (ed.). *Essays in Agrarian History*. 2 vols, Newton Abbot (Devon), 1968.
Ministry of Agriculture, Fisheries and Food (U.K.). *Animal Health: a centenary 1865–1965*. London, 1965.
——— *Some Diseases of Farm Animals*. Bulletin no. 1, London, 1936.
Morris, G. Series of newspaper articles in *Werribee Shire Banner*. Werribee, 1962.
Morton, J. C. *The Farmer's Calendar*. 2nd ed., London, 1862 (original edition written by Arthur Young).
Mouritz, J. J. *The Port Phillip Almanac and Directory*. Melbourne, 1847.
Mueller, Baron F. von. *Select Extra-tropical Plants, Readily Eligible for Industrial Culture or Naturalisation* . . . 7th ed., Melbourne, 1888.
Napolitan, L. *Centenary of the Agricultural Census 1866 to 1966*. London, 1966.
Newman, R. J. 'Plant nutrient deficiencies in Victorian pasture soils', *Journal of Agriculture* (Victoria), vol. 54 (1959), pp. 337–45.
Oeser, O. A. and Emery, F. E. *Social Structure and Personality in a Rural Community*. London, 1954.
Orwin, C. S. and Whetham, E. H. *History of British Agriculture 1846–1914*. London, 1964.
Packer, D. R. G. 'Victorian population data, 1851–1861', *Historical Studies, Australia and New Zealand*, vol. 5 (1953), pp. 307–23.
Patterson, G. D. *The Tariff in the Australian Colonies 1856–1900*. Melbourne, 1968.
Peck, H. H. *Memoirs of a Stockman*. Melbourne, 1942.
Peel, L. J. 'Viticulture at Geelong and Lillydale', *Victorian Historical Magazine*, vol. 36 (1965), pp. 154–73.
Perry, T. M. *Australia's First Frontier: the spread of settlement in New South Wales 1788–1829*. Melbourne, 1963.
Philosophical Institute of Victoria. 'Report of the resources of the colony of Victoria', *Transactions of the Philosophical Institute of Victoria*, vol. 4 for 1859, Melbourne, 1860, appendix 1.
Pike, D. 'The smallholder's place in the Australian tradition', *Tasmanian Historical Research Association Papers and Proceedings*, vol. 10 (1962), pp. 28–33.

Pollitt, J. H. *An Historical Record of Melton.* Melbourne, 1962.

Port Phillip Farmers' Society. *Transactions of the Port Phillip Farmers' Society.* Melbourne, 1857–60 (general report published in 1857 and annual reports for the years 1856–7 to 1859–60).

Prescott, J. A. and Thomas, J. A. 'The length of the growing season in Australia as determined by the effectiveness of the rainfall', *Proceedings of the South Australian Branch of the Royal Geographical Society of Australasia,* vol. 50 (1949), pp. 42–6

Price, C. A. *Jewish Settlers in Australia.* Canberra, 1964.

Pullar, E. M. 'Foot and mouth disease in Australia with particular reference to the Victorian incident of 1872', *Victorian Veterinary Proceedings,* vol. 23 (1964–5), pp. 12–18.

——— 'Contagious bovine pleuropneumonia in Victoria 1858–61: fate or folly?', *Victorian Veterinary Proceedings,* vol. 24 (1965–6), pp. 12–17.

——— 'The Victorian Royal Commission on contagious bovine pleuropneumonia of 1863–64 and the essay prizes of 1864–65', *Victorian Veterinary Proceedings,* vol. 25 (1966–7), pp. 12–17.

Rasmussen, W. D. *Readings in the History of American Agriculture.* Urbana, Ill., 1960.

Riddell, J. 'Shorthorns' in Department of Lands and Agriculture (Victoria), *Third Annual Report of the Secretary for Agriculture.* Melbourne, 1875.

Roberts, S. H. *History of Australian Land Settlement 1788–1920.* Melbourne, 1924.

——— *The Squatting Age in Australia 1835–1847.* Melbourne, 1935.

Russell, (Sir) E. J. *A History of Agricultural Science in Great Britain 1620–1954.* London, 1966.

'Rusticus', *How to settle in Victoria: or, instructions on the purchase and occupation of the land; with observations on gardening and farming . . .* Melbourne, 1855.

Scott, E. 'Hume and Hovell's Journey to Port Phillip', *Journal of the Royal Australian Historical Society,* vol. 7 (1921), pp. 289–380 (this includes W. H. Hovell, Journal Kept on the Journey from Lake George to Port Phillip, 1824–1825).

Serle, G. *The Golden Age: a history of the colony of Victoria 1851–1861.* Melbourne, 1963.

Serle, P. *Dictionary of Australian Biography.* 2 vols, Sydney, 1949.

Shann, E. *An Economic History of Australia.* Australian ed., Melbourne, 1948.

Shaw, A. G. L. *The Economic Development of Australia.* 5th ed., Melbourne, 1966.

Short, B. F. and Carter, H. B. *An Analysis of the Records of the Registered Australian Merino Stud Flocks.* C.S.I.R.O. bulletin no. 276, Melbourne, 1955.

Smith, J. (ed.). *The Cyclopaedia of Victoria.* 3 vols, Melbourne, 1903–5.

Snedecor, G. W. and Cochran, W. G. *Statistical Methods.* 6th ed., Ames, Iowa, 1967.

Story, W. 'Essay upon the agriculture of Victoria' in *The Victorian Government Prize Essays 1860.* Melbourne, 1861.

Sutherland, A. *Victoria and Its Metropolis Past and Present.* 2 vols, Melbourne, 1888.

Sutton, C. S. 'A sketch of the Keilor Plains flora', *Victorian Naturalist,* vol. 33 (1916), pp. 112–23, 128–43.

Sutton, G. L. 'The invention of the stripper', *Journal of the Department of Agriculture* (Western Australia), vol. 14 (1937), pp. 194–247.

Thompson, F. M. L. 'The second agricultural revolution, 1815–1880', *The Economic History Review,* vol. 21 (1968), pp. 62–77.

Thomson, W. 'On diseases among stock' in Department of Lands and Agriculture (Victoria), *Second Annual Report of the Secretary for Agriculture.* Melbourne, 1874.

Trow-Smith, R. *A History of British Livestock Husbandry 1700–1900.* London, 1959.

Tully, J. 'Agricultural education for extension workers', *Agricultural Education.* Papers presented to the Third National Conference, Australian Institute of Agricultural Science. Hobart, 1965.

Turner, H. G. *A History of the Colony of Victoria.* 2 vols, London, 1904.

von Mueller, Baron F., *see* Mueller, Baron F. von.

Wadham, S. M. *Australian Farming 1788–1965.* Melbourne, 1967.

—— *History of Victoria's Wheat Industry*. Melbourne, 1951 (reprinted from *Chamber of Agriculture Year Book*, 1951).

Wadham, S. M., Wilson, R. K. and Wood, J. *Land Utilization in Australia*. 3rd ed., Melbourne, 1957.

Waterson, D. B. *Squatter, Selector and Storekeeper: a history of the Darling Downs 1859–93*. Sydney, 1968.

Wekey, S. *The Land, Importance of its Culture to the General Prosperity of Victoria* . . . Melbourne, 1854.

Whitworth, R. P. *Baillieres Victorian Gazetteer*. Melbourne, 1865 and 1879.

Wibberley, G. P. *Agriculture and Urban Growth*. London, 1959.

Williams, D. B. *Economic and Technical Problems of Australia's Rural Industries*. Melbourne, 1957.

Williams, W., et al. *A History of Bacchus Marsh and Its Pioneers 1836–1936*. Bacchus Marsh, 1936 (mainly newspaper extracts to 1896).

Wright, Stephenson & Co. Ltd. *A Guide to Better Pastures*. 2nd ed., Melbourne, 1957.

Wright, W. T. *The Live Stock Annual of Australia 1905*. Melbourne, 1905.

Youatt, W. *Cattle: their breeds, management and diseases*. London, 1834.

—— *The Complete Grazier and Farmer's and Cattle-Breeder's Assistant*. 11th ed., London, 1864.

—— *Sheep, Their Breeds, Management, and Diseases*. New ed., London, 1875.

THESES

Barley, K. P. A History of Two Victorian Farmers' Organisations, the Royal Agricultural Society and the Chamber of Agriculture. M.Agr.Sc. thesis, University of Melbourne, 1950.

Bartlett, G. R. Political Organisation and Society in Victoria 1864–1883. Ph.D. thesis, Australian National University, 1964.

Broughton, J. A. S. and Walter, N. F. A General Survey of the Early Settlement and Architecture along the Maribyrnong between Bulla and Keilor. History of Architecture thesis, University of Melbourne, 1963.

Brownfield, G. The Land and Its Users: a history of the Dandenong–Cranbourne–Berwick–Pakenham area from the beginning of white settlement until about 1870. History IV thesis, Monash University, 1965.

Condon, L. Point Cooke. History of Architecture thesis, University of Melbourne, 1964.

Howard, G. R. and Philip, R. A. The History and Settlement of the Bulla District. History of Architecture thesis, University of Melbourne, 1963.

Jordan, T. G. A Geographical Appraisal of the Significance of German Settlement in Nineteenth Century Texas Agriculture. Ph.D. thesis, University of Wisconsin, 1965.

Parnaby, J. E. The Economic and Political Development of Victoria 1877–1881. Ph.D. thesis, University of Melbourne, 1951.

Wilson, R. K. Type of Farming Areas in Victoria, Australia. Ph.D. thesis, Australian National University, 1959.

Index

Index